Explorer
New York

Mick Sinclair

 Publishing

Front cover
Top *an iconic yellow cab in Times Square* (Clive Sawyer); Centre *(left to right)* (a) *the Fuller Building* (Richard Elliott); (b) *playing baseball in Central Park* (Paul Kenward); (c) *Circle Line cruises for a water-based view of the city* (Douglas Corrance); (d) *bagels* (Simon McBride); (e) *the Guggenheim Museum* (Clive Sawyer)
Spine: *Empire State Building* (Simon McBride)
Back cover
Left: *Christmas lights at Macy's department store* (Clive Sawyer); Right: *the Statue of Liberty* (Clive Sawyer)

All pictures from AA World Travel Library

Written by Mick Sinclair
Updated by Mick Sinclair. Hotels and Restaurants updated by Melisse Gelula

Published by AA Publishing, a trading name of Automobile Association Developments Limited, whose registered office is Southwood East, Apollo Rise, Farnborough, Hampshire, GU14 0JW. Registered number 1878835.

ISBN-10: 0 7495 4378 7
ISBN-13: 978-0-7495-4378-5

A CIP catalogue record for this book is available from the British Library.

Colour separation by Fotographics Ltd
Printed and bound in Italy by Printer Trento Srl

Find out more about AA Publishing and the wide range of travel publications and services the AA provides by visiting our website at www.theAA.com/bookshop.

Revised sixth edition 2005
First published 1994

Titles in the Explorer series:
Australia • Boston & New England • Britain • Brittany
California • Canada • Caribbean • China • Costa Rica • Crete
Cuba • Cyprus • Egypt • Florence & Tuscany • Florida
France • Germany • Greek Islands • Hawaii • India • Ireland
Italy • Japan • London • Mallorca • Mexico • New York
New Zealand • Paris • Portugal • Provence • Rome
San Francisco • Scotland • South Africa • Spain • Thailand
Tunisia • Turkey • Venice • Vietnam

Opposite: *New York skyscrapers*

A02140

How to use this book

ORGANIZATION

New York Is, New York Was

Discusses aspects of life and culture in contemporary New York and explores significant periods in its history.

A–Z

Breaks down the city into regional chapters, and covers places to visit, including walks and drives. Within this section fall the Focus On articles, which consider a variety of subjects in greater detail.

Travel Facts

Contains the strictly practical information vital for a successful trip.

Accommodations and Restaurants

Lists recommended establishments throughout New York, giving a brief summary of their attractions.

KEY TO ADMISSION CHARGES

Standard admission charges are categorized in this book as following:

Inexpensive under $7
Moderate $7–$13
Expensive   over $13

ABOUT THE RATINGS

Most places described in this book have been given a separate rating. These are as follows:

▶▶▶   **Do not miss**

▶▶   **Highly recommended**

▶   **Worth seeing**

MAPS

To make each particular location easier to find, every main entry in this book has a map reference to the right of its name. This comprises a number, followed by a letter, followed by another number, such as 48B3. The first number (48) refers to the page on which the map can be found, the letter (B) and the second number (3) pinpoint the square in which the main entry is located. The maps on the inside front cover and inside back cover are referred to as IFC and IBC respectively.

Contents

5

Sign-cleaning on the corner of Seventh Avenue and Broadway

Statue of Liberty

New York fire engine

*Lower Manhattan—
post-September 11—seen
from Brooklyn Heights*

Foreword

Whether they loath or loathe it, few can deny that New
York is among the most stimulating cities in the world,
and perhaps the only one where so much is so familiar
even at first sight. The Statue of Liberty, the Empire State
Building and Central Park are just three New York landmarks well known to visitors before they set eyes on
them. Equally familiar are New York images such as
creamcheese bagels and yellow cabs that could exist anywhere but which the media have made icons of the city.

The destruction that befell Manhattan on 11 September
2001, reminded everyone that New York is a symbol as
well as a city. The twin towers of the World Trade Center
embodied the entrepreneurial spirit on which the city,
and the nation, grew. They marked New York's place at
the heart of a global economy and underlined the city's
role as a flag-carrier of American values.

New York might never be quite the same as it was
before that day but as the impact softens with time, it
becomes possible to think of New York less for the
destruction unleashed upon it and more for the things
that have attracted visitors for decades: architecture of
genius, museums stocked with many centuries-worth of
treasures from around the world, galleries showcasing
art from the established to the cutting edge. Still thriving,
too, are the department stores and specialist outlets that
carry consumerism into a higher dimension and the
restaurants that set world standards for fine dining.

New York also continues to provide gist for the inquisi-
tive traveler. How many people know the Statue of
Liberty was originally intended for the Suez Canal? Who
can name the hard-headed 19th-century financier who
consulted an astrologist for decision-making assistance?
And how many visitors can explain how profits from the
notorious slums of the Lower East Side helped give New
York one of the world's greatest reference libraries?

One of the pleasures of writing this book was discovering the answers to such questions and in so doing peeling
back the layers of myth that disguise the true city. New
York stripped bare is not always a pretty sight but is
more believable than the city of cliché and media hype. If
only to encourage others to explore and uncover something new in this seemingly familiar, but also strange and
mysterious place, the undertaking was a worthwhile one.
Mick Sinclair

New York Is

Incredible museums, fantastic architecture, luxurious hotels and every kind of restaurant—New York has them all. But it is only by stepping out among the sights, smells, and sounds that fill its streets that you will begin to feel the true pulse of the city.

NONSTOP STREETS A New York street can be a lonely place but seldom is it an empty one. Around 5am, the first batches of briefcase-carrying commuters emerge from the city's subway stations, just in time to see the nightclubbers heading for home. A few hours later, young people make their way to school; soon after, the first lunch-seeking office workers begin filing onto the sidewalks. By early afternoon, some commuters are already making for the stations and by dusk Midtown Manhattan is buzzing with pre-theater diners. In Greenwich Village and the East Village, bars and clubs prepare for another long, busy night.

Despite the zero tolerance policy in New York, graffiti is still visible on some city streets

❏ The 12,000 yellow taxis that cruise New York's streets are much more than merely a quick (traffic permitting) way of traveling from A to B. Enshrined in city mythology, taxis have inspired a TV series (*Taxi*, which made a star of Danny DeVito), been represented as small yellow rectangles in a major painting—Mondrian's *Broadway Boogie-Woogie* (displayed at New York's Museum of Modern Art)—and, like taxis the world over, are infamously hard to find when it rains. Why are they yellow? Because John Hertz, who founded the Yellow Cab Company in 1907, read a survey carried out by the University of Chicago which concluded that yellow was the color most people found easiest to spot. ❏

OFF THE STREET One contributory factor to the round-the-clock hubbub on New York's streets is the size and price of the apartments that rise above them. Most Manhattan apartments are small and, except for a few rent-controlled properties, extremely expensive. Rather than stay indoors cooking in a tiny kitchen, New Yorkers will welcome any opportunity to eat, drink and socialize outside their apartments.

STREET DEALS Free enterprise rules the New York streets. An abundance of foodstands can be found all around the city and appetites can be satisfied—often surprisingly well—without ever venturing inside a restaurant. Bookworms can shop at makeshift outdoor tables, which offer for sale all kinds of reading material ranging from brand-new discounted hardbacks to used paperbacks. Many New York apartments have been furnished by various purchases from street markets, where the merchandise ranges from eccentric junk to valuable pieces of matching furniture.

Even if it rains, there is no need to duck inside for shelter. As the first drops start to fall, street-corner traders appear, as if from nowhere, bearing armfuls of inexpensive umbrellas.

STREET TRAFFIC Listen to bike riders and truck drivers locked in verbal combat at traffic lights, after jostling for prime position the length of the last block. Careful eavesdropping may even provide you with useful ammunition if *you* ever find it necessary to exchange insults with a New Yorker.

Watch out for rollerbladers who tempt death by weaving through Fifth Avenue's frantic rush-hour traffic—sometimes they will even grab hold of passing vehicles for a free tug.

IMPROVING STREETS After decades of cost-cutting in city services had left some city streets potholed and socially unsafe, New York's Times Square and the area around Grand Central Terminal underwent dramatic changes during the 1990s.

Designated as BIDs, or Business Improvement Districts, under a nationwide scheme funded by a tax on local businesses, both neighborhoods now employ unarmed security forces to heighten safety and provide visitor-friendly services such as information desks and street maps. Both New York BIDs offer free walking tours of the area to highlight their success.

Walking along Fifth Avenue during rush-hour is a memorable experience

❏ Everyone knows New York is nicknamed the Big Apple but nobody is sure of the origins of the term. Musicians, gangsters and horse-racing devotees have all been cited as its source, but the phrase's recent popularity stems from a tourism campaign launched in 1971. ❏

SAFER STREETS Through the 1990s, levels of crime in New York fell sharply. Between 1993 and 2003 there was a 55 percent drop in "serious" crime. Murders fell from 1,952 to 538. Subway offences also declined by a significant amount. However, as in most of the world's big cities, it is wise to be cautious and New York is no different. If you have particular concerns, or for further guidance, refer to page 249.

11

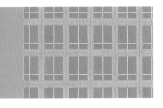

For anyone, anywhere, with aspirations and dreams, New York is the place to be. Whether you want to sing and dance your way to fame, make a mint on Wall Street, or start a new life in a new land, New York is—as it has always been—the beacon of opportunity.

HIGH FINANCE For those who can stand the stresses and strains, the heady world of New York high finance offers rewards unimagined and a level of power that few outside international politics ever experience.

Even without the World Trade Center twin towers, the glass-and-steel high-rises of the Manhattan skyline make it clear that this is a linchpin of the US economy, a city that provides over 3 million jobs, 80 percent of them in the private sector.

However, there is no doubt the WTC attacks of September 2001 had a terrible impact on Lower

❑ While it had long dominated the US financial markets, New York also became the heart of the global economy that emerged during the 1980s and 1990s. As such, Financial District high-flyers found themselves acquiring significant performance bonuses as well as, in world terms, some of the sector's best salaries. Soaring stock prices through the bull market of the mid-1990s saw, in one year, an *average* bonus payout of $54,000 per employee. Such sudden increases in disposable income have a knock-on affect across the city as demand for goods and services rises, and property prices escalate. A downturn in the world markets can reverse the trend just as sharply. ❑

Cab driving: a steady living

(88ha) of office space—equivalent to the whole of Atlanta—and their loss necessitated temporary relocation for many major players. It remains to be seen how many will return.

Manhattan's role as the center of the financial world. While it still stands that many industrial giants with workers across the globe are driven by decisions made in their Manhattan boardrooms, it is also the case that many such companies moved their headquarters away from the decimated center of the financial district. The twin towers alone housed some 50,000 workers in 218 acres

TAXI DRIVERS Shortly after the internal combustion engine replaced the horse on the New York streets, driving a taxi became the staple first job of arriving immigrants. Less than 11 percent of applications for cab-driving jobs are from native-born New Yorkers. Many of these newly arrived taxi-drivers may have a university degree or years of experience in some profession in their native land, but cannot find work. Being a cabbie in New York at least means

12

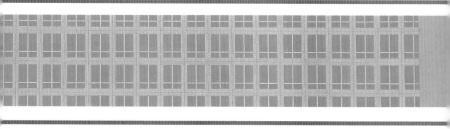

steady wages and a chance to provide their children with an education.

UNCONVENTIONAL LIFESTYLES

Many come to New York simply for the opportunity to live as they want to. Multicolored hair and bizarre attire seldom raise eyebrows on Manhattan's seen-it-all-before streets. Avid night clubbers can go out and enjoy themselves all night

New Yorkers have learned to take the eccentric in their stride

every night, stay in bed all day and never feel that New York life is passing them by in this city that never sleeps.

New York also promises a supportive infrastructure for gays and lesbians, many of whom come to escape discrimination elsewhere.

PUBLISHING The New York-based *Wall Street Journal* and *The New York*

❏ An estimated 770,000 college graduates move to New York annually. ❏

Times lead the country for quality reporting and carry journalism's most prestigious jobs—coveted by ambitious news-gatherers across the country. Some New York-based magazines enjoy worldwide esteem. The *New Yorker*, *Vanity Fair*, and *Vogue* have had little trouble in luring overseas talent and in the past have raised eyebrows by appointing British editors. Most of the country's major publishers are based in New York, which attracts writers—both American and émigré—to the city and gives agents and editors the chance to work with some of the world's most celebrated literary names.

THE STAGE Those intent upon a career in the performing arts ignore New York at their peril. A major early boost is to be one of the thousand students accepted every year into the city's highly rated Juilliard School of Music and Performing Arts.

For thespians, New York's place is clearly at the heart of US theater, whether it is Broadway blockbusters or the dozens of Off-Off-Broadway productions. New York also offers acting opportunities away from live audiences: The majority of TV soap operas and commercials are cast in Manhattan, although most TV and film work is centered in Los Angeles.

New York's ballet, orchestras, and opera companies, are among the world's most highly rated.

Everybody knows, or thinks they know, New York long before they actually arrive there, having seen the city depicted—be it lovingly or with loathing—in innumerable movies. Here is a highly selective list of the most revealing, famous, or simply the most enjoyable, movies set in New York. (Woody Allen's New York movies are detailed on page 188.)

Breakfast at Tiffany's (1961). On screen New York has never appeared more romantic than in this adaptation of the Truman Capote novella; Audrey Hepburn stars as the free-spirited Holly Golightly who—dressed in a chic black evening gown—drinks coffee shortly after dawn as she admires the jewels in the store window of Fifth Avenue's Tiffany and Company.

The Crowd (1928). Two years after Fritz Lang's futuristic *Metropolis*, inspired by the Manhattan skyline, came King Vidor's expressionistic study of the ordinary man's struggle in the seething city: memorable New York scenes abound.

Do The Right Thing (1989). In what might be Spike Lee's best movie, the director uses the setting of a New York ethnically mixed community—such as the Korean grocer and Italian pizzeria owner who operate in a predominantly African-American neighborhood—in a witty and provocative exploration of complex racial issues.

❏ Thomas Edison may have electrified the city but a combination of factors—royalties due on Edison-patented cinematic equipment, the demands of actors' unions, and inclement weather—encouraged fledgling moviemakers to leave New York (where movies were a natural offshoot of Broadway theaters) in the early 1900s for the sunshine of southern California. ❏

I Shot Andy Warhol (1996). A fact-based evocation of Warhol's Factory and the insularity of the 1960s New York art world as seen through the eyes of Valerie Solanas, played in marvelously intense style by Lili Taylor, whose rising anger culminates in her shooting of Andy Warhol.

King Kong (1933). The conflict between man and nature reaches its climax as the giant ape swats planes while flirting with Fay Wray beside the Empire State Building.

The Lost Weekend (1945).The bar in which Billy Wilder's alcoholic weekend began still exists—P. J. Clarke's, Third Avenue at 55th Street.

Mean Streets (1973). Martin Scorsese had a bigger hit in 1976 with *Taxi Driver*, but this movie contrasts the New York of hippies and flower-power with the macho traditions of young Italian-Americans on the make.

On the Town (1949). One of the first MGM musicals shot on location, this fast-paced movie follows three sailors (Gene Kelly, Frank Sinatra and Jules Munshin) on a 24-hour pass as they dash around the city, stopping at the Rockefeller Center, the Statue of Liberty, the Bronx Zoo, Brooklyn Bridge and other sights.

Portrait of Jennie (1948). A lovely and appropriately haunting movie in which a troubled artist is enchanted by a young girl in Central Park only to discover later on that she is a ghost.

The city's best-known screen moment: King Kong and Fay Wray in 1933

Q—The Winged Serpent (1982). Witty, low-budget piece in which a giant bird flies out of Aztec mythology to terrorize New Yorkers. It lays an egg inside the Chrysler Building, only to be discovered by a hoodlum who tries to cash in on his amazing find.

Saturday Night Fever (1977). A product of 1970s disco mania that gives a taste of the culture of young Italian-Americans in Brooklyn's Bensonhurst neighborhood. It launched John Travolta's career.

Serpico (1973). In real life, Frank Serpico was an honest cop whose efforts to stamp out corruption in the New York police force met with intimidation and violence. Serpico's stand eventually led to a massive clean-up campaign—and to Al Pacino playing him in this highly charged thriller, which has great location shots.

Seven Year Itch (1955). Probably Marilyn Monroe's finest screen moment: her skirt is lifted by air rising from the subway grate at the junction of 52nd Street and Lexington Avenue.

Sweet Smell of Success (1957). A brilliant Tony Curtis plays the sleazy press agent currying favor with the Broadway gossip columnist, Burt Lancaster.

The Thomas Crown Affair (1999). An ingenious theft from the Metropolitan Museum is the cue for a cat and mouse game between an artloving playboy and a wily nonconformist detective.

❏ An unknown 18-year-old actress called Lauren Bacall was crowned Miss Greenwich Village in 1942. ❏

Saturday Night Fever *in Brooklyn*

From Broadway shows to live bands in Bowery basements, New York resonates with music and has frequently attracted the composers, lyricists, musicians and those simply seeking stardom, who have reshaped popular music and created some of the world's most memorable songs.

TIN PAN ALLEY The sound of pianos resembling the rattling of tin pans earned a section of 28th Street the nickname Tin Pan Alley from the 1890s. George Gershwin began his career as a Tin Pan Alley composer with the song "Swanee" (1918). The pianos belonged to music publishing companies, many of which later moved to the Brill Building (1619 Broadway; see page 17).

RHAPSODIES IN BLUE Migration of African-Americans to New York underpinned the city's emergence as a jazz center during the 1920s when emerging talents took jazz far beyond its roots. Among the innovators were Duke Ellington, pianist, composer and band leader in Harlem's Cotton Club; and jazz-influenced classical composers such as Gershwin, whose "Rhapsody in Blue" became synonymous with New York. The city also provided a launch pad in the 1940s for bebop, a new improvisational style with the glorious Charlie Parker, Thelonious Monk and Dizzy Gillespie among its practitioners.

LULLABIES ON BROADWAY In the early 1900s, Broadway's vaudeville shows beckoned aspiring songwriters. After working in Chinatown as a "singing waiter," Irving Berlin found success with the Ziegfeld Follies and composed classics such as "White Christmas," "There's No Business Like Show Business," and "Everybody's Doin' It." George M. Cohan's "Give My Regards to Broadway" and "I'm a Yankee Doodle Dandy" both originated in Broadway shows. Howard Arlen penned reviews for Harlem's Cotton Club, including "Stormy Weather," before heading for Hollywood and "Somewhere Over The Rainbow."

16

❏ Penned at the Brill Building were: "The Locomotion," "One Fine Day," "Da Wah Diddy," "Baby I Love You," "Hound Dog," "You've Lost That Loving Feeling," "Da Doo Ron Ron" and "Oh Carol." ❏

Irving Berlin at his piano

FOLK AND ROCK Through the late 1950s and early 1960s, Greenwich Village coffee houses and folk clubs provided the breeding ground for a new batch of young folk singers, often dealing with topical issues and inspired by luminaries such as Woody Guthrie and Pete Seeger. Those who emerged to wide success included Judy Collins and Bob Dylan.

Dylan's switch from folk to rock music pre-empted the psychedelic era. The streetwise cynicism characteristic of New York was at odds with the sensibilities of psychedelia, however, but provided a perfect setting for the Velvet Underground. Using violas alongside guitars, cymbal-less drumming and songs about the seedier side of urban life, the Velvet Underground (and their main singer and songwriter Lou Reed) became one of the city's most enduring influences on rock music, despite lack of commercial success during their short life.

BRILL The Brill Building was home to songwriters Carole King, Jerry Goffin, Neil Sedaka, Neil Diamond, Barry Mann and Cynthia Weill, who created some of the famous hits of the 1950s and 1960s (see panel).

NEW WAVE A Bowery basement club, CBGBs, became a venue for nascent bands of the New Wave movement from the mid-1970s.

Mr Tambourine Man, Bob Dylan

17

Musically diverse but sharing an attitude, Blondie, The Ramones and Talking Heads all regularly appeared here, as did other seminal figures such as Patti Smith and Richard Hell. Blondie evolved into the biggest-selling band in the world, reforming in the 1990s to still more success.

RAP AND HIP-HOP Also in the mid-1970s, DJs in the predominantly African-American-populated South Bronx began forging the turntable style known as "scratching," often adding beats from their own drum machine and sometimes joined by an MC providing an improvised vocal "rap" over the music.

Scratching, rap, and the associated break dancing, and graffiti art (collectively known as hip-hop) evolved into a worldwide phenomenon during the 1980s, with first hits from the Sugarhill Gang and Grandmaster Flash and the Furious Five and then by the Beastie Boys and Run DMC. By the late 1990s, rap-related music had a global audience, and, in the US.was outselling the commercially dominant country music.

Run DMC in concert

Few areas of New York stay the same for long. Not only do entire districts undergo staggering transformations—socially, architecturally, and commercially—within a few years, but sometimes a whole new neighborhood can suddenly arise where previously there was nothing but a hole in the ground.

TIMES SQUARE AND 42ND STREET

A major program of regeneration and development got underway under the banner of the Times Square Business Improvement District, in the mid-1980s in and around Times Square, previously a rundown area dominated by porn theaters and pickpockets. The now transformed area—patrolled by its own security force and kept clean with frequent garbage collection—succeeds in its intention of being a safe and welcoming part of the city to shoppers, tourists and legitimate businesses alike.

New construction work over recent years has seen high-rise hotels, shopping complexes and office buildings appear and a number of the area's historic theaters have also received much-needed renovations.

Nonetheless, the new-look square has drawn a mixed response from New Yorkers. While most are happy to see crime levels reduced and relish a much-improved subway station, many fear Times Square's "Disneyfication," its character buried beneath theme restaurants and major retail franchises.

BATTERY PARK CITY Yet another testament to New York's powers of metamorphosis is Battery Park City, a $4-billion project combining commercial, residential and recreational areas on a 92-acre (37-ha) land-fill site situated on the western edge of the Financial District.

Conceived in the 1970s, Battery Park City gave a new lease of life to an abandoned stretch of Hudson River waterfront, while finding a use for the thousands of tons of earth and rock excavated during the building of the World Trade Center.

Battery Park City has evolved through the labors of several prestigious architects working within a single master plan: to re-create the atmosphere of an elegant, traditional Manhattan neighborhood.

The redeveloped Times Square

The residential buildings hold luxury apartments while the commercial structures include Cesar Pelli's World Financial Center. This was completed in 1986 and noted for its palm-decorated Winter Garden atrium, which was severely damaged in the World Trade Center attacks. Escaping almost undamaged, however, was the mile-long Esplanade, with Victorian-style lampposts and wooden benches, which restored public access to this section of the Hudson River for the first time in several decades.

The Esplanade in Battery Park City

now consider Chelsea to have replaced SoHo as the city's art center.

On Chelsea's western edge, beside the Hudson River, four early-1900s cruise-ship docks have been redeveloped into Chelsea Piers, a beehive of sports activities, dining and shopping.

Many early landmarks remain, not least the Chelsea Hotel (see page 85) and those of the Chelsea Historical District, which has examples of the diverse residental styles of 19th-century New York.

CHELSEA Approximately bordered by 14th and 29th streets and Sixth Avenue and the Hudson River, the Chelsea neighborhood began collecting the residential overspill from the increasingly upscale Greenwich Village through the 1980s. By the early 1990s, the neighborhood—a prominent shopping area during the 1890s and now a mixture of town houses and apartment buildings, industry and commerce—was an increasingly important nightlife and restaurant area, with a strong gay contingent among its residents and business owners.

A growing number of galleries that have appeared in the area have made Chelsea a serious rival to the longer-established SoHo art scene and have encouraged more and more stores and restaurants to open up. Many

RE-ENERGIZED Elsewhere, previously stagnant areas such as NoLiTa (abbreviated from North of Little Italy) and the Flatiron District have been re-energized, most noticeably with an influx of stylish stores and restaurants.

❑ The continuing eastward migration of New York's unknown and lesser-known artists from Greenwich Village, through SoHo and the East Village neighborhoods, now finds them located across the East River, creating loft studios in the former factories of Brooklyn's Williamsburg. Here they form a striking contrast to the area's orthodox Jewish community. ❑

Thanks to a unique combination of wealthy collectors and a wartime influx of modern European artists, New York has amassed some of the world's finest pieces of art—displaying them in several world-class museums—and evolved into a showcase for new artistic ideas and directions.

FIRST COLLECTIONS Founded in 1804, the **New-York Historical Society** (see page 165) became the city's first repository for art, acquiring a singular collection of Early American works, including many commissioned by Robert Lehman, a New Yorker who opened part of his town house as a gallery and brought American artists such as Thomas Cole to public attention.

The paintings collection of New York's **Metropolitan Museum of Art** (pages 142–148) began with a modest purchase of 174 Dutch and Flemish canvases in 1870 and grew—aided by bequests and donations—into a world-class stock, including many major pieces by Van Gogh, Turner, El Greco and Vermeer.

BUSINESSMEN BECOME COLLECTORS Having amassed wealth through their control of the industralization of the United States, and with newly built Fifth Avenue mansions in need of decoration, New York's 19th-century millionaires began raiding the art collections of Europe. One such was Henry Clay Frick, who acquired the phenomenal hoard now known as the **Frick Collection** (see page 110).

PATRONS Many affluent New Yorkers commissioned artists to paint their portraits, but one who did a great deal more to encourage the creativity of American artists was Gertrude Vanderbilt Whitney.

Displaying and promoting emergent artists such as Edward Hopper and John Sloan, Whitney also established an influential Parisian-style salon during the early 1900s. Her legacy, the **Whitney Museum of American Art** (page 191), continues to champion the country's unknown artists regardless of fashion and has many of the finest, long-established American artists of the 20th century represented among its permanent stock.

The Metropolitan Museum of Art

Art for Sale—a private SoHo gallery

> ❏ New York is said to be home to 90,000 artists and to hold over 1,000 art galleries. ❏

As Gertrude Whitney was busy furthering appreciation of American art, wealthy industrialist Solomon R. Guggenheim was discovering the art and artists of modern Europe. Guggenheim's purchases of early Cubist and abstract canvases were displayed on the walls of his suite at the Plaza Hotel and later became the basis of the **Guggenheim Museum** (pages 122–124). Frank Lloyd Wright designed the building, which is as remarkable as the innovative works of art it holds and worth a visit just to see the edifice.

AN INTERNATIONAL ART CENTER
As war loomed in Europe, New York found itself acquiring not only European art but European artists as well. By the 1940s, many of modern art's major names resided in the city, as an attempt to escape the fighting. They were to have a colossal impact on the New York art scene.

New York surpassed Paris (then under Nazi occupation) as the center for international art dealing and the city's preeminence was confirmed by the emergence of abstract expressionism (see pages 128–129). Meanwhile, the **Museum of Modern Art** (see pages 158–160), founded in 1929, was evolving into the world's most prestigious and most popular modern art museum.

NEW YORK NOW New York spawned pop art, op (or optical) art, which is designed to persuade the viewer that static images are in fact moving, and minimalist art during the 1960s, and by the late 1970s the shabby warehouses of SoHo (see page 175) had been transformed into pristine galleries showcasing new trends and new talents.

In the economically buoyant 1980s, New York art became big business. The artists in vogue then—Julian Schnabel, David Salle and Eric Fischl—could expect poverty to be a thing of the past.

Today, artist-run galleries can be found in the East Village, Chelsea and on the Lower East Side. While still energetically showcasing emerging New York artists, the larger galleries also reflect interest in the relatively under-acknowledged art of Latin America, Africa and Asia.

> ❏ Around the city you will find a veritable outdoor art museum. There are many public sculptures, but among the best are: Barbara Hepworth's 1964 *Single Form* by the pool of the UN Secretariat Building; Louise Nevelson's 1972 *Night Presence IV* on Park Avenue at 92nd Street; and Henry Moore's 1965 *Reclining Figure* at the reflecting pool in the Lincoln Center. ❏

Not only is New York the center of US publishing, it has also provided more material for 20th-century writers than perhaps any other city. Literary landmarks are plentiful and several New York neighborhoods have carved out special places for themselves in the annals of literary achievement.

A PUBLISHING CAPITAL Geography made New York the publishing capital of the US in the 1850s. Before the US recognized international copyright laws in 1891, any book could be copied, printed and sold, earning its publisher fat profits as no royalties were due.

To maximize earnings, publishers vied with one another to be first with the latest foreign manuscripts. As New York became the nation's major seaport, the city's publishers could get their hands on new books and produce pirate versions of them faster than rivals elsewhere.

THE CITY OBSERVED New York has long provided rich pickings for observant writers. From a bar-stool vantage point in the early 1900s, O. Henry (the pen name of William Sydney Porter) wrote short stories drawing on the seamy side of city life. In a similar vein a few decades later, the characters on

Damon Runyon

the fringes of Broadway theaterland were described by Damon Runyon. Truman Capote's *Breakfast at Tiffany's* was fine-tuned to 1950s New York high life, while J. D. Salinger's *Catcher in the Rye* followed its young narrator through a New York night and became a benchmark of adolescent angst.

The strains and stresses of 1980s New York underpinned Tom Wolfe's comic novel, *Bonfire of the Vanities* and the same decade saw the emergence of writers such as Tama Janowitz and Jay McInerney. Their cocaine-fueled tales were followed by more introspective, if similarly drug-centered work, such as Elizabeth Wurtzel's *Prozac Nation*. The 1990s ended with Kurt Andersen's *Turn of the Century*, satirizing New Yorkers' attempts to reconcile morals and money, a theme taken and twisted in 2004 by Plum Sykes's *Bergdorf Blondes*.

❏ Born in Manhattan in 1783, Washington Irving might well be considered New York's first home-grown writer. His satirical *A History of New York* was written under the memorable pseudonym of Diedrich Knickerbocker. ❏

LITERARY NEIGHBORHOODS In the mid-1880s, New York literary life revolved around the fashionable drawing rooms of Greenwich Village town houses, where heavyweights like James Fenimore Cooper rubbed shoulders with the publishers of literary journals. Such times were described in Edith Wharton's *The Age*

*Washington Square and (below right)
Henry James*

❏ Rejected writers in New York have included some notable names. Born in Lower Manhattan in 1819, Herman Melville was a customs officer on the East River after his *Moby Dick* received scathing reviews. Only after his death was it acclaimed as a masterpiece. Edgar Allan Poe's poems and short stories were admired in Europe, but in New York he scraped a living from journalism before dying in a state presumed to be drunkenness. Walt Whitman penned eulogies to Manhattan and the Brooklyn Bridge in the 1840s, but every publisher in the city turned down *Leaves of Grass*, eventually acknowledged as one of the great works of American poetry. ❏

of Innocence and by Henry James in *Washington Square.*

As Greenwich Village rents fell, it drew a host of talented but impoverished writers—as diverse as Willa Cather, John Reed, Theodore Drieser, John Dos Passos, Robert Frost, Eugene O'Neill and Thomas Wolfe—who left the area filled with literary landmarks (see pages 112–118). The East Village and the Lower East Side began attracting impecunious scribes in the 1950s, when Beat writers such as William Burroughs and Allen Ginsberg moved in alongside émigrés such as W.H. Auden. Another arrival was Norman Mailer, who had previously lived in Brooklyn Heights (where he currently lives). Mass African-American migration into Harlem helped to stimulate the Harlem Renaissance of the 1920s, bringing black writers such as Langston Hughes and Zora Neale Hurston to public notice. In the 1950s, Harlem-born James Baldwin created a stir with *Go Tell It on the Mountain* as did Ralph Ellison with *The Invisible Man.* More recently, Chester Himes used Harlem as the setting for a series of thrillers.

A history of New York's Jewish population can be found in *World of Our Fathers*, by Irving Howe; *Call It Sleep*, by Henry Roth; *The Promise*, by Chaim Potok; *The Assistant*, by Bernard Malamud and *Enemies, a Love Story*, by Isaac Bashevis Singer.

The Manhattan skyline is the stuff of dreams. The city's colonial structures may have almost vanished, but New York's existing buildings are a thrilling mixture, encompassing styles from the country's formative years to the contemporary adventures in postmodernism.

THE FEDERAL STYLE From 1760 to 1830, the Federal style became the first genuine American building style, though it drew heavily on British Georgian and treated public buildings to columns and domes reminiscent of ancient Rome: **City Hall** (see page 89) is a prime example.

Federal-style applied to residential architecture was distinguished by duplex houses of brick and wood, with fanlights above the entrances and dormer windows. **Gracie Mansion** (see page 111) is one example. A grander specimen is the former James Watson residence, now the **Shrine of Elizabeth Ann Seton** (see page 66).

> ❏ The zoning law of 1916, which outlawed new buildings rising sheer from their plot to rob the streets of light, shaped the look of the Manhattan skyscraper. The law led to the widespread use of cutbacks (also called step-backs), a tapering effect that has been interpreted by architects in various ways and perhaps most memorably demonstrated by the well-known profile of the Empire State Building. ❏

REVIVALS As New York enjoyed an economic surge during the 19th century, the Greek revival style—bringing floral-patterned ironwork and porticoes to the facades of the new rows of town houses, such as those facing **Washington Square Park**—was the first of a spate of revivals, which included Italianate, Renaissance and Gothic.

BROWNSTONES A cheap form of sandstone quarried in New Jersey, brownstone was used to build swiftly and at low cost during the mid-1800s and brownstone town houses became the main residences of the middle classes. Brownstones enjoyed a surge of popularity from the 1950s and those that remain are highly prized.

LUXURY APARTMENT HOUSES By the turn of the century, property prices in Midtown Manhattan had risen beyond the pockets of the middle classes, who began colonizing the new luxury apartments on the Upper West Side. Sumptuously appointed and with anything up to 10 rooms, the apartments also boasted futuristic extras such as built-in refrigerators and pneumatic mail-delivery systems. The **Dakota** (see page 96) was the first such building; several others remain nearby.

EARLY SKYSCRAPERS The **Flatiron Building** (see page 106) was the city's first "world's-tallest" structure and was also the first to be supported by a steel frame—a technique that showed the way for creating even taller buildings. A 1920s building boom gave Manhattan the **Chrysler** and **Empire State buildings**, both of which not only reached record

heights but bore the hallmarks of art deco (see pages 162–163).

THE INTERNATIONAL STYLE The towers of steel and glass above Manhattan resulted from the arrival in New York of Europe's most creative architects, who fled Nazism and brought with them the antitraditional ideas of the International Style.

The **Museum of Modern Art**, its original facade designed by Goodwin and Stone in 1939, gave New York a taste of the International Style. Among later examples was Mies van der Rohe's 1958 **Seagram Building** (Park Avenue between 52nd and 53rd streets), which gave New York its first plaza.

THE 1980S BOOM In the 1980s, Manhattan gained its first modern buildings not bearing the International-Style stamp. Philip Johnson's **AT&T Building** (Madison Avenue between 55th and 56th streets) became known as the Chippendale skyscraper and the

❏ The beaux-arts style arrived in New York in 1890 and is exemplified by Carrère and Hastings' **New York Public Library** (see page 168), Cass Gilbert's **US Custom House** (see page 190) and works by the firm of McKim, Mead, & White, such as **Washington Memorial Arch** (see page 116). ❏

World Financial Center filled its atrium with palm trees.

THE 1990S AND BEYOND Regeneration of neighborhoods was a key theme of the 1990s. The new millennium saw the **Rose Center for Earth and Space** (see page 64), an enlarged Museum of Modern Art, and plans for a new Guggenheim Museum and the Freedom Tower, due to rise on the World Trade Center site.

The Chrysler Building and its futuristic neighbors

There is usually some kind of festival taking place in New York, whether a traffic-stopping parade along Fifth Avenue or a low-key neighborhood get-together. These are just a few highlights from an exceptionally busy festivals and events calendar. For precise dates and details, check the local newspapers or contact the New York Convention and Visitors' Bureau (tel: 484-1222 or 800/NYC-VISIT).

JANUARY
Chinese New Year Celebrated by giant dragon and lion dances through the streets of Chinatown. Festive banquets are offered by the neighborhood's restaurants. (The exact date of this depends on the lunar cycle; however, it usually takes place in February.)

❏ With a 150-year history, the St. Patrick's Day Parade (along Fifth Avenue between 44th and 86th streets) is by far the biggest of New York's parades.

Green proliferates in many of the city's bars, which often mark the day with a variety of special events, as do other institutions through the city.

Tens of thousands take part in the parade itself and many more join in other St. Patrick's Day-related activities. ❏

Winter Antiques Fair At Seventh Regiment Armory, Park Avenue at East 66th Street. Upscale antiques and their dealers; browsers are also welcome (see page 226).

FEBRUARY
Black History Month Lectures and exhibitions on African-American themes are held throughout the city.
Empire State Building Run-Up Indoor joggers dash from the landmark building's lobby to its 86th floor by way of 1,575 stairs; the winner usually climbs all the steps in approximately 12 minutes.

MARCH
Greek Independence Day Parade On Fifth Avenue between 59th and 79th streets. Honors the regaining of Greek independence in 1821: a sea of blue and white as school bands and

Chinese New Year celebrations: the Lion Dance

Greek-Americans dressed in their national costume march jovially along the route.

Parade of Circus Animals
Creatures from the Ringling Bros. and Barnum & Bailey Circus trek from a railroad siding at Twelfth Avenue and 34th Street to Madison Square Garden.

St. Patrick's Day Parade (see previous page).

Check the daily papers for parade routes and arrive early for the best view

❑ The Puerto Rican Day Parade, along Fifth Avenue between 44th and 86th streets on the first Sunday in June, brings New York's huge Puerto Rican population onto the streets to celebrate their nation's Independence Day. Red, white and blue Puerto Rican flags are everywhere, traditional foods are sold from stalls, and live bands playing on floats provide a nonstop soundtrack of salsa music to wildly appreciative audiences. ❑

APRIL
Easter Day Parade Participants stroll on Fifth Avenue near St. Patrick's Cathedral wearing extravagant Easter bonnets. On the Saturday before Easter a children's egg-rolling contest takes place on Central Park's Great Lawn. Check out Macy's first floor the week before Easter—it's wall-to-wall flowers.

Japanese Cherry Blossom Festival
Highlights bloomtime in Central Park's Conservatory Garden and at the Brooklyn Botanic Garden.

MAY
Martin Luther King Memorial Day Parade Along Fifth Avenue from 44th to 86th streets. Marchers celebrate the life and achievements of the civil rights leader and highlight other African-American issues.

Ninth Avenue International Food Festival A two-day feast of the city's ethnic cuisines, on Ninth Avenue between 37th and 57th streets.

27

Ukrainian Festival In the East Village along 7th Street on the weekend closest to May 17: traditional foods, crafts and folk dancing.

Washington Square Outdoor Arts Show A gathering of local artists showing and selling their wares over three successive weekends.

JUNE
American Crafts Festival Lincoln Center. Over two successive weekends, exhibitors from all over the country show their skills.

Welcome to Brooklyn Festival Stalls and events along Eastern Parkway provide a focal-point while happenings throughout the borough mark local history and culture.

Feast of St. Anthony of Padua Little Italy. More restrained than the neighborhood's Feast of St. Gennaro (see September), with food stalls along Sullivan Street, the feast culminates with an image of the saint carried through the streets after dark.

Puerto Rican Day Parade See box.

Lesbian and Gay Pride Day Parade
Along Fifth Avenue to Washington Square Park and around Greenwich Village. New York's gay and lesbian community stands together for this assertion of strength through unity.

Museum Mile Celebration The museums ranged along Fifth Avenue hold special events and stay open later than usual.

The Metropolitan Opera A number of free performances in city parks, including Central Park; continues all through the summer.

Shakespeare in the Park Staged for free at Central Park's Delacorte Theater throughout the summer.

SummerStage Varied events at Central Park's Naumburg Bandshell during July and August.

JULY

Feast of O-Bon Japanese music and dance in the Upper West Side's Riverside Park, timed to mark the full moon.

Independence Day celebrations Including Macy's firework display, the site of which varies.

The horrors of Halloween

Mostly Mozart Festival At Lincoln Center's Avery Fisher Hall (see page 235); continues into August.

AUGUST

Harlem Week A two-week celebration of Harlem's history and culture.

New York Philharmonic Open-air concerts in city parks.

SEPTEMBER

New York Is Book Country Fifth Avenue between 48th and 59th streets. Major—as well as numerous minor—publishers are represented at stalls along the avenue and many well-known authors give readings and signings.

New York Film Festival At Lincoln Center (see page 234).

Feast of St. Gennaro Lasts ten days along Little Italy's Mulberry Street. Makeshift kitchens serve sausages and hunks of pizza; final night sees a shrine to the saint carried through the streets and showered with dollar bills. (See also page 135.)

Washington Square Outdoor Art Show Stands with locals' artworks and ethnic food sold from stalls.

OCTOBER

Columbus Day Parade Fifth Avenue between 44th and 72nd streets. As awareness of indigenous American cultures grows throughout the US, this parade to commemorate Christopher Columbus' "discovery" of the New World has become increasingly controversial. Many Native American and Hispanic groups—and others—actively oppose the event.

Halloween Parade Outrageous drag queens and others in freakish costumes parade up Sixth Avenue in Greenwich Village to Washington Square Park.

NOVEMBER

New York Marathon From Verrazano-Narrows Bridge to Central Park's Tavern on the Green, through all five boroughs.

Macy's Thanksgiving Day Parade Along Central Park West and Broadway starring the famous helium-filled balloons. The area around the American Museum of Natural History is mobbed the night before when the balloons are inflated.

DECEMBER

Rockefeller Center The lighting of the Rockefeller Center Christmas Tree in December begins NYC's festive season, when many stores mount magical window displays.

❏ Thousands of New Yorkers gather in Times Square to see in the New Year. As midnight approaches, an illuminated ball (disguised as a big apple) slides down Times Tower. ❏

During the 16th century, the eastern seaboard of North America was steadily explored by European seafarers, not with the expectation of locating the site of the future major metropolis but in the hope of finding the North West Passage—a shortcut to the spice islands of the Pacific. Many years were to elapse between the European discovery of the land that now holds New York and its eventual settlement.

EARLY EXPLORERS The first European sighting of what became New York was made in 1524 by Giovanni da Verrazano, a Florentine merchant employed by the French. Verrazano described the land he found as having "commodiousness and beauty" and its native inhabitants uttering "loud cries of wonderment" as they spotted the vessels of the Europeans.

It was not until 1609 that a more thorough navigation of the area was made, this time by Henry Hudson, an Englishman working for the Dutch East India Company. Hudson's voyage was made along the river that now bears his name as far north as present-day Albany.

New Amsterdam (New York), 1673

❏ Before European settlement, the New York area was inhabited by several Native American groups, most being of the Algonquin tribe. The Native Americans, who survived by farming, hunting and fishing, did not share the European concept of land ownership but they did share the European enthusiasm for trading, which helped keep early relations fairly cordial.

A sustained series of Dutch-led attacks eventually forced the natives away from the settled areas. European diseases, to which Native Americans lacked immunity, also took their toll. ❏

30

Like Verrazano, Hudson failed to find the fabled North West Passage, but he did note that the Native Americans were rich in beaver, mink and otter pelts and were also eager to trade them.

THE FIRST NEW YORKERS Attracted by the prospect of commerce with the Native Americans, the Dutch West India Company was founded in Amsterdam and launched several North American settlements. In 1625, one such settlement—named

The arrival of Henry Hudson in 1609 at the mouth of what is now the Hudson River

New Amsterdam—was founded in what is now Lower Manhattan. It was made up of Dutch and French-speaking Walloon families and their African slaves. In 1626, the leader of the Dutch colony, Peter Minuit, bought Manhattan (a native term possibly meaning "Island of Hills") from a local tribe for a box of tools and trinkets worth the equivalent of $24.

Though established as a colonial trading base, Dutch New Amsterdam—soon to become British New York—quickly acquired a charac-ter of its own, partly through the ethnic and religious diversity of its inhabitants and partly through the fact that many of them came to share a desire to rid themselves of their Old World links for good.

NEW AMSTERDAM—SUCCESS AND FAILURE Much to the delight of the Dutch West India Company, New Amsterdam soon began to flourish as a trading center. New settlers arrived, taking advantage of the com-pany's generous land grants. Some came to escape religious persecution, seeking the freedom of worship that the company had promised.

New Amsterdam was far from being the tranquil replica of a Dutch town that the company might have hoped for, however. Violence and lawlessness were rife, unmarried couples cohabited, pigs ran wild in the streets and—with a tavern for every 12 adults—many of the population spent their spare time drinking to excess.

A NEW GOVERNOR In 1647, the corrupt governor was dismissed and the job of bringing order to bear on the wayward colony was given to a noted disciplinarian, Peter Stuyvesant. Under his iron rule, and with a new city charter providing for elected officials, New Amsterdam doubled in population and in size, gaining its first hospital, prison, school, post office, and its first real commer-cial institutions.

The colony also gained a protective northern wall, which would later prove ineffectual at halting British advances but did give rise to the thoroughfare named Wall Street.

Peter Stuyvesant

THE BRITISH ARRIVE Stuyvesant's unpopularity, coupled with excessive tax demands by the Dutch West India Company, caused the population of New Amsterdam to offer no resistance when four British warships blockaded the harbor in 1664. Under British rule, the colony was renamed New York, after James, Duke of York, brother of King Charles II.

Set between the major British bases to the south and north, and at the mouth of the strategically important Hudson River, it is not surprising that New York became a prominent sea-port. Nonetheless, the British proved no more able to stamp their authority on the everyday life of the colony than had the Dutch, and New York remained as socially robust as ever.

By 1700 New York had acquired a population numbering 20,000, com-posed of a mix of nationalities and a variety of religions.

THE AMERICAN REVOLUTION After the 1763 Treaty of Paris confirmed their dominance over the 13 American colonies, the British imposed a series of punitive taxes on the settlements. Previous anticolonial uprisings had been quashed by the British, but with the world entering a postcolonial age and the theories of republicanism being universally discussed, the idea of independence became increas-ingly attractive to the economically thriving colonies.

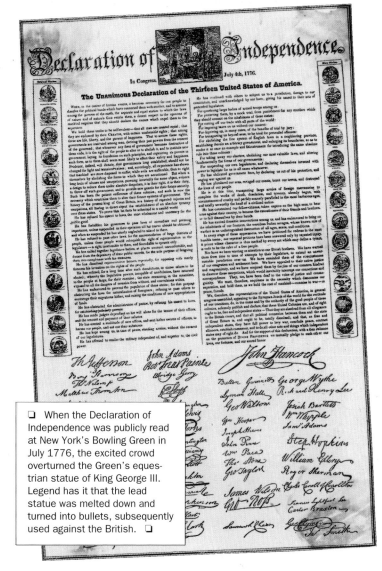

The Declaration of Independence

33

❏ When the Declaration of Independence was publicly read at New York's Bowling Green in July 1776, the excited crowd overturned the Green's equestrian statue of King George III. Legend has it that the lead statue was melted down and turned into bullets, subsequently used against the British. ❏

Following the Declaration of Independence in 1776, General George Washington led the war against the British. Many British troops were billeted in New York, where they commandeered food supplies, terrorized locals and imprisoned captured rebel prisoners on board ships in which hunger and disease were rife.

New York was to remain the last toehold of British rule in the New World. Although the 1783 Treaty of Paris formally ended the War of Independence, it was not until Washington's march from Harlem down to the Bowery in November of that same year that the last remnants of the British troops were finally withdrawn from the area.

The last act of defiance carried out by the British was to grease the flagpole to hinder the raising of the Stars and Stripes.

As the country's major seaport, New York was the gateway to the New World. Through the 19th century it received the largest migration in human history: a mass movement of people which not only transformed the city but shaped the future of the entire nation.

New York's population had been markedly cosmopolitan from the earliest days of settlement, and a steady influx of immigrants continued after the Revolution.

Some new arrivals were attracted by the prospect of shaping the first democratic mixed-nationality society, others were radical intellectual rebels driven into exile by governments who feared them, and a few were simply adventurers or fortune-seekers.

In the mid-19th century, however, came the great waves of mass immigration into New York that were to change the city completely.

MASS MIGRATIONS There were three major factors all of which contributed to the mass waves of European migration into New York during the first half of the 19th century: the social upheaval which had been caused by the Napoleonic wars, the potato famines in Ireland and Germany and the industrial revolution, which spread across Europe and robbed many skilled craftsmen and farmers of their livelihoods.

Arriving in the New World: an engraving of 1892

❏ Immigration into 19th-century New York:
1820s 150,000
1840s 1.7 million
1850s 2.5 million ❏

On the receiving end of a mass movement of people on a scale never before known, New York's overstretched Castle Garden (now called Castle Clinton) immigrant processing center was replaced in 1890 by the federally funded Ellis Island complex. The new receiving center, which was a pristine, state-of-the-art affair, was a far cry from the slums that awaited most new arrivals once they set foot in New York as American citizens.

While not all of the new arrivals stayed in New York, many did; and they placed a massive burden on the city's resources. The 1860s saw the creation of tenements in an effort to fit more people into small areas—five- or six-story buildings where an entire family would sometimes occupy a single windowless room. These tenements earned the nickname "lung blocks" due to the high incidence of tuberculosis among their inhabitants. Inadequate drainage and sewage systems made diseases such as yellow fever and cholera a constant threat.

In a city of immigrants, a mix of guile, initiative and extremely hard work in appalling conditions usually bore rewards and the major ethnic groups became assimilated and began climbing the city's social ladder comparatively swiftly (particularly as child immigrants reached adulthood fully conversant with the ways of the New World).

The northward spread of Manhattan's grid-style streets was matched by a steady northward flow of wealth. As the city's rich occupied the newest, most northerly homes, their previous dwellings were occupied by prospering ethnic groups while the poor—the latest

immigrants—were housed in the south, usually in the tenements of the Lower East Side.

ANTI-IMMIGRATION LAWS
Established and powerful groups campaigned for tighter immigration controls. They feared loss of jobs, the spread of disease and the decline of Anglo-Saxon supremacy (after the Revolution, 60 percent of Americans had been of English origin). In 1882, the Chinese Exclusion Act banned further Chinese immigration into the US The Act reflected an anti-Chinese feeling that also led to lurid stories about New York's Chinatown.

The US entered the 20th century as the world's richest industrial power and the calls for protecting its economic position and well-being grew much stronger.

The outbreak of World War I encouraged the isolationist stance that paved the way for the immigration curbs of the 1920s (although the granting of US citizenship to Puerto Ricans in 1917 was an exception). Mass immigration as seen in earlier decades came to an end.

35

❑ Immigration into New York is not a thing of the past. Easing of immigration restrictions in the 1960s caused a dramatic expansion of Chinatown (where many inhabitants are now actually Vietnamese or Cambodian). Indians, Koreans, West Indians, Filipinos, Latinos, Middle Eastern nationals and Eastern Europeans from the former Iron Curtain countries are among the 90,000 people who still settle in New York every year. ❑

Seldom has the entrepreneur (or the rogue) had such opportunities to make a name and a fortune for himself as in 19th-century New York. The city, rapidly evolving from an outpost to a great metropolis, was alive with speculation, sharp dealing and money-making. From those heady times, a handful of names are still remembered—fondly or otherwise.

JOHN JACOB ASTOR (1763–1848)

A fur-trade millionaire, John Jacob Astor switched his attentions to property in 1834, buying New York land while currying favor with city politicians and ingratiating himself into New York high society. Profits from slum housing helped Astor become the country's richest man by the time he died in 1848. In a rare act of generosity, however, Astor bequeathed $400,000 for the creation of the US's first public library, now the Public Theater in the East Village.

ANDREW CARNEGIE (1835–1919)

Andrew Carnegie started in industry as a cotton-factory worker and rose to become a magnate with interests spanning iron, coal, steel, ships, and railroads. Believing in the motto "a man who dies rich, dies disgraced," Carnegie financed numerous trusts, some 2,000 libraries, and gave $2 million for the building of Carnegie Hall—yet still had $23 million when he died in 1919. The Carnegie mansion on Fifth Avenue is now the home of the Cooper-Hewitt National Design Museum.

From mill-worker to multimillionaire: Andrew Carnegie

❏ When Caroline Schermerhorn married into the Astor family in 1853, she became the fabled "Mrs Astor," a New York high-society legend whose annual balls were regarded as the city's definitive social barometer. The 400 people invited (the number of people in New York who, it was thought, would fit into her ballroom) could consider themselves "in"; those not invited—which included anyone who worked for a living or who had made their millions through railroads—were definitely "out." ❏

HENRY CLAY FRICK (1849–1919)

A partner of Andrew Carnegie in the Carnegie Steel Company, Henry Clay Frick was credited with few redeeming qualities. He instigated the blackest event in the history of US labor relations: hiring a mob to bring a steel-mill strike to a violent and murderous end. Some of Frick's fortunes went into acquiring the great stash of European art that now forms the Frick Collection, housed in his Fifth Avenue mansion (see page 110).

JAY GOULD (1836–1892)

Robber baron, dealer and socialite, Jay Gould made his first fortune at 21. He would bet on the outcome of Civil War battles, having learned the result by tapping telegraph lines. In 1869 he manipulated the price of gold, made himself a hefty profit of $11 million on the gold market and brought about the calamitous "Black Friday" financial crash.

36

JOHN PIERPONT MORGAN

(1837–1913) Much of the European money invested in the US during the 19th century was channeled through banker and financier John Pierpont Morgan. Able to wield influence on every new project that needed money, Morgan gained considerable wealth and importance. He had a finger in every entrepreneurial pie and oversaw the creation of the US Steel Corporation, which became the world's first billion-dollar business in 1901.

Morgan spent $25 million buying gold to help save New York—and the nation—from bankruptcy in 1907. He is the founder of the library that carries his name: the Pierpont Morgan Library (see page 169).

CORNELIUS VANDERBILT

(1794–1877) Beginning with a ferry service between Staten Island and Manhattan in the early 1800s, Cornelius Vanderbilt built a steamship empire that dominated transportation across New York Bay and plied routes as far afield as Latin America and—at the height of the Gold Rush—to California. In 1864, Vanderbilt diversified, placing some of his $20 million into railroads. Tracks were laid that linked the steel-producing factories of Pittsburgh and the dairy farms of rural New York state to the city's docks, where his cargo ships awaited loading: Vanderbilt had once again cornered the market.

When he died in 1877, Vanderbilt was worth $105 million.

> ❏ J. P. Morgan fully deserved his reputation as a hard-headed businessman, but he regularly consulted society astrologist Evangeline Adams before making decisions. Evidence of the banker's interest in astrology is easy to find at the Pierpont Morgan Library, where symbols of the zodiac are incorporated into the lavish decoration. ❏

37

The Pierpont Morgan Library

Unusually for a major city, the pattern of New York's expansion is easy to trace. The city's growth was a simple case of the long, narrow island of Manhattan being smothered with urban development, starting at one end and working systematically toward the other.

The European settlement of the island of Manhattan began at its southern tip, the easiest place for ships to berth. Here the first businesses and homes became established. As the settlement grew, therefore, it could only expand northward. In the process, it acquired the haphazard street pattern which remains largely intact in today's Financial District.

THE GRID PLAN In 1811, the Board of Commissioners ratified a rectangular, grid-style street plan formulated by a surveyor, John Randel. Ignoring all existing streets except for Broadway—a track that followed an ancient Native American route—the design called for numbered streets (intended for residence) running east–west and numbered avenues (intended for commerce) running north–south.

The new Brooklyn Bridge must have seemed a miracle in its day

The grid plan provided a blueprint for Manhattan's development. In 1820, with a population of 123,000, New York was already the US's largest city, despite barely extending beyond Canal Street. North of Canal Street, a few villages had taken root in what are now Chelsea and Greenwich Village, and the areas that now comprise the Upper East Side and the Upper West Side were a mixture of farms, wasteland and squatters' camps.

When the Erie Canal opened in 1825, it linked New York to the Great Lakes and the agriculturally productive Midwest and left the city unchallenged as the major American seaport—the gateway to lucrative international trade. This, coupled with the waves of mass immigration, which began in the 1840s, set the scene for New York's rapid expansion throughout the 19th century.

élite. By the 1860s, several hundred millionaires were calling Manhattan home. Many of them occupied the luxury apartment houses recently erected along Fifth Avenue, facing the newly created Central Park—and the Upper East Side became the lasting domain of the rich.

A METROPOLIS IS BORN Steadily, the city gained an infrastructure worthy of the metropolis it was becoming. In 1868, the first "El" (or Elevated) train went into service. Two years later the first subway line was drilled. Work on the Brooklyn Bridge—the engineering miracle of its day—began in 1870 and was completed in 1883. Thomas Edison's company began the electrification of the city, opening its first generating station in 1882.

In 1898, the creation of Greater New York linked the five boroughs—Manhattan, Brooklyn, the Bronx, Queens and Staten Island—under a single municipal government. New York City's population was now 3.8 million, making it the second largest city in the world.

39

Harlem was speedily developed by 19th-century speculators

MONEY MOVES NORTH Property developers wasted little time in moving northward through Manhattan, flattening hilly land and erecting new buildings. In the mid-1800s, the first of the city's handsome brownstones appeared, which provided comfortable accommodations for New York's expanding moneyed classes on the city's northerly fringes.

In the Lower East Side, meanwhile, the first tenement houses were erected, sheltering penniless immigrants and swiftly maturing into desperate slums.

As its poor toiled in sweatshops, New York generated incredible wealth for its already well-heeled

❏ When work began on New York's City Hall in 1803, the building stood on what was then the city's northern edge. Marble was used for the building's front and sides, but the north-facing rear was made from cheap red sandstone in the expectation that nobody would ever see it. Such was the rate of New York's expansion, however, that by the time of its completion in 1812, City Hall was already encircled by new buildings. ❏

The USA's early years were colored by frequent financial uncertainties, but none of the early banking troubles quite prepared the city for "Black Tuesday," the Wall Street crash of 1929, which dragged the country—and the world—into the Depression.

New York lasted only a year as the capital of the US, but the financial institutions on and around Wall Street—most notably the Stock Exchange, which began as a trading place for the $80 million-worth of bonds created to pay Revolutionary War debts—remained at the heart of the nation's monetary system.

As unscrupulous investors played on the insecurities and inexperience inherent in the new nation's financial systems, crashes were numerous. The panic of 1837 wiped $60 billion off the value of shares and left 50,000 people without jobs; 20 years later, another crash put 40,000 out of work. A further stock-market tumble occurred in 1873 and in 1907 New York's banks had to be saved from insolvency by the wealthy financier J. P. Morgan.

THE ROARING TWENTIES As the federal government came to replace independent financiers and the US emerged from World War I as a rich and powerful nation, financial uncertainties seemed to be very much a thing of the past.

The economy boomed and rumors of fortunes being made overnight caused the stock market to trade faster than ever before, its ticker-tape machines struggling to keep up with the developments.

Even economically irrelevant events, such as Charles Lindbergh's successful first solo flight across the Atlantic in 1927, were enough to quicken dealing. Trading levels regularly broke new records during 1928.

THE CRASH OF 1929 Although the warning signals had been observed—industrial production was declining and the economy was beginning to stagnate—few people paid any heed

until the third week of October 1929 when everyone began selling at once. Millions of shares were traded at a loss, causing 11 dealers to kill themselves and the date 29 October 1929, to go down in history as "Black Tuesday"—the day the Depression began.

> ❏ "Sooner or later a crash is coming, and it may be terrific"—financial expert Roger W. Babson, speaking in September 1929. ❏

By 1932, the Depression's bleakest year, more than a third of New York's 29,000 manufacturing firms had closed down, leaving a quarter of the city's work force idle. Many people, unable to afford rent, lived in the shanty towns that appeared in Central Park (dubbed "Hoovervilles" after the incumbent president, Herbert Hoover) and lined up for free food provided by soup kitchens.

Many of the city's most enduring skyscrapers had appeared through the buoyant 1920s, but now the building boom ground to a halt. The Empire State Building, opened in 1931, had to pay for its upkeep on the proceeds of tourist visits rather than office rents.

LA GUARDIA LEADS RECOVERY
For New Yorkers, the woes of the Depression were made worse by the incompetence of their mayor, Jimmy Walker, better known for his songwriting skills than for his political abilities. Not the first—nor the last—city mayor to be embroiled in a corruption scandal, Walker departed from office in 1932 and fled to Europe. His replacement was Fiorello

La Guardia, a young, credible politician who pledged to end corruption and lead the city out of the Depression.

While La Guardia engineered the social policies which did lift New York from the Depression, it was Robert Moses who oversaw city planning and development from the 1930s to the 1960s and gave New York a new look. Old neighborhoods were razed to make way for the expressways, tunnels and bridges of the modern city, as well as for specific projects that included the creation of the Lincoln Center and Battery Park City.

Below: the drama of the Wall Street crash, as illustrated by an Italian magazine of the day

Staged in Queens, the 1939 World's Fair was intended to be a symbol of New York's emergence from the Depression, but it was the country's entry into World War II in 1941 that really restored the city's finances, as tens of thousands of soldiers and streams of tanks, trucks and planes passed through New York on their way to Europe.

❏   In 1940, the capital budget of New York City was $1.   ❏

Police being paid off by criminals and the mayor using public funds for private gain are enduring images of New York—and with good reason. Corruption was part of New York life from the city's earliest days and has proved hard to shake off, even in recent times.

THE TWEED RING A former volunteer fireman and street-gang member, William Marcy "Boss" Tweed got himself elected in 1851, age 21, as assistant alderman to a council body popularly nicknamed "The 40 Thieves."

Tweed quickly rose to the top of the thuggish faction of New York's Democratic Party (called Tammany after a Native American chief) by promising (and delivering) jobs and money to people—often freshly arrived immigrants—in return for votes.

The administration was soon under the thumb of the "Tweed Ring," a coterie of corrupt officials who, during their brief reign, are estimated to have helped themselves to $300 million of public money. As commissioner of public works, Tweed extracted fat commissions from construction companies as a reward for giving them lucrative contracts and extorted large sums from businesses in return for providing essential services. A share of the ill-gotten gains was earmarked for bribes to the police and others, to dissuade them from speaking up.

Tweed's most spectacular swindle involved the construction of the New York County Courthouse (now known informally as the Tweed Courthouse). Having started in 1862 with a budget of $250,000, the courthouse eventually cost New York taxpayers $14 million, of which the Tweed Ring creamed off around $12 million.

Eventually, an angry City Hall clerk (who is said to have been offered a $500,000 bribe to keep quiet) passed incriminating documents to *The New York Times*. While in jail, Tweed was allowed out each day for lunch and escaped to Chile before being recaptured. He died in 1878, in a jail which his corrupt regime had commissioned.

THE "BRAINS"

The secret of success: one 1871 cartoonist's view

❏ Since most of the people who voted for him were illiterate, Tweed claimed to have little interest in what newspapers wrote. He considered the satirical cartoons published in *Harper's Weekly*—which he called "them damn pictures"—to be more damaging to his career than reports on his dirty dealings documented in words. ❏

Mayor William O'Dwyer at his desk in City Hall (below)

MAYORS Quaker Fernando Wood was viewed as the man who would end corruption at City Hall in 1844, despite previous accusations of fraud and the fact that he was elected mayor with more votes than there were voters. In fact, Wood sold the job of city commissioner for $50,000 and provided guarantees of natural-ization to immigrants in return for their electoral favors.

A symbol of the booming 1920s, songwriter and playboy Jimmy Walker was elected mayor in 1925. Walker dressed in white suits, frequented nightclubs, and never arrived for work until the afternoon. After raising his own salary from $25,000 to $40,000, Walker skipped town in 1932 as the news broke that he had taken $1 million in payoffs for city contracts.

After the term of the admired mayor Fiorello La Guardia, it was dirty business as usual at City Hall. The subsequent incumbent, William O'Dwyer, made a swift exit to Mexico in 1951 as his links with organized crime were about to be exposed.

THE POLICE In a city corrupt from head to toe, it was little surprise that 19th-century New York police similarly veered off the straight and narrow. Patrolmen routinely acted as

paid lookouts for illegal gambling dens and brothels, while higher ranks improved their salaries with bribes and the proceeds of bank robberies. Crimes were liable to "disappear" in return for payments and many rob-beries were investigated only if a reward was offered.

Actual arrests were usually intended to improve the appearance of the city for its affluent classes, removing any "lewd women," beggars, or homeless people from well-to-do areas.

Within the force, payments secured a popular beat and would bring promotion. According to a newspaper report of 1892, a fee of $300 was required to become a patrol-man, while $14,000 was the asking price for a precinct captain's job.

It may be a bastion of big business, high finance, the media and the arts, but New York's lofty position in the hierarchy of world cities is largely due to the simple matter of possessing an outstanding natural harbor. This stroke of geographical good fortune made possible its rise from an obscure colonial trading post to the world's greatest port.

EARLY DAYS New York's discovery by Europeans stemmed from the search for the North West Passage, a shortcut to the Spice Islands of the Pacific. Early explorers did not find the shortcut, but they did record that New York Bay provided a safe, sheltered anchorage in an area that enjoyed a comparatively mild climate and was relatively free of fog. With the Hudson River, the bay also provided access to a navigable route inland.

Even so, New York was but one of several moderately busy ports on the continent's east coast and was fortunate when the British—then ruling over the American colonies—chose it in preference to Boston as the main recipient of their exports.

THE ERIE CANAL The trigger of New York's phenomenal rise as a seaport—and its subsequent emergence as a major world city—was the building of the Erie Canal. The Hudson River provided a transportation route between the city and the

44

❏ New York's waterside streets were traditionally among the dirtiest, most dangerous and crime-ridden in the city. The glamour accorded to Fifth Avenue partially derived from its geographical position: plumb in the center of Manhattan and as far from the rivers as it was possible to be. ❏

upstate farms (and the important towns of New England), but the Erie Canal—begun in 1817 and completed in 1825 at a cost of $7 million—connected the Hudson to Lake Erie and thereby opened a swift, direct line of communication between New York and, via the Great Lakes, the newly settled farmlands of the Midwest.

Using the canal, the 500-mile (804-km) journey between Buffalo (on Lake Erie) and the city could be completed

Manhattan and several of its numerous busy piers in the 1860s

The 20th-century port: South Street Seaport today (above) and (right) the Queen Mary *at 51st Street Pier*

in ten days. With the American heartland opened up, ships from almost every nation converged on New York bearing products destined for the interior.

THE PORT EXPANDS By the turn of the 20th century, the southern end of Manhattan was lined by 22 miles (35km) of docks, with 270 piers extending along both the East River and the Hudson River.

The advent of the railroads did more to improve New York's transportation links. Many freight lines ran directly to the docks, while Grand Central Station (now Grand Central Terminal) became the country's foremost rail passenger station.

By the 1930s, "the freighter, the river boat, the ferry and the soot-faced tug" plied the city's rivers—making the Hudson River itself barely viewable below 23rd Street. These craft were among the 3,500 vessels that berthed in New York each month.

OCEAN-GOING LUXURY Cargo may have been the bread and butter of the city's docks, but its place among the world's great ports was symbolized by the graceful ocean liners of the 1910s to the 1950s. Greeted by low-flying planes and water jets, the *Queen Mary* arrived in New York for

the first time in 1936 as one of several vessels regularly ferrying the rich and famous between Europe and the US, where New York welcomed them in a blaze of publicity.

GRADUAL DECLINE Changing patterns in international trade caused New York's port to lose its commercial importance. Also the rising popularity of air travel reduced the demand for ocean-going liners and the great passenger ships made their last farewells to New York, although the *QE2* (as well as modern cruise ships) is still a regular visitor. Nonetheless, the city's port is the third busiest in the US (after New Orleans and Houston) and annually handles around 118 million tons of freight. Meanwhile, the fall in passenger routes failed to deter the construction of a new passenger ship terminal on the Hudson River in 1974.

Nobody waking up on 11 September 2001, an ordinary Tuesday, was remotely prepared for what was about to happen: New York City and Washington D.C. were under terrorist attack, and the world stood still to watch the tragedy unfold.

Just before 9am, TV and radio programs were interrupted: A plane had flown into the north tower of the World Trade Center, ripping a great burning gash in its top floors. Then, exactly 15 minutes later, as New Yorkers stared in disbelief, the top of the south tower exploded in flames. It took several minutes before footage was found and replayed on television: It was another jet, apparently a commercial flight. Suddenly it was clear this was no freak accident. New York had been attacked.

A MORNING OF TOTAL HORROR Two Boeing 767-200s left Boston's Logan airport at 8am, both loaded with fuel for their flights to Los Angeles. At 8.48am, American Airlines Flight 11 crashed into the north tower, slicing into floors 96 to 103; and at 9.03am, while the whole world watched, United Airlines Flight 175 destroyed floors 87 to 93 of the south tower. At 9.59am the south tower crumpled, taking a mere 12 seconds to sink, its steel trusses and exterior columns having softened and buckled like spaghetti in a furnace thought to have reached 2,000°F. A lethal tidal wave of smoke, dust and debris thundered up the narrow streets of the Financial District, shrouding it in blackness. As office workers continued to evacuate the north tower, they passed hundreds of firefighters grimly mounting the narrow stairways. When, at 10.28am, that tower also collapsed, it consumed 343 members of the New York City Fire Department.

New York did not suffer alone. Reports came in of other hijackings: one plane was flown into the Pentagon in Washington DC, another crashed in Pennsylvania after passengers apparently tried to regain control. All on the flights died, with more loss of life on the ground.

A TERRIBLE TOLL New York mobilized instantly. The Manhattan hospitals' emergency rooms prepared for a huge influx of wounded; in all five boroughs hopeful blood donors queued up for hours; doctors rushed to what had become known as Ground Zero to help with triage. But the hordes of injured never materialized. Spouses, children, relations and friends of the twin towers' 50,000 occupants roamed from hospital to hospital desperately scouring lists for their loved ones' names. Some had had their hopes raised by cell phone calls after the towers' collapse. Soon, photocopied notices appeared all over Manhattan—the vital statistics, WTC office location and a smiling snapshot of the missing person. Around the hastily set up Lexington Avenue Amory disaster center, twenty blocks were papered with these heartbreaking posters. At Union Square, New Yorkers congregated in an impromtu vigil, gazing at the posters of the missing, praying, unrolling half a mile of paper to write messages of hope. Across the East River, the Brooklyn Heights Promenade, with its famous panoramic view of the Lower Manhattan skyline, was packed with people staring in silent disbelief at the gigantic plume of

> ❏ "US ATTACKED. Hijacked Jets Destroy Twin Towers"—13th September *New York Times* headline. On 14th September "Stunned Rescuers Comb Attack Sites, But Thousands Are Presumed Dead." ❏

dense, acrid smoke billowing from the place where the towers had stood since 1973, obscuring their absence. Everywhere flowers were stuck in railings and candles burned. But the temporary morgue in the Brooks Brothers store at Ground Zero remained ominously empty.

It was more than two weeks before Mayor Giuliani could bring himself to announce that the gruesome round-the-clock labor of clearing twisted steel, flattened fire trucks, masonry and human remains from the 16-acre (6.5ha) disaster site was no longer a search-and-rescue operation. DNA testing was used to verify identity whenever a shard of bone was found in the rubble, but a huge number of the missing seemed to have vaporized. The city offered the bereaved an urn filled with dust from the site in lieu of a body where no trace was found.

❏ "I don't know what the gates of hell look like, but it's got to be like this. I'm a combat veteran, Vietnam, and I never saw anything like this." A WTC firm's security director, quoted in the *New York Times.* ❏

THE DAY REMEMBERED As soon as the site was cleared, debate began to rage over its future. In particular, how to combine a memorial to the 2,752 who died with the practicalities of providing office space. Whatever happens, the events of the day will live on with New Yorkers for many years to come.

Smoke drifts over the city from the damaged twin towers after the impact

47

New York City

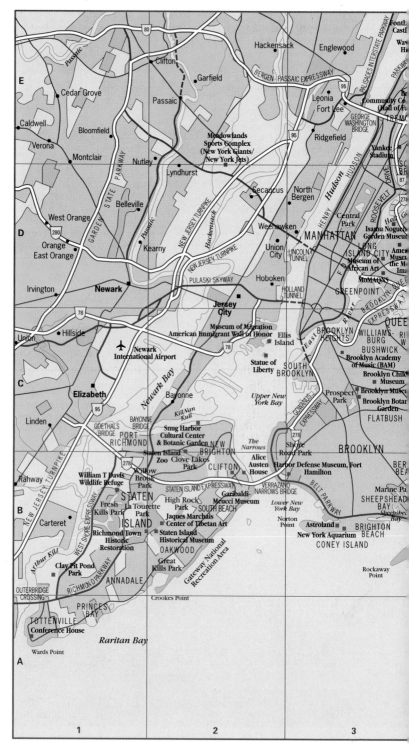

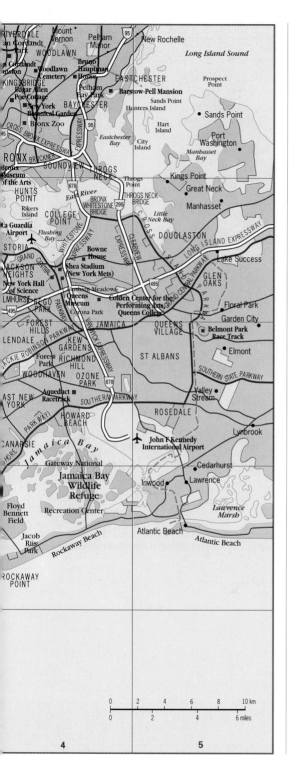

RIVERDALE
Mount
Vernon
Pelham
Manor
New Rochelle
n Cortlandt
Park
WOODLAWN
Long Island Sound
n Cortlandt
nsion
Woodlawn
Cemetery
Bruno
Hauptman
House
EASTCHESTER
KINGSBRIDGE
Pelham
Bay Park
Prospect
Point
Edgar Allen
Poe Cottage
BAYCHESTER
Barstow-Pell Mansion
Sands Point
New York
Botanical Garden
Hunters Island
Sands Point
Bronx Zoo
Hart
Island
Port
Washington
CROSS
BRONX
EXPRESSWAY
Eastchester
Bay
City
Island
Manbasset
Bay
BRONX
BRUCKNER
SOUNDVIEW
THROGS
NECK
Kings Point
Bronx
Museum
of the Arts
678
Throgs
Point
Great Neck
HUNTS
POINT
East River
BRONX
WHITESTONE
BRIDGE
295
THROGS NECK
BRIDGE
Manhasset
Rikers
Island
COLLEGE
POINT
Little
Neck Bay
La Guardia
Airport
Flushing
Bay
CROSS
DOUGLASTON
LONG
ISLAND
EXPRESSWAY
STORIA
GRAND
WHITESTONE
Bowne
House
Lake Success
JACKSON
HEIGHTS
CENTRAL
EXPRESSWA
Shea Stadium
(New York Mets)
495
GLEN
OAKS
New York Hall
of Science
Flushing Meadows
Queens
Museum
Colden Center for the
Performing Arts
Queens College
Floral Park
LMHURST
REGO
PARK
495
Corona Park
Garden City
FOREST
HILLS
VAN WICK EXPRESSWAY
JAMAICA
QUEENS
VILLAGE
Belmont Park
Race Track
LENDALE
KEW
GARDENS
ST ALBANS
Elmont
JACKIE ROBINSON PARKWAY
Forest
Park
RICHMOND
HILL
WOODHAVEN
OZONE
PARK
678
SOUTHERN STATE PARKWAY
AST NEW
YORK
Aqueduct
Racetrack
SOUTHERN PARKWAY
Valley
Stream
CANARSIE
PARK WAY
HOWARD
BEACH
ROSEDALE
Lynbrook
SHORE
Jamaica Bay
John F Kennedy
International Airport
Gateway National
Cedarhurst
Jamaica Bay
Wildlife
Refuge
Inwood
Lawrence
Floyd
Bennett
Field
Recreation Center
Lawrence
Marsh
Jacob
Riis
Park
Atlantic Beach
Atlantic Beach
Rockaway Beach
ROCKAWAY
POINT

0   2   4   6   8   10 km
0   2   4   6 miles

4
5

Browsing in Greenwich Village makes good entertainment: Stores here range from the mildly quirky to the completely outlandish

Not for nothing did they name New York twice. What most people think of as being New York is really Manhattan, a long, narrow island squeezed between two rivers. Manhattan is the kernel of New York life, home to much of the city's affluence and élan. Most New Yorkers live in the so-called Outer Boroughs that form the remainder of New York City: Brooklyn, the Bronx, Queens and Staten Island.

MANHATTAN As far as the rest of the world is concerned, the island of Manhattan—just over 12 miles (19km) long and for the most part 2.5 miles (4km) wide—is everything that defines New York, with its towering skyscrapers, teeming streets, ceaseless noise and giant neon advertisements that turn night into day. But it quickly becomes apparent to visitors traveling beyond Midtown that only a fraction of Manhattan actually fits this image. The island divides into numerous separate areas and each has its own distinctive history, looks, atmosphere and residents.

Lower Manhattan At Manhattan's southern extremity, the modern high-rise towers of the **Financial District** rise above the oldest part of New York. It was here that the first Dutch settlement took root and, while few markers of the colonial days remain, the entrepreneurial spirit with which the colony was founded remains very much alive—from the floor of the New York Stock Exchange to the street-side foodstands dispensing all kinds of ethnic food to power-dressed brokers.

Pressed hard against the Financial District's northern edge, the short busy streets of **Chinatown** make up one of New York's longest-established ethnic areas. Lately, Chinatown's banks, bakeries and dim sum houses have spread across the traditional boundaries into **Little Italy**— a tiny area where freshly made cappuccino and creamy pastries can still be consumed at sidewalk tables.

To the west, the ethnic atmosphere gives way to artiness in compact **SoHo** and **TriBeCa**, trendy locations that, not long ago, were derelict industrial areas—prime examples of the neighborhood transformations that are a New York specialty, as is the thriving **Chelsea** farther north.

By contrast, the elbow of land jutting toward the East River is consumed by the **Lower East Side**, a long-time first base of newly arrived immigrants and now the home of cut-rate stores and street markets where the work-hard-and-prosper ethos that built the city remains strongly in evidence despite a substantial number of newer stores and bars.

Greenwich Village is packed with restaurants, cafés, bars and clubs. This area also has some fine houses, intriguing narrow streets and, even today, a knack for attracting the writers and artists who, historically, have shaped American culture.

Across Broadway—which runs the length of Manhattan—the **East Village** provided a less costly alternative for those dispossessed by Greenwich Village's rising rents and gentrification during the 1980s. With offbeat stores and cafés, the area still has a modestly radical atmosphere, although the writers and artists who once colonized it are being replaced by trendy professionals.

H. G. WELLS ON NEW YORK
"To Europe, she was America, to America she was the gateway of the earth. But to tell the story of New York would be to write a social history of the world."

Choose from a few skyscraper viewing galleries to contemplate the almost unbelievable panorama of Manhattan and beyond

51

Areas of New York

THE WPA GUIDE TO NEW YORK CITY (1939)
The guide, which was commissioned during the Depression to create jobs for writers, gave this description of the scene around the Hudson River docks: "A surging mass of back-firing, horn-blowing, gear-grinding trucks and taxis."

OGDEN NASH ON THE BRONX
"The Bronx? No thonx." wrote Ogden Nash in 1931, his four words summing up many a New Yorker's attitude to this particular Outer Borough. Nash later offered an apologetic update: "The Bronx? God Bless Them." Unfortunately for the Bronx, few remember the latter verse as well as the former, which is usually the one to be quoted.

LEON TROTSKY ON NEW YORK
"New York impressed me tremendously because, more than any other city in the world, it is the fullest expression of our modern age."

Little Italy—one of several ethnic areas that make up New York's complex cosmopolitan patchwork

To the east of Fifth Avenue are **Murray Hill** and **Gramercy**. There is an air of elegence here and the various squares and parks, including **Gramercy Park**, offer a respite from city life. The **Flatiron District** is just across Fifth Avenue and another of New York's regions, similar to Chelsea, that has seen a revival in its fortunes, becoming a chic place to eat and shop.

Midtown Manhattan Unlike Lower Manhattan, where the streets tend to have names and to be short and crooked, Midtown Manhattan is all numbered streets and avenues that fortunately make the visitor's life a simple one. These broad, busy thoroughfares, with their dizzying pace of life, hold many of the city's highlights.

Midtown's northern border is defined by the southern perimeter of **Central Park**, an imposing and precisely rectangular chunk of greenery that re-creates a piece of the country in the heart of the city. At this, Central Park succeeds admirably.

Upper Manhattan To the east of Central Park, gaining much of its long-lasting prestige from the mansions and apartment houses erected to face the bucolic expanse, the **Upper East Side** is far and away Manhattan's wealthiest neighborhood, a fact borne out by its exclusive clothing stores, gourmet restaurants and sizeable gathering of upscale art galleries.

Three of the city's major art museums are located here: the Metropolitan Museum of Art, the Guggenheim Museum and the Whitney Museum of American Art. To enjoy art in a luxurious setting, it is hard to beat the Frick Collection, still housed in Henry Clay Frick's 19th-century mansion.

Across Central Park, the **Upper West Side** offers the Lincoln Center, the Cathedral of St. John the Divine and the American Museum of Natural History as its major attractions. The neighborhood's tall apartment houses—among them the Dakota, which has been home to celebrities ranging from Judy Garland to Leonard Bernstein and John Lennon—were the height of luxury

living at the turn of the century and are still coveted addresses in what has grown into a vibrant bastion of the upper middle class.

Stretching across the northern reaches of Upper Manhattan, **Harlem** has played a key role in the history and culture of black America from the turn of the century. The economic and social infrastructure that had traditionally held back African-Americans also contributed to Harlem spending many years in decline.

Similar problems derived from institutionalized racism have been experienced in **East Harlem**, above the Upper East Side, a major base for the city's enormous Hispanic population. Like Harlem, however, local initiatives as well as the passing of time have helped reduce long-held assumptions that the area is off-limits and has nothing to interest those from outside the resident community.

THE OUTER BOROUGHS Locals would no doubt disagree but, unless your time is limitless, the Outer Boroughs probably merit only day-trip excursions from Manhattan.

Brooklyn, with the exceptional Brooklyn Museum, the enjoyable Brooklyn Heights neighborhood and Prospect Park, has most in its favor. On the coast, Brooklyn also has Coney Island. Its glory days are gone, but the amusement area and boardwalk remain a curious piece of Americana. The latter leads to the New York Aquarium and to the lively Russian community of Brighton Beach.

Staten Island is also worth a visit, partly for the fun of the ferry ride to reach it, but also to enjoy the pastoral pace and the scattering of low-key museums.

In the **Bronx**, the Bronx Zoo (also called the Wildlife Conservation Park) is an excellent stop for children. The New York Botanical Garden is just next door. A more somber relic is the cottage in which author Edgar Allan Poe resided for two troubled years.

The predominantly residential surburbia of **Queens**, named in honor of the wife of England's King Charles II, includes thriving ethnic communities and the American Museum of the Moving Image.

The Wollman Memorial Rink in Central Park

LE CORBUSIER ON NEW YORK
"A hundred times I have thought New York is a catastrophe and fifty times: it is a beautiful catastrophe."

New York may appear to be a complicated city to navigate, and due to its past reputation, may even daunt some travelers. However, by following some simple advice and guidelines, visitors can be confident of enjoying all that the city has to offer without feeling too much like a stranger in a strange land.

MANHATTAN ADDRESS CALCULATOR

To find the cross street of any avenue address:
1. DROP the last figure of the building number (944 Third Avenue becomes 94).
2. DIVIDE the remainder by 2 (94 divided by 2=47). If a number is not evenly divisible, this indicates it is between two streets (46.5 is between 46th and 47th streets).
3. ADD or SUBTRACT the number on the following chart (47+10=57 or 57th Street).

Avenue	Number
1st	+4
2nd	+3
3rd	+10
6th	-12
7th	+12
8th	+9
9th	+13
10th	+13
A,B,C,D	+3
Amsterdam	+59
Columbus	+60
Lexington	+22
Madison	+27
Park	+34
Park South	+8
West End	+59
Fifth Avenue	
to 200	+13
to 400	+16
to 600	+18
to 775	+20
to 1286	-18
Broadway	
755–846	-29
to 953	-25
above 953	-31
Central Park West	all +6

The subway is a great way to travel

Addresses Walking is the best way to explore Manhattan, but before you start, take time to orient yourself and to learn a few basic rules about how New York's grid system works. First, work out which way is north, which way is south, and so on. North of Houston (pronounced *how*-ston) Street, where the streets and avenues are numbered this is relatively easy: streets run east to west, avenues run north to south. Broadway is like an avenue, in that it runs north to south, but cuts diagonally through the length of the island. Fifth Avenue is the dividing line between East and West in Manhattan. On each side, street addresses start at 1 and climb higher the farther you go toward either river. New Yorkers usually give addresses in terms of intersections: Third Avenue at 50th Street, for example, or 29th Street between Park and Lexington. Below Houston Street, the West Village is a tangled web of tiny streets. Without a map, there is no foolproof method to maneuver your way around, although its labyrinthine quality is part of the area's charm.

The subway Using the subway is the cheapest and fastest way to get around during the day. There are over 620 miles (1,000km) of track in the subway system, which is open 24 hours a day and can be traveled on at any one time for $2. For more information on tickets see page 257. Study the Metropolitan Transit Authority (MTA) map, which is free from the ticket booths and posted in

the stations and on the trains. Before you go through the turnstile, check that you are taking the train going in the right direction and whether you need an express or local train. Signs above the tracks will indicate this, as will the train number: 1, 6 and 9 are always local, while 2, 3, 4 and 5 are always express.

Many New Yorkers feel the subway in Manhattan is safe around the clock, although waiting for the infrequent trains at night can be very frustrating, particularly if construction work affects services (check signs in the stations). However, if at night you are traveling alone or going to the outer boroughs, consider taking a taxi.

Take a bus instead of the subway if you're not in any special hurry. You will see a lot more of the city and, because buses are air-conditioned, will be more comfortable in summer (if the bus isn't crowded). Buses are particularly useful to go across town above 59th Street, where there is no east-west subway service. Be aware that on weekdays at rush hour (8–9.30 and 4.30–6) all buses and trains are packed. During these times be careful on subway platforms and safeguard your purse or wallet. Whenever you are on the street, especially in Midtown where business people are rushing about, stay with the flow and be careful not to stop suddenly or stand still for too long in the middle of the sidewalk, as it is considered discourteous.

After dark No matter how safe New York may seem during the day, you should always be more careful at night. If you are in a group, a dark or deserted street may not feel threatening. However, if you are out walking alone or in a couple, remember to use your common sense and stick to busy and lighted streets. Several areas that you might visit with comparative nonchalance in daylight hours are considered to be potentially unsafe after dark. These areas include Alphabet City beyond Avenue C (avenues A and B are fine), Central Park, Riverside Park, Harlem and parts of the Lower East Side, just north of Canal Street.

To help orient yourself within the city, remember to use the bridges

CROSSING THE WATERS
New York's bridges are useful landmarks for navigating around the city. Among them are the Queensborough Bridge (or 59th Street Bridge), which crosses into Queens and is to the northeast of Manhattan island, level with the bottom of Central Park; the Triborough Bridge, which is farther north, past the top of Central Park and close to East 125th Street; the Manhattan Bridge, which stretches from the Lower East Side to Brooklyn; and the Brooklyn Bridge, to the southeast of the island in the Financial District.

New York

WALKING TOURS
A number of organizations run walking tours of various Manhattan neighborhoods (see Travel Facts, page 260). Historical walks led by Columbia University historians are run by Big Onion (tel: 439-1090) and walks through the Lower East Side are organized by the Lower East Side Tenement Museum (see page 138).

Itineraries

You could spend your entire life in New York and never feel you had seen the whole city. Nonetheless, these itineraries will provide a balanced view of New York.

Weekend itinerary
Day one In the morning, visit the Empire State Building and continue on foot to the New York Public Library, Rockefeller Center and St. Patrick's Cathedral. Have lunch in Midtown Manhattan and spend the afternoon at the Museum of Modern Art.
Day two Take an early morning ferry to the Statue of Liberty and Ellis Island. Lunch at the World Financial Center and then spend the afternoon in Greenwich Village.

Despite losing its world-record status, the Empire State Building is still a magnet for visitors

STATUE OF LIBERTY FERRY
Due to the events of September 11, the ferry service to the Statue of Liberty and Ellis Island is subject to change. It is advisable to call ahead for the latest information (tel: 269-5755) or visit www.statueofliberty ferry.com. You will also need to allow plenty of time (currently about an hour) to pass through the new security system. Don't take backpacks, coolers or packages with you.

One-week itinerary
Day one As day one of weekend itinerary.
Day two Take an early morning ferry from Battery Park to the Statue of Liberty and Ellis Island. After returning, take the subway to Union Square for lunch and then spend the afternoon traveling through the universe at the Rose Center for Earth and Space.
Day three Spend the whole day at the Metropolitan Museum of Art. If a whole day seems too long, spend part of it shopping for clothes in Midtown and along Madison Avenue, or in the discount outlets of Lower Manhattan.
Day four In the morning, you can explore Central Park. Travel to Greenwich Village for lunch and spend the afternoon exploring Greenwich Village, SoHo, Little Italy and Chinatown.
Day five On the Upper East Side, tour the Frick Collection or the Cooper-Hewitt National Design Museum. After lunch, continue to the Guggenheim Museum or the Whitney Museum of American Art.
Day six Travel by subway to the Brooklyn Museum. Spend the day here, pausing to eat a picnic lunch in the Brooklyn Botanic Garden. Alternatively, spend the day exploring Brooklyn Heights, dropping into the Brooklyn Historical Society and continuing to the New York Transit Museum.
Day seven Tour the Lower East Side and the East Village. After lunch, explore the Gramercy Park area and then conclude at the Pierpont Morgan Library.

Two-week itinerary

Day one As day one of weekend itinerary.

Day two As day two of week itinerary.

Day three As day three of week itinerary.

Day four In the morning, explore Central Park. Have lunch on the Upper West Side before visiting the American Museum of Natural History.

Day five Spend the whole day on Staten Island, visiting the Snug Harbor Cultural Center, the Richmondtown Historic Restoration and the Jacques Marchais Center of Tibetan Art.

Day six Tour the Lower East Side and Chinatown. Have lunch in Chinatown and spend the afternoon exploring Greenwich Village.

Day seven As day six of week itinerary.

Day eight On the Upper East Side, zip through either the Frick Collection or the Cooper-Hewitt National Design Museum. After a late lunch, continue to the Museum of the City of New York.

Day nine Visit the Forbes Galleries and idle away the rest of the morning in Washington Square Park. Have lunch at a café in Greenwich Village and then continue on to the East Village, or explore the Gramercy Park area and conclude your sightseeing at the Pierpont Morgan Library on 36th Street.

Day ten Explore Harlem and the museums of the Audubon complex on West 155th Street. After lunch, tour the Columbia University campus and the Cathedral of St. John the Divine.

Day eleven Pay a visit to the Bronx Zoo and the New York Botanical Garden.

Day twelve Divide the day between the Whitney Museum of American Art and the Guggenheim Museum.

Day thirteen Travel by subway to Coney Island, tour the New York Aquarium and continue to Brighton Beach.

Day fourteen Spend the morning at the Cloisters, returning to Midtown for lunch and to visit the Museum of TV and Radio, or the Museum of American Design—and any landmark building you have yet to view at close quarters.

The Statue of Liberty is essential viewing, even if you're on a flying visit to the Big Apple

GUIDED TOURS OF HARLEM

Harlem is one of New York's most celebrated areas but can be intimidating for the first-time visitor. One way to see Harlem without worries is with a guided tour. Harlem Spirituals, Inc. (tel: 391-0900) offers a choice of several: a Sunday or weekday tour that combines a gospel church service with a tour of historic Harlem, another that offers a soulfood lunch and a local history commentary and an evening fling based around several hours of jazz at a local venue.

The ultimate New York viewing platform is no more, but even without the magnificent panorama that was available from the World Trade Center's Tower Two, New York has views that no other city comes close to matching. The sun setting and the lights going on across Manhattan as seen from the Empire State Building is still as breathtaking as ever. Another option is to leave Manhattan itself and view it from afar. The Staten Island Ferry or the Brooklyn Heights Promenade both afford stunning vistas of the famous skyline.

58

Empire State Building This is the star of virtually every Manhattan view except those from its own 86th-floor observation level. On a clear day, the eagle-eyed can see through the wire mesh into Massachusetts and Pennsylvania and peer down at jets swooping into New York's airports. Come after dusk to see nighttime Manhattan: The building is open until midnight at weekends.

Waterside Restaurants Fewer restaurants than you might suppose have staked a claim to the best dinner show in town: the New York skyline. One, however, is rightfully famous for its food as much as for its prime vistas of lower Manhattan: Brooklyn's River Café. Several top-rated chefs have made their reputations devising menus to compete with that view—Larry Forgione, Charlie Palmer and Rick Laakkonen are just three—and ensuring the steep check is money well spent. In Queens, the Water's Edge affords a different take on Manhattan, the Midtown east skyline. Finally, a barge on the East River called the Water Club lets you see in both directions, though, being tethered just off 34th Street, Queens is the easier shore to spot.

Rockefeller Center Look out from the 65th-floor windows of the Rainbow Room restaurant complex in the GE (formerly RCA) Building and you will see the Empire State Building rising regally to the south. Look north, and the green rectangle of Central Park cuts between the stately apartment buildings of the Upper East Side and the Upper West Side toward Harlem.

STATUE OF LIBERTY VIEWS
At the Statue of Liberty, which sits on an island between Manhattan and New Jersey, the outlook is stirring; at time of press Liberty Island was open to visitors though the statue itself was closed. This may well change—check on arrival.

Above the East River From its terminal at the intersection of Second Avenue and 60th Street, the cable car that crosses the East River to Roosevelt Island gives clear views of the island's former hospitals and lunatic asylums. The memorable views, though, are in the other direction, taking in a lengthy swath of riverside Manhattan from Midtown's United Nations complex northward, far into the Upper East Side. A bonus is a bird's-eye view of any passing river traffic.

Fort Tryon Park Close to the northern tip of Manhattan, Fort Tryon Park offers not only the unexpected sight of a reassembled medieval European monastery (the Cloisters) but also, from the hilltop site of the fort itself, views across the Hudson River to New Jersey's Palisades Park and, on the other side of Manhattan, the Harlem River.

Brooklyn Some of the most rewarding views of Manhattan are found by leaving it. From Brooklyn Heights Promenade, the eastern edge of the Financial District—the so-called Water Street corridor, a heady mix of glass, steel, limestone and marble—walls the East River. In the foreground are the tall ships of South Street Seaport. Behind Water Street's forest of high-rises, you should be able to pick out the world's one-time highest building, the Woolworth Building, while two more, the Chrysler Building and the Empire State Building, are visible in the cluster of skyscrapers marking Midtown Manhattan.

Brooklyn Bridge Be sure not to use up all your film on the Promenade: Returning to Manhattan on foot across the Brooklyn Bridge reveals the same scenes from continually shifting perspectives behind the struts of the bridge, providing endless scope for inventive photographers. The outlook is familiar from countless movies and TV shows.

Staten Island Ferry
Look across the harbor from Brooklyn Heights to see the green hills of Staten Island rising to the south. You might also spot the Staten Island Ferry as it plies between the island and the southern tip of the Financial District.

Riding the ferry is much more interesting than looking at it, however. Dramatic views of Manhattan's skyline can be seen from the vessel (best on the return leg, when the skyscrapers appear to grow bigger and bigger) as well as slightly less dramatic ones of Governors Island (occupied by the US Coast Guard), the Statue of Liberty and one of the world's longest suspension bridges, the Verrazano-Narrows Bridge, which forms a link from Staten Island to Brooklyn.

H. G. WELLS ON NEW YORK VIEWS, 1906
"Suddenly as I looked back at the skyscrapers of lower New York a queer fancy sprang into my head. They reminded me quite irresistibly of piled-up packing cases outside a warehouse. I was amazed I had not seen the resemblance before."

View over Midtown—one of the most recognizable skylines in the world

59

THE TOMPKINS SQUARE PARK RIOT

In the heart of Alphabet City, Tompkins Square Park was the scene of a heavy-handed police operation on a steamy August night in 1988, when 12 mounted police, soon joined by 400 re-inforcements, battled for four hours to clear the 16 acre (6.5ha) park of the homeless people who were occupying it.

The incident was recorded on video by a local artist and the police brutality that the playback showed triggered outrage across the city, and nightly violence at the park. Mayor Dinkins closed the park for major renovations, posting police guards to keep out anyone but dog-walkers and basketball players. Reopened, the park is now fairly peaceful during the day.

Tompkins Square Park, in Alphabet City, has seen its share of problems, but it is now a fairly safe and peaceful place in daylight

▶ Abyssinian Baptist Church   *IBCC2*

132 West 138th Street (tel: 862 7474; www.abyssinian.org)
Open: Sunday services at 9, 11.
Subway: 2, 3, B, C; 135th Street

Founded in New York in 1808 and steadily moving north, as did its predominatly black congregation, until arriving in Harlem and occupying this purpose-built Gothic/Tudor bluestone building in the 1920s, the Abyssinian Baptist Church first flourished under the leadership of Adam Clayton Powell and gained the largest congregation of any protestant church in the US. Powell's son, Adam Clayton Jnr., continued in his father's footsteps, delivering powerful sermons during the Depression years and in 1945 becoming the nation's first black Congressmen and a noted civil rights campaigner.

The Sunday morning services offer, besides the opportunity to praise the Lord and listen to the striking oratory of the Reverend Calvin O. Butts, the current long-serving pastor, the chance to hear the church's acclaimed gospel choir in full voice.

▶ Alphabet City   *IFCC3*

Subway: B, D, F, N; Second Avenue

The process of gentrification that spread through Greenwich Village in the 1970s continued into the East Village. By the mid-1980s it had reached Alphabet City (so-called for having lettered rather than numbered avenues), which lies east of First Avenue between Houston and 14th streets. With its restaurants offering cuisines from Asia to Eastern Europe, the area draws mainstream New Yorkers in search of new dining experiences. Among its resident population are those wealthy enough to inhabit a classy, if usually small, renovated apartment in one of the many former tenement blocks.

Most of Alphabet City's population, however, are Puerto Ricans who have informally dubbed the area "loisaida"

(pronounced "low-ees-SIDE-ah"), a phrase reputedly first used by a local poet and playwright. The neighborhood suffered from urban blight into the 1980s, but the efforts of the local community and a major police initiative—and the rising interest of property developers—all contributed to regeneration. Much poverty remains though, and the area east of Avenue B can seem intimidating.

▶ American Academy and Institute of Arts & Letters IBCD2

Broadway at 155th Street (tel: 368-5900)
Open: Thu–Sun 1–4. Admission: free
Subway: C, D, 1; 155th or 157th streets
Two august cultural bodies—the National Institute of Arts, founded in 1898 and the American Academy, founded in 1904—unified in 1977 and jointly honor American achievements in art, writing and music.

Although much of its activity seems little more than mutual backslapping, the organization also administers grants to deserving artistic causes and stages temporary seasonal exhibitions highlighting individual members. If your favorite author, painter or composer is being featured, it could be worth a visit.

▶ American Bible Society 151D1

Broadway at 61st Street (tel: 408-1500; www.americanbible.org)
Open: Mon, Wed and Fri 10–6, Thu 10–7, Sat 10–5. Admission: free
Subway: A, B, C, D, 1, 2, 3, 9; 59th Street
A 1960s cast-in-place concrete structure a bagel's throw from busy Columbus Circle makes an unlikely home for the American Bible Society, founded in 1816 in order to circulate the Bible "without note or comment."

Over the years, historic bibles from near and far have been collected to form the society's extensive library and archive. The collection includes an illustrated Armenian account of the Four Gospels dated to the early 1400s and also a 16th-century bible translated by a New England preacher into Massachusetts (an Algonquin Native American dialect).

A few changing selections are displayed on the second-floor level, alongside a reconstruction of a Gutenberg printing press and a feature on the Dead Sea Scrolls.

AUDUBON TERRACE
The American Academy and Institute of Arts & Letters occupies one section of Audubon Terrace, a Renaissance Revival complex planned in 1908 and intended to provide a suitably imposing setting for several venerable national institutions—others among them including the American Numismatic Society (see page 65) and the Hispanic Society of America (see page 126).

Situated between Riverside Drive and Broadway and 155th and 156th streets, the plan was never entirely successful: Not only a poor architectural job, it also left its tenants in a humdrum residential area far removed from the ebb and flow of New York life.

The terrace was built on a part of the estate of John James Audubon, the eminent American naturalist of the early 1800s.

The American Natural History Museum

MUSEUM OF AMERICAN ILLUSTRATION
Within a few steps of the American Federation of the Arts, the Society of Illustrators (63rd Street between Lexington and Park avenues, tel: 838-2560; www.societyillustrators.org), established in 1875, holds the small but interesting Museum of American Illustration. Through lively temporary exhibitions, the museum highlights the contribution made to Americans' self-image through cartoons, advertising, book and magazine drawings, and much more.

▶ **American Federation of Arts**   *151D2*
65th Street, between Park and Madison avenues (tel: 988-7700; www.afaweb.org) Call for opening times and admission fee. Subway: 6; 68th Street
The American Federation of the Arts arranges traveling exhibitions for the small museums of the U.S., often finding time to display tasters of some in its own galleries. It is potluck what might be on display but a look inside also reveals the building's lavishly decorated interior, a 1960s restoration of what was originally the home, built around 1910, of a successful stockbroker.

▶▶ **American Museum of Natural History**   *IFCF2*
Central Park West and 79th Street (tel: 769-5100; www.amnh.org) Open: daily 10–5.45. Admission: moderate Subway: 1, 9, B, C; 79th Street or 81st Street
With 36 million exhibits, this is one of the world's best-stocked museums. Whether you are gazing at a sabre-toothed tiger or an ancient Guatemalan inscription, there is a strong chance it will be among the foremost examples of its kind on show anywhere in the world.

Darwin's theory of evolution and Mendel's law of heredity were two of the natural science breakthroughs that provided the stimulus for the museum's founding in 1869. Within a decade, the collections had acquired a specially built home, a stately Romanesque structure beside Central Park.

The sheer size of the collections of the American Museum of Natural History makes it a daunting prospect even for the most enthusiastic visitor. One way to discover the best of the museum without fatiguing your-self too much is to join a free hour-long guided Highlights Tour. These depart several times daily and details can be obtained from any of the museum's information desks. Greatly improved by a $30 million restructuring, the museum's fossil collection—which was already among the best in the world—now forms part of a six-room, state-of-the-art complex revealing the intricacies of the evolutionary relationships as far back as the Jurassic period (180–120 million years ago). The museum's Tyrannosaurus Rex, guilty of scaring generations of New York school children whose aggressive stance became an emblem of the museum, provided the focal-point of the Dinosaur Hall until scientific reassessment prompted a repositioning of the bones to better reflect the likely pos-ture of the creature. Still providing shock potential is the towering skeleton of a Barosaurus, a plant-eating dinosaur alive 140 mllion years ago, although again there are doubts as to whether the creature ever reared up in quite such an imposing manner. An intriguing adjunct to the skeletons and fossils is the tracing of mammalian development, beginning with curious fin-backed lizard-like creatures contemporaneous to the earliest dinosaurs, and a tracing of the lineage of mankind that reveals startling similarities between humans and bats.

Native American life and the evolution of animal and bird species in North America are outlined by fairly dreary, but comprehensive, habitat dioramas. More enjoyable, however, are the excellently arranged anthro-pological collections on Africa, Asia and Central and

CARL AKELEY
The Akeley Gallery at the American Museum of Natural History is named after Carl Akeley, a naturalist, explorer, and inventor. Akeley twice narrowly escaped death by dangerous animal. In 1911, he was gored by an elephant but saved him-self by swinging beneath the creature's body; on another occasion, he ran out of bullets while con-fronted by an angry leopard but saved himself by strangling it. Among his many technical innovations was a new taxidermy technique, which he employed on the seven elephants that stand in the gallery. Ironically, Akeley died in 1926 from complications arising from a gnat bite.

63

Massive exhibit in a massive museum—the Barosaurus at the Museum of Natural History

THE ROSE CENTER

A 138-ft (42-m) steel and glass cube provides a striking (particularly so when illuminated) transparent exterior for the Rose Center for Earth and Space. Inside, a giant sphere orbited by models of the planets of our solar system holds the Hayden Planetarium and a series of walkways and galleries offering displays on astronomical subjects, from the mysteries of black holes to the birth of a star. The state-of-the-art planetarium offers 3D trips through the universe and temporary presentations for imminent astral phenomena such as eclipses. The Center's design is especially bold when viewed alongside the main museum's 19th-century architecture and the neighboring apartment buildings. For planetarium tickets tel: 769-5200.

64

South America. This last section is particularly strong, including thousands of curious religious, ceremonial and everyday objects. Look for the Aztec musical instruments made from human bones, the 17th-century sheet metal ornamental llamas from the Andes and shrunken heads from the Amazon rain forest.

The Hall of Human Biology and Evolution studies the workings of the human body, traces ancestors over the centuries and features a computerized archeological dig, a see-thru woman and an electronic newspaper with information on human evolution.

Measuring 94ft (29m) in length and weighing 10 tons, what is thought to be the world's largest museum exhibit replicates the world's largest mammal—the blue whale—above the Milstein Hall of Ocean Life. The fiberglass whale steals the show, although the room's dioramas and fish skeletons do a commendable job in unraveling the mysteries of reproduction, feeding and self-defence far beneath the ocean's waves. Rocks of a different kind provide the substance of the Hall of Meteorites, bringing insights into the origins of the solar system and the opportunity to leave your fingerprints on the 4.5 billion year old Cape York Meteorite that crashed into Greenland thousands of years ago.

Moving on, even the mindbogglingly priced gems of Midtown Manhattan's jewelry stores pale into insignificance when compared with the contents of the Hall of Minerals and Gems, a collection valued at $80 million. A great chunk of crystal-impregnated copper and scores of

The gorilla diorama at the American Museum of Natural History. Few aspects of the world's wildlife are left untouched by the museum's vast collections

darkened display cases filled with sparkling stones are part of a cleverly planned exhibition on the natural forces that create the world's most prized pieces of rock. Some of the stones are the size of a pinhead, others are as big as your fist; the 21,000-carat Brazilian Princess Topaz weighs a quarter of a ton and is the world's largest uncut gem.

Even further back, the Ancient Oceans displays emphasize the importance of seas to the planet's ecosystem, describing how the bodies of water that covered a young Earth sustained the single cell organisms that, some scientists believe, became the basis for all life on earth. Entered directly from the museum, the **Nature Max Cinema** has screenings on natural history themes using the giant-screen IMAX system. Adjacent is the museum in the **Rose Center for Earth and Space** (see panel).

▶ American Numismatic Society   *IBCD2*

Broadway at 156th Street (tel: 234-3130; www.amnh.org/ museum/welcome/) Open: Tue–Sat 9–4:30. Admission: free Subway: C, D, 1; 155th or 157th streets

A vast hoard of coins and medals that is unsurpassed anywhere in the world, the collections of the American Numismatic Society are primarily intended to aid the research of devoted coin collectors and academics. There are, however, two engaging second-floor exhibitions. The first is a documentation—using maps, photographs, and remarkable specimens of very ancient money—of the origins of, and the spread of, coins throughout the world.

After viewing the coins, you may not have sufficient energy left to do justice to the extensive display of medals housed in the second exhibition. Upstairs, there is a public information desk where you can find out whether the unusual coin you have just found in your change is likely to improve your lifestyle dramatically.

▶▶ Asia Society   *151D3*

Park Avenue at 70th Street (tel: 228-6400; www.asiasociety.org) Open: Tue–Thu and Sat–Sun 11–6, Fri 11–9. Admission: inexpensive Subway: 6; 68th Street

Founded in 1956 with a pledge to improve understanding between Asia and America, the Asia Society hosts conferences, concerts, workshops and film shows, and mounts stunning temporary exhibitions of Asian art drawn from the world's foremost collections. Displays from the society's own collections include Chinese ceramics from the 11th century BC, some very fine pre-Angkor Cambodian sculpture, and wonderful Japanese Edo-period prints, all donated by John D. Rockefeller III. The decorative lion above the entrance is based on an 18th-century bronze of a Nepalese guardian lion.

ST. JAMES CHURCH
The Sunday services at St. James Episcopal Church (861–863 Madison Avenue), a short walk from the Asia Society, draw many of New York's wealthiest believers from their Upper East Side homes. Drop in during the week to admire the church's impressive stained glass and reredos.

The bright interior of St. James Church on Madison Avenue—one of several notable places of worship on the Upper East Side

ST. ELIZABETH ANN SETON

The well-preserved Federal-style building at 7 State Street (tel: 269-6865)—its columns said to be cut from ships' masts—was erected in 1783 for the prominent Watson family but has found longer-lasting fame as the Shrine of Elizabeth Ann Seton. She founded the Sisters of Charity, the first order of nuns in the US, in 1812, and in 1975 she became the first native-born American woman to be canonized by the Roman Catholic Church. This was her home from 1801 to 1803. Usually *open* Mon to Fri 6.30–5, on weekends and holidays. *Admission: free*; ring bell for attention.

Above and right: Battery Park, the gateway to the Statue of Liberty, combines history and small-time commerce

▶ Battery Park 104B1

Subway: 4; Bowling Green

A welcome open space on the edge of the Financial District, Battery Park provides 22 acres (9ha)of greenery with outstanding harbor views. Historical texts are pinned to its lampposts, leaving you with no excuse for not discovering something of early New York simply by strolling the tree-lined pathways. The park took its name from the row of cannons that the British stored during the 17th century along State Street, which now borders the park but which then marked the Manhattan shoreline.

If you are taking the ferry to the Statue of Liberty and Ellis Island, you will enter Battery Park's most interesting structure to reach the ticket booth, which is situated on the one-time parade ground of **Castle Clinton** (tel: 344-7220, www.nps.gov/cacl; *Open:* daily 8.30–5. *Admission free*). This circular fortification, finished in 1811, was built to repulse British attack.

Though there is little evidence of the fact today, Castle Clinton—which originally stood some 300ft (90m) offshore and was linked to land by a causeway—has enjoyed a prominent place in New York life. As its defensive importance declined, the fort was planted with floral gardens and became the scene of well-attended concerts (some presented by 19th-century showman P. T. Barnum) and exhibitions; subsequently, it predated Ellis Island as a landing and processing point for immigrants, almost 8 million of whom came ashore here between 1855 and 1889. The castle also served a 46-year stint as aquarium for the city.

Elsewhere in Battery Park is the pint-sized Peter Minuit Plaza named after the Dutchman who bought Manhattan from its Native American inhabitants for the equivalent of $24 paid in the form of tools and trinkets. Occupying a granite building topped by a distinctive six-tiered roof in nearby Battery Park City (see page 18), the **Museum of Jewish Heritage** (18 First Place; tel: 437-4200, www. mjhnyc.org; *Open:* Sun, Tue and Thu 10–5.45, Fri 9–5. *Admission: moderate*) traces Jewish life through persecution in Europe to the creation of Israel, and the growth of Jewish communities throughout the US.

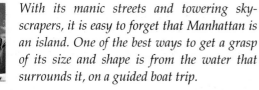

With its manic streets and towering sky-scrapers, it is easy to forget that Manhattan is an island. One of the best ways to get a grasp of its size and shape is from the water that surrounds it, on a guided boat trip.

Most boat-tour operators seem to be offering much the same thing—a sightseeing trip along the Hudson and East rivers that includes a stop at the Statue of Liberty and a view of any New York landmarks visible from the water. There are variations, however, so consider all the options to find the trip that suits you best.

In-depth sightseeing The most comprehensive of the sight-seeing cruises is run by **Circle Line** (tel: 536-3200). This comprises a two- or three-hour narrated circumnavigation of Manhattan Island, passing beneath seven major bridges on the way. The same company operates a two-hour cruise after dark and several other options including a speedboat ride. **NY Waterway** (tel: 902-8700) also offer a full circumnavigation of Manhattan, this one lasting two hours and, for those smitten by the waves, all-dayers along the Hudson River into rural New York state. By contrast, the Fantastic Friday Dance Cruise comprises a night of dancing to salsa and merengue.

Other options The 75-seater bright yellow catamarans of **New York Water Taxis** (tel: 742-1969) ply stops around the West Side, Lower Manhattan and Brooklyn; an all-day pass allows unlimited hopping on and off. Much more decadent are the eating and sight-seeing trips of **Spirit Cruises** (tel: 727-7735). The company offers a two-hour Tropical Lunch Buffet cruise daily except Sunday, voyaging around Manhattan's southern tip and passing some of the city's major sights. On Sundays, the champagne-fueled Jubilee Lunch Cruise follows a similar route. Dinner and dance cruises (with a substantial buffet and live music), depart nightly and offer memorable views of Manhattan by moonlight.

EAT AS YOU GO
Visitors love to sightsee but New Yorkers love to eat and they are the people most in evidence on the lunch, brunch and dinner cruises offered by World Yacht (tel: 630-8100). These are not calorie-counting affairs: Lunch and brunch are lavish buffets and dinner is a four-course treat followed by dancing.

67

Even on a short stay, sightseeing by boat can make a pleasant change from hot sidewalks and traffic jams

New York

BROADWAY'S FIRST BEND

Broadway's angular scythe through Manhattan's otherwise largely grid-style street plan gave rise to squares such as Union, Madison, and Times. Its first bend—after traveling for 3 ruler-straight miles (5km) north from Bowling Green—was due to the refusal of a Dutch landowner, Jacob Brevoort, to allow it to cross his property, a site now occupied by Greenwich Village's Grace Church.

Broadway's nerve center: the theater district near Times Square

TIMES SQUARE TOURS

Stop in the Times Square Visitors Center, inside the Harris Theater, 1560 Broadway, for the story of Times Square, told with posters and assorted memorabilia. Each Friday at noon, the center is the starting point of a free two-hour walking tour of the neighborhood, pointing out places of interest.

►► Broadway   151C2

The story of Broadway is the story of New York. This is the city's oldest and longest thoroughfare—in one guise or another, Broadway not only runs north–south through Manhattan but continues for 140 miles (225km) to Albany. It has witnessed every good, bad, and indifferent phase in the city's growth, while its internationally famous theater district of Times Square and adjacent streets is, for many, what New York is all about.

Originally part of a Native American trail, Broadway was known to early Dutch settlers as De Heere Straat, or Main Street. It has remained New York's major (and perhaps most famous) artery ever since.

Broadway acquired the city's first numbered housing in 1793 and was also the first New York street to see its residential properties put to commercial uses. The commerce came in contrasting forms, with seedy bars, brothels and gambling dens alongside the city's finest retail outlets. In the 1880s, a popular saying held that if you fired a shotgun in any direction at the intersection of Broadway and Houston Street, you would not hit an honest man.

In the days before traffic signals and one-way streets, Broadway was bedlam. Holding the city's major businesses and being the main route north, Broadway's sidewalks were packed with pedestrians and its center a crush of handcarts and horse-drawn wagons. Police had to physically intervene to prevent the thoroughfare becoming completely blocked. Walkers took their lives in their hands when attempting to cross Broadway. The intersection with Fulton Street was so hazardous that, in 1867, the authorities erected a footbridge—only for it to be torn down at the insistence of store owners fearful of losing their side's share of captive pedestrians.

What evolved into New York's theater district began in Broadway's southern reaches and steadily moved north, one of the first theaters opening in 1798 at the intersection with present-day Park Row. Broadway's theaters quickly forged a reputation for entertaining the city's well-to-do classes with productions of artistic merit and were therefore considered a cut above their Bowery counterparts, popularly regarded as offering low-brow titillation for the consumption of the masses.

By the 1880s, the heyday of vaudeville and the age of stars such as Lillie Langtry, the Broadway theaters had pushed north to Union Square. Around this time, however, the Metropolitan Opera House opened on an unlikely site 26 blocks north and began drawing the city's élite to an area then dominated by livery stores and stables. Broadway crossed this area at Longacre Square.

Ten years passed before a theater opened at Longacre, but by then a section of Broadway around 34th Sreet had been famously labeled "the Great White Way" on account of its giant advertising billboards lit by hundreds of electric light bulbs.

Soon, **Times Square**—as Longacre Square was renamed after the publisher of *The New York Times* got permission to build an office tower above it—was similarly illuminated. Once joined to the subway system, it quickly became the heart of the city's theater district.

Broadway continued north but the theater district stayed where it was. By the 1920s many of the theaters were showing movies and, 50 years on, the oldest of them were demolished in a spate of office building.

As if to echo the sleaziness of an earlier Broadway, the area around Times Square degenerated into a center for porn shops, prostitution and drug dealing—though the sheer gaudiness of the place and the many legitimate theaters showing hit plays and musicals continued to attract crowds of tourists.

With the help of several billion dollars, a different Times Square began to appear through the 1990s: Numerous new commercial developments and considerable improvements in appearance and safety have utterly transformed the area (see page 18).

The night-time neon of Broadway—still as dazzling to visitors as it was the day the electricity was switched on

*Above and opposite:
riding above it on the
Skyfari aerial tramway is
a good way to view the
re-created habitats found
at the Bronx Zoo*

**BRONX ZOO
PRACTICALITIES**
The zoo's Browndale
entrance is a short
walk from the Pelham
Parkway subway stop.
An alternative route from
Manhattan is with the
Liberty Lines Express Bus
(BxM11), which runs
from Madison Avenue to
the Bronxdale entrance
(for details, tel: 718/
652-8400).

Though busy, early on
summer days is the best
time to visit (*Open* Mon–Fri
10–5, Sat and Sun
10–5.30). During the
winter (Nov–Mar) many
of the zoo's open-air sections are closed and the
animals moved indoors
(opening hours are then
10–4.30). Admission is
inexpensive but free on
Wednesdays. For general
information on the zoo,
tel: 718/367-1010.

▶ **The Bronx**   49E4

That the Bronx has had a worse press than any other New
York borough is largely because one section, the South
Bronx, became an international symbol of the most
extreme forms of urban decay. Since the 1970s, abandoned buildings stripped clean of their fittings and
regularly targeted by arsonists have littered the area. A
major injection of funds for the building of affordable
housing for the predominantly low-income population
and widespread community initiatives are steadily, if
slowly, having an impact, but the South Bronx's image as
a place depressed is a hard one to lose.

The rest of the Bronx is quite different. Off **Grand
Concourse**, a stately thoroughfare laid out in 1892 and
still (though no longer deserving of its title) cutting south-
north through the borough, lie safe and tidy residential
areas, immense parks and the **Bronx Zoo** (see below).

In the South Bronx, **Yankee Stadium** (161st Street and
River Avenue; tour info tel: 718/579-4531, www.yan-
kees.com) has been the home of the New York Yankees
since its completion in 1923. A $100-million renovation
program carried out in the mid-1970s was intended to
improve the area as much as the building. If you visit the
stadium, continue to the **Bronx Museum of the Arts** (1040
Grand Concourse; www.bxma.org). Opened in 1971, the
museum has exhibitions of local art and Bronx-related
cultural topics.

If they are not fans of the Yankees, many New Yorkers
visit the Bronx for just one thing: the **Bronx Zoo**▶ (officially called the **Wildlife Conservation Park**), the largest
city zoo in the nation. Spanning 265 acres (107ha), the zoo
puts its emphasis on herds and flocks rather than single
animals and on re-created natural habitats rather than

cages. The indoor rain forest of JungleWorld, for example, finds gibbons and monkeys leering at their human visitors from across artificial rivers. You should also spot a few Indian gharials, a type of alligator whose ancestry goes back 180 million years. Rare snow leopards are the highlight of the Himalayan Highlands, while World of Darkness—where day is transformed into night—allows glimpses of aardvarks, bushbabies and bats (including the vampire variety, which receive a daily ration of blood).

The animals of the zoo's principal open space, Wild Asia, can be viewed only on a 25-minute narrated monorail ride. The open-sided cars glide above a plain roamed by antelopes, elephants, rhinoceroses and sika deer—a species now extinct in its native habitat.

More traditional exhibits include the ape and reptile houses, and the MouseHouse, its cages inhabited by innumerable tiny furry things. There is also a Children's Zoo, intended to provide young minds with an insight into animal behavior and offering plenty of cute and cuddly creatures for stroking.

Beginning across Fordham Road from the zoo, the **New York Botanical Garden▶** (tel: 718/817-8779, www.nybg. org/; *Open:* Tue–Sun 10–6, 10–5 in winter. *Admission: inexpensive*) is a wonderful mixture of formal gardens, rock gardens and rugged woodlands—including a 40-acre (16ha) hemlock forest. In the northwest corner, the Enid A. Haupt Conservatory is filled by a glorious array of banana

plants, palm trees, cacti and other vegetation and stages seasonal flower shows. Stop for refreshment at the Snuff Mill Terrace Café (*Open:* summer only), invitingly shaded by trees and overlooking the Bronx River.

The **Edgar Allen Poe Cottage▶** (off Grand Concourse at East Kingsbridge Road, tel: 718/881-8900; *Open:* Mon–Fri by appointment, Sat 10–4, Sun 1–5) is where the writer lived for two years during the 1840s, in the hope that the country air would improve his wife's health. In the unheated dwelling, Poe's tubercular spouse died during the first winter. Holding a few of the Poes' sparse furnishings, the cottage is an aptly bleak memorial to a man whose short life was seldom a happy one.

In the grounds of the **Bronx Community College▶** (181st Avenue and University Avenue) is the **Hall of**

New York

RIVERDALE

When New Yorkers talk of the Bronx, they are not usually thinking of Riverdale, part of which is the site of enviable homes and which reaches from the eastern edge of Van Cortlandt Park to the Hudson River.

One place worthy of a visit is the 1846 Fonthill Castle, a Gothic Revival structure modeled on an English folly and originally the home of actor Edwin Forrest. It now serves as the admissions office for the College of Mount St. Vincent, at Riverdale Avenue and 263rd Street. Another is Wave Hill (675 West 252nd Street; tel: 718/549-3200), 28 acres (11ha) above the Hudson River holding two 19th-century mansions with gardens and green-houses. It is the site of horticultural exhibitions and summer concerts.

The New York Botanical Garden

Fame for Great Americans. Here the bronze busts of around 100 prominent Americans are lined up along an open-air colonnade. The neo-classical style of the Hall of Fame is noteworthy and is replicated across the campus, much of which is credited to the prominent turn-of-the-century New York architect Stanford White (of the firm McKim, Mead, & White).

Predating the college, as well as most other buildings in the Bronx, the **Van Cortlandt Mansion▶** (off Broadway, between 240th and 242nd streets, tel: 718/543-3344, www.vancortlandthouse.org; *Open:* Tue–Fri 10–3, Sat and Sun 11–4. *Admission: inexpensive*) was built in 1748 for a family that was prominent in politics and farming, their land holdings consuming what are now the wild expanses of **Van Cortlandt Park**. The mansion, built in Georgian style with Dutch adornments, also provided a part-time base for George Washington, who marched from here into Manhattan to celebrate the end of the Revolutionary War. The mansion does an excellent job of highlighting its English, Dutch and Colonial furniture, and a few other 18th-century odds and ends.

Strange as it may sound, a more intriguing stop than the mansion is **Woodlawn Cemetery▶** (East 223rd Street and Webster Avenue). Rather than raid the art collections of Europe or finance Manhattan skyscrapers, some ultra-rich early New Yorkers chose to spend their fortunes on extravagant mausoleums. Among those buried here are merchants Richard H. Macy, J. C. Penney, and F. W. Woolworth—whose sphinx-guarded, pseudo-Egyptian palace defies belief. Smaller monuments honor writer Herman Melville and jazz giant Duke Ellington.

72

New York's first black immigrants were slaves who arrived with the Dutch, by whom they were treated with comparative benevolence. A change for the worse occurred during the era of British dominion, when the colony's new rulers showed no respect for people whom they regarded merely as chattels. They responded to slave uprisings with public hangings and burnings. Since then, the struggle for civil rights has been a long, uphill battle.

Early racism After the Revolutionary War, a few freed slaves attained respectable social positions, but others were illegally transported to the Deep South. All were subject to racial hostility.

By the early 1800s, New York's African-Americans encountered segregation in public places and were prevented from obtaining the necessary work skills to be employed as anything other than laborers and servants.

The rise and fall of Harlem In response, the first black churches and mutual aid societies were formed and, after years of enduring racism in the city's slums, it was amid the stylish brownstones of Harlem (originally built for wealthy whites) that New York's blacks first felt they had found a secure and self-supporting enclave.

Harlem's population doubled during the 1920s, a period when its art, music and literature flowered into the "Harlem Renaissance." Swiftly, however, the Depression made Harlem a ghetto, and its problems, along with those of African-American communities in other boroughs, were never tackled by the authorities. The Civil Rights Movement—and the Harlem speeches of Malcolm X—brought racial issues into the public spotlight during the 1960s.

Modern times David Dinkins became New York's first black mayor in 1990, as Harlem was evolving into one of Manhattan's newest areas of tourist interest. Meanwhile, Harlem institutions such as the Schomburg Center of Research in Black Culture have earned widespread recognition.

73

The raising of black consciousness in the 1960s was helped by public campaigners such as Malcolm X, seen here addressing a Muslim meeting in Harlem. He was assassinated in 1965

GREEN-WOOD CEMETERY

Henry Pierrepont, the man who developed Brooklyn Heights, was not only concerned with providing homes for the living. With Green-Wood Cemetery (main entrance at Fifth Avenue and 25th Street), he created a 478-acre (193ha) landscaped plot to be enjoyed by some of the most prominent New Yorkers on their earthly demise. The cemetery drew 100,000 visitors a year in its Victorian hey-day to wander its 20 miles 32km) of footpaths, take in the views over New York harbor, and contem-plate the many richly decorated tombs. Richard Upjohn's remarkable Gothic Revival gate and gatehouse, at the Fort Hamilton Parkway entrance, just marks the beginning. Among the 500,000 interred are Henry Ward Beecher, William Marcy "Boss" Tweed, Peter Cooper and Samuel Morse.

Absorbed into New York City in 1898, fiercely independent Brooklyn at least has its own view of the Statue of Liberty

▶ ▶ ▶ Brooklyn

48C3

Brooklyn was once a full-fledged city in its own right, with an affluent population and revered cultural institu-tions. In 1898, buoyed by the opening of the Brooklyn Bridge spanning the East River, it decided (by a narrow majority) to become part of New York City.

The decision has been cursed by Brooklynites ever since. Post-independence humiliations have been many: The Depression and a huge influx of immigrants turned many of Brooklyn's stylish neighborhoods into slums and cre-ated breeding grounds for organized crime; the naval shipyards were closed down; Brooklyn's award-winning *Daily Eagle* newspaper bit the dust after a strike. Perhaps most galling of all, the Brooklyn Dodgers moved to Los Angeles in 1955.

Despite these setbacks, Brooklyn does remain the most distinctive and enjoyable of the Outer Boroughs. The moderate tempo of its streets comes as a welcome relief after the bustle of Manhattan.

If it were still a city, Brooklyn would be the sixth most populous in the US. Within its metropolitan sprawl are four pockets of special interest. Downtown Brooklyn and the historic Brooklyn Heights lie closest to Manhattan. To the north, Fort Greene is gaining a reputation as the home of the new black artistic community. South of downtown, the elegant Eastern Parkway leads past the massive Brooklyn Museum and the Botanic Garden; farther south, on the coast, is the Russian-dominated Brighton Beach and the fabled but faded Coney Island amusement park.

From the Brooklyn Bridge, any turning to the right leads into the short leafy streets of **Brooklyn Heights▶ ▶ ▶**. The 1814 invention of the steam-powered ferry made this dis-trict, set on bluffs above the East River, a residential area coveted by the bankers and speculators active in Manhattan's Financial District, just across the water.

(Continued on page 76)

Where Brooklyn meets the Atlantic Ocean you will find not only a coastline but two contrasting images of New York life: Coney Island amusement park, world-famous but now a pale shadow of its former self, and Brighton Beach, a declining seaside resort energized and transformed since the 1970s by a massive influx of Russian émigrés.

Coney Island Up until the mid-1940s, this was many New Yorkers' idea of heaven. For a nickel subway fare they could spend a day of fun beside the ocean, munching cotton candy, making themselves dizzy on the roller coasters, or lurking around the side shows. Coney Island is undoubtedly a legend, but today it is also—in every sense— history. In the amusement park area between Surf Avenue and the Boardwalk and West 8th and West 16th streets, little more than run-of-the-mill fairground rides suggest the old days, though a 1927 rollercoaster, the fearsome Cyclone, is still in business, offering an 85-ft (26-m) drop at a 60-degree angle.

On summer days, Coney Island's beach still gets plenty of users, while remaining surprisingly clean, and the Boardwalk beside it is as atmospheric as ever—windswept, breezy and with an exhilarating polyglot flavor.

CONEY ISLAND'S NAME
The most plausible of many theories as to how Coney Island acquired its name is that it derives from the Dutch *Konijn Eiland*—Rabbit Island.

New York Aquarium (tel: 718/265-FISH; www. nyaquarium.com; *Open:* daily 10–4.30/5, until 6/7 in summer. *Admission: moderate*) Sharks, beluga whales, dolphins and sea lions are among the inhabitants here, accessed from the boardwalk. You will also find the Sea Cliffs exhibition, a re-creation of a rocky coastal habitat populated by walrus, seals, penguins and sea otters.

Brighton Beach Continue east along the Boardwalk to reach this revitalized area where between 10,000 and 20,000 ex-Soviet immigrants form the largest Russian community in the US, beneficiaries of the USSR's relaxing of restrictions in the years before its collapse. With caviar and ice-cold vodka advertised in Cyrillic script, and the riotous restaurants along Brighton Beach Avenue known to round off the evening with frenzied dancing and the odd drunken brawl, so-called Little Odessa (many settlers arrived from the Black Sea port) is becoming one of the most celebrated areas of New York City. Bakeries and restaurants here offer Russian culinary specialties.

MAXIM GORKY ON CONEY ISLAND, 1906
"Fabulous and beyond conceiving, ineffably beautiful, is this fiery scintillation."

From its beginnings as an ash dump, the Brooklyn Botanic Garden has developed into an inspiration and delight for its visitors

STROLL: BROOKLYN HEIGHTS
An enjoyable way to walk off a good lunch is with a stroll along the Brooklyn Heights Promenade. Also called the Esplanade, this wide pathway overlooks the East River, and has views of Manhattan strong enough to draw Brooklyn office workers with picnic lunches and to push the prices of west-facing penthouse apartments along nearby Columbia Heights into the realms of the phantasmagoric.

(Continued from page 74)

Brooklyn Heights subsequently became covered with brownstone dwellings—Gothic, Greek or Romanesque in style—which largely survive intact in an area that became a National Historical Landmark in 1965.

Structure your explorations sufficiently to include Orange Street and its **Plymouth Church of the Pilgrims▶** (tel: 718/624-4743, www.plymouthchurch.org for opening hours). It was here during the 1800s that abolitionist minister Henry Ward Beecher (see panel on page 78) delivered eloquent and impassioned sermons against slavery and made the church a platform for the leading abolitionists. He is remembered by a statue in the adjoining garden. **Brooklyn Historical Society▶** (128 Pierrepont Street, tel: 718/221-4111, www.brooklynhistory.org; *Open:* Wed–Sun 12–5, Fri 12–8. *Admission: inexpensive*), with its exhibits of local memorabilia, is another worthwhile stop.

Below the Heights, downtown Brooklyn spills along Fulton Street, which bends around Borough Hall, an unappealing Greek Revival building erected in 1848. Of far greater interest, the **New York Transit Museum▶▶▶** (tel: 718/243-8601, mta.info/mta/museum/index.html; *Open:* Tue, Thu and Fri 10–4, Wed 10–6, Sat and Sun 12–5. *Admission: inexpensive*) occupies a former subway station at the intersection of Boerum Place and Schermerhorn Street. Inside, art deco air-vent coverings and mosaic-tiled station name plates recall the care that went into the early years of what became the world's second-largest mass transit system.

Between downtown Brooklyn and the former naval dockyards, **Fort Greene▶** is another district well endowed with leafy streets and elegant brownstones, now owned by Brooklyn's more affluent blacks among others. Many became rooming houses during the Depression, causing the area to fall into neglect.

Though signs of inner-city poverty remain apparent, Fort Greene is very much on the rise. African-Americans still make up 70 percent of the district's population, a significant number of them being successful in the arts. Artist Ernest Critchlow is a long-established local;

another is movie-maker Spike Lee, who resisted the lure of Hollywood and located his production company here. Lee grew up in Fort Greene and his 1986 movie, *She's Gotta Have It*, made use of a local landmark: **Fort Greene Park**, designed in 1860 by Olmsted and Vaux (better known for Manhattan's Central Park). The Doric column was added later in memory of the 12,000 American patriots who died on British prison ships during the Revolutionary War and lie buried beneath the park.

Fort Greene sees comparatively few tourists. It would be sensible to keep to the area south of the park, where you will find the most impressive of the brownstone buildings and also several churches (visit on Sunday morning for the best atmosphere).

There are many more brownstones to be viewed in the surrounding residential streets between Flatbush Avenue and Sixth Avenue, which is an upscale section of the Park Slope neighborhood. A much more spectacular sight in this area, however, is located at the center of Grand Army

BORN IN BROOKLYN
Mae West (1892), George Gershwin (1899), Aaron Copland (1900), Clara Bow (1905), Phil Silvers (1912), Veronica Lake (1919), Mickey Rooney (1922), Woody Allen (1935), Mary Tyler Moore (1937), Philip Glass (1937), Elliot Gould (1938), Neil Sedaka (1939), Barbra Streisand (1943), Barry Manilow (1946).

Brooklyn

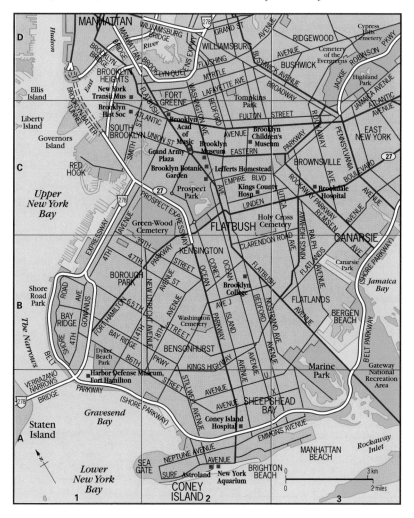

New York

THE HASIDIC JEWS
Since the 1940s, Brooklyn's Williamsburg district (north of Downtown) has been a base of the ultrastrict Hasidic community. Men wear beards, side curls, dark frock coats and hats; the heads of married women are shaven and covered by a wig. The Hasidim adhere rigidly to kosher diets, and some eschew TV and radio. Another large Orthodox Jewish community in Brooklyn is the Lubavitchers, adherents to a Hasidic sect that originated in 18th-century Russia.

HENRY WARD BEECHER
Clergyman at the Plymouth Church of the Pilgrims for some 40 years in the latter half of the 19th century, Henry Ward Beecher spoke out against slavery and in favor of women's suffrage. Equally controversial for the time, Beecher's writings supported Darwin's theory of evolution. His later years were dogged by allegations of adultery, charges of which he was cleared only after his death in 1887.

Plaza: the oversized Soldiers' and Sailors' Memorial Arch, raised in 1892 to commemorate the Union forces who died during the Civil War. This can be found on Flatbush Avenue by the main entrance to Prospect Park (see below).

This Brooklyn version of an imperial Roman arch was designed by John H. Duncan, who was also responsible for the similarly grandiose General Grant Memorial (see pages 110–111). The memorial's sheer size makes it much more of an architectural curiosity than a fitting shrine to the dead. The sense of pomposity is compounded by the heroic sculptures added to the memorial in 1898, though some amends are made by the finely detailed bas-reliefs that decorate the walls on the inside of the arch.

Prospect Park▶ itself is a broad and bucolic open space completed in 1874. With none of the restraints that were imposed with Central Park (such as incorporating major traffic arteries) architects Olmsted and Vaux gave their imaginations free rein here and considered Prospect Park their finest work.

The grand streets and landscaped open spaces—as well as the triumphal monuments—that Brooklyn acquired during the late 19th century were the hallmarks of a city very much on the rise. In keeping with the optimism of the times—and in an effort to create a symbol of

Brooklyn Heights. Not all of the city's best skyscrapers are in Manhattan

Brooklyn's cultural superiority over Manhattan—the **Brooklyn Museum▶▶▶** (200 Eastern Parkway, tel: 718/638-5000, www.brooklynart.org; *Open:* Wed–Fri 10–5, Sat and Sun 11–6, 11–11 first Sat of the month. *Admission: inexpensive*) was founded in 1897 with the intention of becoming the largest museum in the world. Such great ambitions were never fulfilled, however, and this fine museum does play second fiddle to the better-known Manhattan museums. It is probably most renowned as the resting place for the world's third largest stock of ancient Egyptian artifacts.

The museum's sixth floor has an exceptional collection of 19th-century American portraiture, including Gilbert Stuart's iconographic image of George Washington. Elsewhere, Francis Guy's airy *Winter Scene in Brooklyn* of 1817 stands out, and a quality selection from the Hudson River School culminates in Albert Bierstadt's *Storm in the Rocky Mountains, Mt. Rosalie*, an intense landscape of rugged granite beneath brooding storm clouds.

The fifth floor of the museum has colonial-period ceramics and interiors ranging from 17th-century farmhouses to 1920s art deco lounges. Note the Moorish Room: a dreamy conglomeration of patterned tiles, gold-brocaded walls, oak panels and velvet drapes which once graced John D. Rockefeller's Manhattan mansion.

Other floors have comprehensive Asian art collections, while the second floor holds pottery, figurines and votive objects from Africa, Oceania and Central and South America. Most striking among the latter is the Paracas Textile, a 2,000-year-old Peruvian burial cloth. The Native American collections, on the same floor, feature diverse tribes and exhibits from buckskin jackets to totem poles.

To the rear of the museum is the divinely landscaped **Brooklyn Botanic Garden▶▶** (tel: 718/622-7200, www.bbg.org; *Open:* Tue–Fri 8–4.30, Sat and Sun 10–4.30, extended hours during summer. *Admission: inexpensive*).

The quiet charm still to be found in parts of Brooklyn Heights contrasts with the frenetic streets of Manhattan, just across the East River

LITERARY BROOKLYN HEIGHTS
Brooklyn Heights has strong literary associations. Poet Hart Crane and novelist John Dos Passos both lived at 110 Columbia Heights during the 1920s (Crane also resided briefly at 77 Willow Street). Henry Miller spent a short time at 91 Remsen Street during the 1920s and Truman Capote wrote *Breakfast at Tiffany's* in the basement of 70 Willow Street. Norman Mailer wrote *The Naked and the Dead* while living with his parents at 102 Pierrepont Street (he now lives elsewhere in Brooklyn Heights). At the same address Arthur Miller wrote his play *All My Sons*, before moving to 155 Willow Street, where he is remembered by a plaque—though he wrote *Death of a Salesman* at 31 Grace Court.

BAD LUCK AND THE BROOKLYN BRIDGE
In its early years, the Brooklyn Bridge saw more than its share of tragedy. Its designer, John A. Roebling, died following an accident before his bridge was complete. His son, Washington, took over, but became paralysed as a result of "the bends," and had to supervise the construction work from his sick bed. Twenty of the 600-strong work force died during the construction. Six days after the bridge opened, the screams of a woman who tripped on the approach caused a panic in which 12 people lost their lives, mistakenly believing the bridge was about to collapse. In 1884, however, circus-owner P. T. Barnum led 21 elephants across it; since then there have been few doubts as to the bridge's strength.

Brooklyn Bridge—"the crowning glory of an age memorable for great industrial achievements"

▶▶ **Brooklyn Bridge** 77D1
Subway: Brooklyn Bridge
Completed in 1883, the Brooklyn Bridge was the world's first steel suspension bridge, and, for 20 years, the longest. It formed the first fixed link between Brooklyn and Manhattan Island.

Enhanced immeasurably by its two Gothic 272-ft (83m) high stone arches (when they were finished, only the spire of Trinity Church rose higher into the New York sky), the bridge is an aesthetic as well as an engineering master-piece. Many writers, including Brooklyn-based Walt Whitman, have waxed lyrical over its beauty.

Bike riders, skaters, joggers and high winds can all be a hazard to walkers on the bridge's pedestrian path, easily the best way to appreciate the structure. From Manhattan, the views used to be of Brooklyn's busy shipyards, a scene re-created by a display beside the footpath, while another recounts the bridge's origins. In the other direction is a fabulous view of Manhattan.

▶ **Carnegie Hall** 151C2
57th Street at Seventh Avenue (tel: 247-7800, www. carnegiehall.org) Guided tours: Mon–Fri 11.30, 2 and 3. Admission: inexpensive
Subway: D, E, N, R; Seventh Avenue or 57th Street
Financed by a $2-million gift from steel magnate Andrew Carnegie, Carnegie Hall opened to the public in 1891 and quickly gained an international reputation for its out-standing acoustics. Its horseshoe-shaped auditorium is modeled on those of Italian opera houses. Refurbishment has restored the hall, best appreciated by attending a concert—a must if you have time. Tours of the building end at the **Carnegie Hall Museum,** which records the hall's origins and the long list of famous names that have graced its boards. Besides Benny Goodman's clarinet and Arturo Toscanini's baton, the museum has a 1964 book-ings diary with a handwritten entry recording the first New York appearance of "The Beetles"(sic).

Gothic vaulting (left) and (below) a sculptural detail of what will, if and when it is completed, be the world's biggest cathedral

▶▶ Cathedral of St. John the Divine   IBCB2

Amsterdam Avenue at 112th Street (tel: 316-7540; www. srjohndivine.org) Open: daily 7–6. Admission: free
Subway: 1; Cathedral Parkway (110th Street)

The cornerstone of the Cathedral of St. John the Divine was laid in 1892, marking the beginning of what is now an immense Episcopalian edifice spread across an amazing 11 acres (4.5ha)—the largest church in the US, and the largest Gothic church in the world, yet still many years short of completion.

The original plans were for a church of Byzantine/ Romanesque design, but delays caused by engineering problems and lack of finance meant that only the choir and four stone arches were completed in the first 25 years. Changing tastes (and the death of the project's original architect) saw the structure remodeled in French Gothic form, and it was given a facade reminiscent of Notre-Dame in Paris.

The nave, covering a staggering 32,000sq ft (3,000sq m), was completed in a comparatively swift 10 years, but the US's entry into World War II again halted progress, as did a decision during the 1960s to divert building money to the needs of the community. Another building program got under way in 1978, when funds were available to import a master stonemason from England to cut the Indiana limestone used in the towers and to train a small army of local apprentices.

As its towers still rise, enclosed by scaffolding, the cathedral's exterior takes on a strangely surreal appearance. Inside, the scale is breathtaking. The clash of Gothic and Romanesque/Byzantine styles is most apparent from the unfinished crossing, where the structure's anatomy is revealed and above which the red-tiled dome, installed as a "temporary" shelter during 1909, remains in place even today.

Foremost among the cathedral's decorations are the Mortlake Tapestries, woven in England during 1623 from cartoons by Raphael, and the 17th-century Barberini tapestries, which were woven on papal looms.

NEW YORK PUBLIC LIBRARY: 115TH STREET BRANCH
The main branch of the New York Public Library on Fifth Avenue (see page 168) is one of the city's greatest architectural delights, and the 115th Street branch (between Seventh and Eighth avenues) is no mere pile either. Dating from 1908, the library was the work of the firm of McKim, Mead, & White, and its imposing Renaissance style was intended to match the grandeur of early Harlem.

1   Charles A Dana Discovery Center
2   El Museo del Barrio
3   Museum of the City of New York
4   International Center of
     Photography
5   Jewish Museum
6   Cooper-Hewitt National
     Design Museum
7   Guggenheim Museum
8   Cleopatra's Needle
9   Delacorte Theater
10   Belvedere Castle
11   Swedish Cottage
12   American Museum of Natural
     History and Hayden Planetarium
13   San Remo Apartment Building
14   Loeb Boathouse
15   Alice in Wonderland Statue
16   Hans Christian Andersen Statue
17   Frick Collection
18   Bandstand
19   Holy Trinity Lutheran Church
20   Tavern-on-the-Green
21   Heckscher Playground
22   Wollman Memorial Rink

▶▶▶ Central Park

From most high points in Manhattan, what holds the eye longest is not the Empire State Building or the Chrysler Building but the great rectangle of greenery in the heart of the dense urban clutter. Central Park (www.central-parknyc.org) fills 843 acres (340ha) and runs for 50 city blocks between the Upper East and Upper West sides.

The candidates in New York's mayoral campaign of 1850 agreed on just one issue: the need for a large public park of the kind civic leaders and journalists had been advocating since poet and newspaper editor William Cullen Bryant raised the idea in 1844. At that time, property developers were breaking all records in their northward streak across Manhattan.

In 1856, the city paid $5.5 million for a tract of land, which was in an area well to the north of the city as then established, dotted with pig farms and squatter camps and mostly used as a refuse dump. Two years later work began on the park, to the plans drawn up by Frederick Olmsted (a farmer-turned-engineer-turned-journalist-turned-landscape architect) and English architect Calvert Vaux.

The park's design called for a major earth-moving project as glades, copses and rock outcrops were created, and some 5 million trees planted. Bridges linked the park's internal thoroughfares and cross-park traffic was carried by sunken roads to keep the pastoral view intact.

With tree-lined driveways for the wealthy to parade in horse-drawn carriages and footpaths for the working classes (who typically at the time toiled in sweatshops and lived in filthy tenements) to experience, as Olmsted expressed it, "a specimen of God's handiwork," the park was an instant success.

Though now fully enclosed by buildings and with far more monuments than Olmsted would have liked, Central Park is still a great escape from the city streets. The Fifth Avenue and Upper West Side apartment buildings that appear above the treetops simply add to the park's country-in-the-city effect. Getting lost temporarily in Central Park is surprisingly easy. Be sure to pick up a map from one of the information kiosks before you enter.

From the south, the first place to make for is the **Dairy**. In pursuit of a romantic rural vision, the Gothic-style Dairy was built here in 1870 as a place where traditionally attired milkmaids would serve fresh milk to mothers and young children. The quaint building now holds the park's main Visitor Center, with displays and several leaflets describing park walks.

North of here, across the 65th Transverse, the 22-acre (9ha) **Sheep Meadow** did indeed hold sheep during the park's earliest years, the resident flock being led across the park's West Drive twice a day to the Sheepfold, which occupied the site of the present Tavern on the Green.

Just east of the Sheep Meadow begins the **Mall**, one of the first completed sections of the park and its only formal area. Many 19th-century New Yorkers got their first taste of European-style promenading along its tree-lined esplanade, and some also gained their first experience of donkey- and goat-cart riding, both of which were offered to visitors here.

Olmsted initially resisted attempts to have statuary in the park but eventually agreed to the memorials of writers—Shakespeare, Robert Burns and Sir Walter Raleigh among them—which are grouped around the Mall's southern end to form the **Literary Walk**. Continuing north, the Mall leads into the **Concert Ground** and the **Naumberg Bandshell**, the scene of free live music on most summer weekends.

Cross the 72nd Street Transverse and you enter **Bethesda Terrace**. At its heart is the Bethesda Fountain and the elegant *Angel of the Waters* statue. One of the few pieces commissioned especially for the park, the statue, inspired by the biblical story of the Bethesda Pool in Jerusalem, was unveiled in 1873 to commemorate the opening of the aqueduct that gave New York its first regular supply of fresh water.

There is more water directly north of Bethesda Terrace, in the form of the **Lake**. A leisurely paddle along this imposingly calm body of water is a fine way to round off a park visit. Boats can be rented from the Loeb Boathouse, on the eastern banks of the lake.

If you are determined to do something more energetic, you could always cross the lake on foot by way of the Bow Bridge—one of Central Park's seven original cast-iron bridges—to **The Ramble**. Comprising 33 acres (13.4ha) of painstakingly re-created rurality, complete with rustic

STROLL: STRAWBERRY FIELDS

From the Upper West Side, entering Central Park on 72nd Street leads into Strawberry Fields, a 3-acre (1.2-ha) section maintained by an endowment from Yoko Ono, as a memorial to her late husband John Lennon.

Overlooked by the Dakota apartment building, where the Lennons lived (see page 96), Strawberry Fields is planted with 161 species of plant, representing 161 nations of the world. The authorities were not unanimous in agreeing to the tribute: conservative elements wanted a memorial to Bing Crosby.

Central Park's Bethesda Fountain

83

CENTRAL PARK IN STYLE
One way of seeing the park is as the city swells of the 1880s did: by horse and carriage. Buy a ticket from the stand at Grand Army Plaza (at the intersection of 59th Street and Fifth Avenue) and climb aboard. Prices have risen over the last hundred years, however: Expect to pay around $34 per person for a 25-minute trot.

birdhouses and beehives, The Ramble is excellent for exploration and for birdwatching. It is not advisable to ramble alone, however, as this is an isolated area. Across the 79th Street Transverse from The Ramble, a replica Scottish castle, **Belvedere Castle** (tel: 722-0210; *Open:* Tue–Sun 10–5. *Admission: free*), was erected in 1869 for no reason other than fun and holds displays on park wildlife.

To the left, a path leads to the **Shakespeare Garden**, planted with trees and plants mentioned in the bard's works, passes the **Delacorte Theater** (scene of a summer Shakespeare festival), and continues to the immaculate **Great Lawn**. Free open-air concerts are given here each year during the summer by the New York Philharmonic.

Central Park has had its share of well-publicised crimes

but is generally no more dangerous than the average New York street, though there are isolated areas where lone wandering is not wise. Do not visit the park after dark, except for a major event.

▶▶ Chelsea

IFCD2

West of Fifth Avenue, between 14th and 34th streets
In the 1990s Chelsea evolved into one of Manhattan's most stylish neighborhoods and a focal point for the city's vibrant gay community. Former warehouses close to the Hudson River have been converted into galleries and Chelsea has become a thriving quarter for new art.

Among the galleries is the **DIA Center for the Arts** (548 West 22nd Street, tel: 989-5566, www.diacenter.org; *Open:* Wed–Sun 12–6. *Admission: inexpensive; due to re-open in 2006*), with low-key exhibitions often featuring major names. Meanwhile, several piers on the water's edge (west of 23rd Street) became the imaginatively designed recreational complex of **Chelsea Piers** offering skating, bowling, river cruises and a promenade.

The commercial heart of Chelsea is around the junction of 23rd Street and Eighth Avenue. The residential areas nearby are a mixture of tasteful townhouses and high-rise apartment blocks.

Top: a sedate tour or (above) the more energetic pastime of rollerblading

The Chelsea Hotel

When the Chelsea opened in 1888 at 222 West 23rd Street, it was the first apartment building in New York to have a penthouse. Its facade featured wrought iron balconies decorated with sunflower motifs. Converted to a hotel in 1905, the Chelsea became famous as a haunt of writers, painters and composers, who gave it an unconventional ambience.

Painter John Sloan and writers Mark Twain and O. Henry (the pen name of William Sydney Porter) were among the Chelsea's early guests, but the hotel hit its artistic stride during the 1930s, after poet Edgar Lee Masters eulogized it in verse and novelist Thomas Wolfe took up residence. Impressed by the size of his suite, Wolfe dubbed his bathroom the "Throne Room" and kept 4,000 loose pages of prose strewn across his floor. Selections from these would be assembled and supplied to his publisher as finished works.

The 1950s and 1960s Its literary links were already established by the time Dylan Thomas made the Chelsea his New York base during the early 1950s. His last conscious hours, after he had claimed to have downed 18 whiskys in a Greenwich Village bar, were spent in room 205, and he died in hospital a few days later of suspected alcohol poisoning.

A decade later, the Irish writer Brendan Behan took shelter at the Chelsea and begged to be commemorated by a plaque—as he now is. Besides Behan, Beat writers William Burroughs and Gregory Corso, expatriate Russian novelist Vladimir Nabokov and abstract expressionist painter Jackson Pollock were among the renegades who gathered at the Chelsea's bar (which is now a Spanish restaurant).

Pop and punk The hotel provided a backdrop for Andy Warhol's rambling split-screen movie *Chelsea Girls* (which starred Warhol acolyte Edie Sedgwick, a Chelsea resident) and through the 1960s its guests included many pop-music icons—among them Bob Dylan, who wrote his epic song *Sad Eyed Lady of the Lowlands* in one of its rooms.

The hotel's most ignominious night came in 1978, when punk rocker Sid Vicious allegedly stabbed his girlfriend to death in their suite—Alex Cox's movie *Sid and Nancy* actually featured the hotel.

Step into the Chelsea's lobby and you will find plaques commemorating its most illustrious residents and many works donated by artist guests. The Chelsea's rooms vary greatly in style, size and price, and many of them are occupied by eccentric long-term guests.

Its decorative design may once have been ahead of its time, but the Chelsea has long been known not as an architectural landmark but as a cultural one

85

PRE-CHINATOWN REMNANTS

On St. James Place you can find the First Shearith Israel graveyard, predecessor of the cemeteries of Greenwich Village and Chelsea. The first Jewish cemetery in the United States, the site was consecrated in 1656, when it was considered to be well outside town.

On nearby James Street, St. James Church is an 1837 Greek Revival edifice. Al Smith, once an altar boy at the church, rose from this poor then-Irish neighborhood to become New York's governor and a 1928 Democratic presidential candidate.

Frenetic but fascinating, Chinatown's streetlife never takes a break

▶▶▶ Chinatown   IFCB3

New York streetlife enters a new dimension on the tightly clustered, densely crowded sidewalks of Chinatown, which lies between the courthouses, Little Italy and the Lower East Side.

Stalls are laden with seafood, vegetables or fruit; herbalist stores dispense wondrous remedies; bakeries concoct sweet cakes; and rows of gaudy neon signs advertise (in both English and Chinese) the noodle stores, tea parlors, and dim sum houses that bring the majority of non-Chinese New Yorkers to the area.

There has been a Chinese presence here since the 1850s, but only with the relaxing of immigration laws in 1965 did Chinatown really begin to expand. Spilling beyond its traditional boundaries, Chinatown now holds around half of New York's estimated 300,000 Chinese population and has been swelled by arrivals from Vietnam and other parts of Southeast Asia.

The handover of Hong Kong to Beijing has also been felt. Hong Kong banks have opened here, and brightly lit shopping malls stuffed with jewelry and electrical goods have spread along Canal Street.

Beyond the business and the people, there is not a lot to see in Chinatown, although an exception is the **Museum of Chinese in the Americas** (third floor, 70 Mulberry Street, tel: 619-4785, www.moca-nyc.org; *Open:* Tue–Sun 12–6, Fri 12–7. *Admission: inexpensive*). This exhibition presents an absorbing documentation of Chinese settlement in the US. The exhibits are a hodgepodge of family photos, items from Chinese-run businesses, and objects of symbolic significance carried from the homeland. Part of the museum's aim is to help young Chinese-Americans understand their history, although the temporary exhibitions examine many aspects of the Chinese Diaspora.

約⋯界慶祝中華民國八十⋯年雙十國慶

THE CHINESE COMMUNITY OF NEW YORK CELEBRATES
THE 81ST "DOUBLE TEN" ANNIVERSARY OF THE FOUNDING OF REPUBLIC OF CHINA

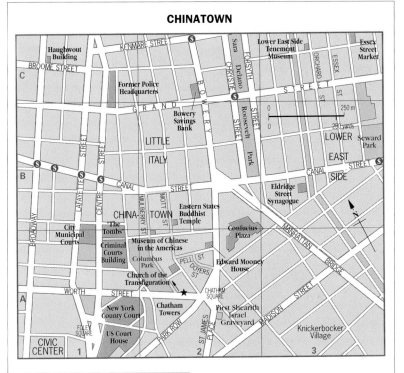

CHINATOWN

Walk

the **Transfiguration**, at 25 Mott Street, predates Chinatown. Not far away, **Doyers Street** was once the

Chinatown streetlife

Effervescent streetlife is the main attraction of Chinatown, which holds few specific sights. This walk covers the main ones and captures the atmosphere of the area.

Begin at **Columbus Park**, which replaced a notorious slum and red-light area of the mid-1800s. Across Mulberry Street is the entrance to the **Museum of Chinese in the Americas**. Walk up to **Canal Street** for Chinatown's biggest and brightest shopping emporiums before reaching Mott Street.

At 64 Mott Street, the **Eastern States Buddhist Temple** is a genuine temple but also sells souvenir Buddha figures, arranged in eye-catching rows. Built in 1801, the Georgian **Church of**

domain of opium dealers and prostitutes, and its bend was used as an ambush point during 19th- and early 20th-century Tong Wars, when rival Chinese gangs fought over who should have control of drug-trafficking, prostitution and gambling. Nowadays perfectly safe, Doyers Street is lined with numerous restaurants.

Chinese faces were few and far between in early 19th-century New York, but nowadays the Chinese community is expanding fast in both size and importance. Whether in academia or business, Chinese-Americans are frequently among the city's most spectacular achievers.

CHINESE IN THE US
Although only a few Chinese were present in New York prior to the late 1800s, they were already established in California where 25,000 had arrived in 1852. Most of them worked in the California gold mines and, subsequently, on the transcontinental railroad that linked the West Coast to the rest of the country. The Chinese gained a reputation as dependable laborers, but in the economic depression that followed the Gold Rush, they found themselves prevented from opening businesses or owning land. Banding together, the Chinese settled in what became the "Chinatown" districts of many California communities, some making the cross-country trip to the less hostile atmosphere of New York.

The 75 Chinese immigrants estimated to be living in New York in 1870 were mostly individuals who had jumped ship and assimilated themselves as best they could into established ethnic groups. By 1890, however, New York's Chinese population had rocketed to 12,000. Many of the new arrivals came here from California, where they had provided labor for the transcontinental railroad.

With their language and culture at odds with European New York, the lone Chinese males (denied the company of their relatives by an anti-immigration law of 1896) rarely strayed from Chinatown. Aided by family-based self-help organizations, they toiled in stores and laundries, sending any spare money back home.

The seamy side The popular imagination saw Chinatown as a neighborhood of exotica. Gambling, prostitution and opium dens did in fact exist, but usually in upstairs rooms or basements. These activities were overseen by the Tongs—an American term for a Chinese-American secret society. Many Tongs claimed long histories to impress recruits and, at a time when the Chinese were excluded from the American legal system, provided a vehicle for settling grievances.

Acceptance and expansion The Japanese invasion of China in 1937 helped unite warring factions in the Chinese community, and the subsequent US–Sino military alliance reduced anti-Chinese feeling among New Yorkers. A bigger change came in 1965, when limitations on Chinese immigration were lifted and waves of new arrivals from Taiwan and Hong Kong came to Chinatown.

The new Chinese were eager to embrace American ways. They quickly made their presence felt in mainstream New York life. Their success and prosperity enabled them to become fully integrated into New York life, and to leave cramped Chinatown for more comfortable homes. Many left the inner city for suburbia as soon as they made the climb up the economic ladder.

Chinese food to go. Chinatown's eateries cover a vast range of styles and regional cuisines

The unmistakable Chrysler Building—New York art deco at its finest, and everyone's favorite skyscraper

THE CHEATING SPIRE
The Chrysler Building's "world's tallest" title was acquired through some slightly devious behavior by its architect, William Van Alen. The needlelike spire that tops its 77 storys was secretly assembled inside the tower and pushed through the roof. In this way Van Alen outwitted his former partner, H. Craig Severance, whose contemporaneously completed Bank of Manhattan Building (40 Wall Street) would otherwise have earned the accolade.

POLICE RIOTS
In 1857, City Hall Park was the scene of violence between New York's two rival police forces, the discredited Municipal and the newly formed Metropolitan. Their battles continued into City Hall and ended only when National Guardsmen drew their bayonets.
   In September 1992, New York's finest again disgraced themselves in the park, when a poorly planned demonstration against Mayor Dinkins culminated in officers (some of them clearly the worse for drink) stepping over the barricades and blockading the entrance to City Hall.

►► Chrysler Building   151B3

42nd Street at Lexington Avenue (tel: 682-3070)
Open: Mon–Fri 7–6. Admission: free
Subway: 4, 6, 7; 42nd Street/Grand Central

The definitive symbol of New York art deco and briefly the world's tallest building, the 1,045-ft (318-m) Chrysler Building was completed in 1930. Its tower is still among the city's most recognizable landmarks. More impressive than the exterior view, however, is the lobby, retaining its walls of red-veined African marble and a mural by Edward Trumbull depicting the glories of world transportation. The elevators, too, still have their original laminated wood, and the entire 77-story building is studded with automobile motifs.

► City Hall   104C2

Broadway and Park Row (tel: 788-3000)
Open: Mon–Fri 9–4. Admission: free
Subway: N, R; City Hall

A cluster of municipal buildings stands near the foot of the Brooklyn Bridge. The oldest, the **City Hall**, a mixture of Federal and French Renaissance styles dating from 1811, is still in use for its original purpose. The barriers that line the front of the building are intended to prevent the frequent demonstrations in City Hall Park from blocking councillors' access to the building. Inside, a circular staircase winds beneath the eye-catching rotunda to the third floor, where the **Governor's Room** is lined by portraits of early New York notables and items of furniture mostly contemporaneous with the building. To the north stands the **Old New York County Courthouse**, intended as a shrine to justice but a building whose financing was one of the biggest swindles in New York history (see page 42). It is now used as municipal offices. Across Centre Street, the present **New York County Courthouse** has a hexagonal shape and a magnificent Corinthian portico.

City dwellers love to root for the home team, and New Yorkers—represented by two professional teams in football, hockey and baseball—are no exception. Loyalties and rivalries run deep, even though the closest most people get to actual games is the TV in their living rooms: Tickets, especially for football games and for playoff games in other sports, tend to be hard to get hold of and expensive.

THE NEW YORK MARATHON

What began in 1970 with 127 runners is now one of the world's largest urban marathons. Its 26-mile (42-km) course is contested by some 22,000 runners and watched by over 2 million spectators. Usually held on the third or fourth Sunday in October, it begins on Staten Island at the Verrazano-Narrows Bridge, passing through each of the city's five boroughs to finish at Central Park's Tavern on the Green.

A great New York sporting event

Baseball The exceedingly successful New York Yankees, with a string of World Series wins echoing the glory days that saw them dominate the sport from the 1920s to the 1960s, play at Yankee Stadium in the Bronx (tel: 718/293-6000; www.yankees.com). The season runs from April to October. Ticket prices range from around $8 (on the day) for the bleachers, where you will hear the New York crowd at its most witty but also get the worst view, to around $90 as you move up into the tiered seating.

The slightly less successful New York Mets (who met and were beaten by the Yankees in the World Series "subway series" in 2000) play at Shea Stadium in Queens (tel: 718/507-8499; www.nymets.mlb.com) where ticket prices range from $5–$48.

Basketball From fall to spring, basketball fans can watch the New York Knicks (short for "Knickerbockers") playing at Madison Square Garden (tel: 465-JUMP; www.nba.com /knicks). The Knicks had an all-win "dream" season in the early 1970s, but their record has been off and on

NEW YORK CITY MARATHON
MILE 16

since. Ticket costs vary, beginning around $10 and rising swiftly to over $300, being particularly difficult to get for the end-of-season play-offs. The advent of professional women's basketball quickly found New York Liberty (tel: 465-6073; www.wnba.com/liberty) among the country's top WNBA sides. Like the Knicks, they play at Madison Square Garden, with tickets priced from $10 to $230.

Hockey The incredible lack of success of the city's New York Rangers was dramatically ended by their winning of the Stanley Cup in 1994. The Rangers face off at Madison Square Garden (ticket info tel: 465-6000; www.nyrangers.com) in a season lasting from late fall to spring. New Yorkers who want to see a local hockey team with a more regular success rate are inclined to travel to Uniondale on Long Island, where the New York Islanders play at the Nassau Coliseum (tel: 516/794-9300; www.newyorkislanders.com).

Football Currently both of New York's two professional football teams play outside the city's boundaries at Giants Stadium, the Meadowlands, East Rutherford, New Jersey (tel: 201/935-8111). Despite being thrashed in the 2001 Super Bowl, the Giants (www.giants.com) have been slightly more successful than New York's AFC team, the Jets (www.nfl.com/jets) who are planning to move to Manhattan's proposed Sports and Convention Center. The season runs from August through December and tickets start at around $25. Particularly for Giants games, tickets are virtually impossible to obtain if not ordered months in advance. Shuttle buses run from Manhattan.

Horse-racing Thoroughbreds can be seen stampeding along the turf at Belmont Park, Elmont, Long Island (tel: 718/641-4700) at daily races held from May to July and from September to mid-October, and from late October to May at the Aqueduct Racetrack, Ozone Park, Queens (phone number as for Belmont Park). During August, the state's horse lovers move upstate to follow a month-long series of meetings at the Saratoga Equine Sports Center (tel: 518/584-2110).

Tennis Early in September the US Open takes place at Flushing Meadows, Queens (ticket info, tel: 1–866-OPEN-TIX). Tickets for the later stages of the Open are snapped up in advance, though it's usually possible to see international stars play at short notice—people with extra tickets sell them outside the stadium area. The springtime Tournament of Champions draws many top players to the West Side Tennis Club in Forest Hills, Queens (tel: 718/268-2300). A variety of lesser tournaments take place virtually year-round featuring rising amateurs and declining former pros. A remarkably long list can be found at www.tennisnyc.com

Student sports Many professionals develop their skills on a sports scholarship. For an early look at tomorrow's stars in sports that range from soccer and golf to fencing and wrestling, explore the forthcoming fixtures listed on the websites of Columbia (www.columbia.edu/cu/athletics) and New York (www.nyuathletics.com) universities.

SCALPERS
Scalpers offering tickets for all major sporting events are usually found on the streets leading to the venue. Be wary of forged tickets and that prices, which can start well in excess of the ticket's face value, will drop as game time approaches.

SPORTS BARS
The city's many sports bars provide alcohol and TV screens tuned to every sports event anyone could possibly want to watch. If a New York team is involved, you can also be sure of loud and frequent partisan comments and suggestions.

Informal basketball

*Altarpieces and chapel
furnishings at the
Cloisters*

▶▶ **The Cloisters**   IBCF1

*Fort Tryon Park, Washington Heights (tel: 923-3700;
www. metmuseum.org) Open: Tue–Sun 9.30–4.45.
Admission: moderate. Subway: A; 190th Street*

Manhattan and medieval European monasteries may
seem an unlikely partnership, but at **Fort Tryon Park**, close
to Manhattan's northern tip and perched on a spectacular
site above the Hudson River, parts of five 12th- to 15th-
century monastic buildings from France and Spain have
been brought together to form the Cloisters, a fitting home
for a large portion of the Metropolitan Museum of Art's
medieval collection and enclosed by beautiful gardens.

Although much of the Cloisters' architecture is new
disguised as old, the genuinely historic parts—assorted
columns, cloisters, chapels, apses and much more—were
gathered by sculptor George Gray Bernard as he roamed
the back roads of Europe during the early 1900s. Bernard
grabbed all the forgotten religious art and architecture he
could lay his hands on—some pieces were discovered
lying in ditches near old churches, others were being
used as garden ornaments. Bernard put the haphazard

collection on show in Manhattan and it was brought to the
Met in 1925 with funds provided by John D. Rockefeller,
who subsequently commissioned the construction of the
Cloisters to put it on permanent show. Rockefeller also
owned the land that became Fort Tryon Park (see panel
page 93) and donated to the Cloisters its most memorable
exhibit—the Unicorn Tapestries (see page 93).

Each section of the Cloisters is arranged more or less
chronologically, and highlights particular aspects of
medieval creativity. The Romanesque Hall, for example,
is entered through one of three sculptured church door-
ways, demonstrating the stylistic shift from 12th-century
Romanesque to 13th-century Gothic. Most impressive of
the three is the latest: a High Gothic masterpiece from
Burgundy, which shows Christ crowning the Virgin,
flanked by Clovis, first Christian ruler of France, and his
son, Clothaire. The two men are so realistically sculpted
they seem almost ready to reach forward and shake
your hand.

92

A "medieval" home for medieval treasures: the Cloisters

Off the Romanesque Hall you will find the apse of the 12th-century Fuentidueña Chapel, which survived as its church crumbled around it: Note the frescoes and the statues of St. Martin and the Annunciation of the Virgin, both of which remain highly impressive despite the ravages of age.

Next door, stroll around the cloisters of the Benedictine Saint-Guilhem Monastery admiring the 12th-century carved capitals before passing through the Romanesque room for the Langon Chapel. During the 12th century, few places produced better wood sculpture than Autun, in Burgundy. Gaze long enough at the chapel's major piece—an Enthroned Virgin and Child—and its many subtleties of form and texture gradually become clear.

Beyond the Langon Chapel are several Gothic rooms and the Cuxa Cloister, its pink arches and columns built in 1188 for a Pyrenean monastery. Across the cloister are the amazing Unicorn Tapestries, probably 16th-century and of Flemish origin. Depicting the hunt for the mythical unicorn as an allegory for Christ's Incarnation, the Unicorn Tapestries are vivid in color and rich in detail. Pick out the images of love and fertility (within the flora and fauna), which mingle with the Christian symbols and suggest that the series may have been commissioned to celebrate a wedding.

The beauty and glowing color of the tapestries tend to outshine everything else in the Cloisters, except for the six glorious stained-glass lancet windows in the adjoining Boppard Room. Produced during the 1400s, the panels originally stood in the Carmelite Church of St. Severinus in Boppard-on-Rhine in Germany. With stunning artistry and craftsmanship, the glass shows several saints occupying canopied niches around the central figure of the Virgin.

Another important exhibit is a few steps away: Robert Campin's *Annunciation* altarpiece, an early Flemish triptych pioneering the use of oils on wood panels and also breaking new ground by using a contemporary domestic setting.

FORT TRYON PARK
This park, in which the Cloisters stands, was the site of the Battle of Washington Heights during the Revolutionary War. The fort that stood here then was renamed Tryon by the victorious British, after the last British governor of New York. Subsequently, its 66 acres (27ha) were divided into private estates which, one by one, were later purchased by John D. Rockefeller. Rockefeller gave the land to the city in 1930, and the Olmsted Brothers (descendants of Frederick Olmsted, architect of Central Park) were commissioned to landscape the lawns, terraces and picnic grounds that stand here now.

RIVERSIDE CHURCH
Just south of the
Columbia University
campus, the Cathedral of
St. John the Divine rises
in its monumental and still
unfinished form (see page
81). Another substantial
example of religious architecture sits just to the
north, between 120th
and 122nd streets off
Riverside Drive, in the very
imposing French Gothic
form of Riverside Church
(www.theriversidechurchny
.org). The church—now
interdenominational—has
championed the under-
privileged, and radical
liberal views have often
been aired from its pulpit.
An elevator runs to the
tower's 20th-story obser-
vation level for views of
the Hudson River and over
Upper Manhattan. Go
after Sunday morning
service to hear world's
largest carillon, housed
in the tower. *Open
Tue–Sun 9–5. Admission:
free (*tel: 870-6700).

Alma Mater, *Daniel
Chester French's statue,
outside Columbia
University's Low
Library*

▶ Columbia University IBCB2

*114th–120th streets, between Amsterdam Avenue and
Broadway (tel: 854-4900, www.columbia.edu; free guided
tours of the campus run most weekdays)*
Subway: 1; 116th Street

Founded in 1754 with a charter from the British king
George II (it was originally named King's College) on a
site in Lower Manhattan, Columbia University was
intended to raise New York's cultural profile at a time
when the fast-growing city was regarded as an uncouth,
money-crazed upstart by the comparatively refined communities of Boston and New Haven, where the
universities of Harvard and Yale were well established.

The campus occupied various locations in Manhattan.
Through its steady movement northward, Columbia
acquired ownership of the land that was later occupied by
Rockefeller Center; it sold the prized plot during the mid-
1980s for $400 million. The university arrived at its
present location in 1897.

The specially designed campus (on the grounds of a
former lunatic asylum) placed the academic buildings
around a series of fountain-dotted plazas at the heart of
which stands the majestic **Low Library**, based on Rome's
Pantheon. This was the gift of Seth Low, a university president and briefly, starting in 1902, mayor of New York.

An elegant three-tiered stairway leads up to the library's
colonnaded entrance. Inside, you will see 16 green marble
columns supporting an impressive octagonal rotunda.
What you will not see is students poring over weighty
tomes: The library is used only for ceremonies and exhibitions. On the third floor, the Columbiana Collection charts
the history of the university with a mass of drawings,
documents, paintings and assorted paraphernalia.

On the library's steps you will pass Daniel Chester
French's symbolic sculpture, *Alma Mater*, which was

covered in gold leaf until 1962 and which formed an unlikely rallying point for the anti-Vietnam War demonstrations that spread across the campus in 1968. Just east of the library is the Italian Renaissance **St. Paul's Chapel,** which has a masterly vaulted interior.

▶▶ Cooper-Hewitt National Design Museum   *187C1*

91st Street at Fifth Avenue (tel: 849-8400; www.si.edu/nmd)
Open: Tue 10–5, Wed–Sat 10–9, Sun 12–5.
Admission: inexpensive
Subway: 4, 6; 86th or 96th streets

Inspired by their 1897 visit to London's Victoria and Albert Museum, the three Hewitt sisters set about creating a visual library of design that would inspire new ideas. From their motley assortment of wallpaper, keys, and unusual jewelry, the Cooper-Hewitt Museum has grown into a collection of more than 250,000 items. It includes ceramics, wall coverings, textiles, decorative arts, drawings and prints, plus encyclopedic reference and picture libraries devoted to design matters.

Selections from the eclectic stocks make up the museum's thematic shows. Whether they feature 17th-century French needlework, contemporary Italian typewriters, Middle Eastern embroidery, American hatboxes or three centuries' worth of maps (to mention a few past shows), this is where you will find some of New York's most imaginative, and sometimes most controversial, exhibitions.

The status of the museum rose greatly in 1967 when its collections, previously displayed in Lower Manhattan, were put into the care of the prestigious Smithsonian Institution and later moved to their present home, the former residence of industrialist Andrew Carnegie.

Carnegie was one of the world's richest men when he announced his intention to have built the "most modest, plainest, and roomiest house in New York": The 1901 Georgian mansion, in red brick and limestone, has 64 rooms and sits amid extensive gardens—intended for Carnegie, his wife and daughter, and their 19 servants.

As you wend your way around the exhibitions, notice the vaulted ceilings, the Tiffany glass windows and the Louis XVI music room furnished with French antiques and with a set of bagpipes molded into the decorations—a reminder of Carnegie's Scottish origins.

▶ Daily News Building   *151B3*

220 East 42nd Street
Open: during business hours (lobby only)
Subway: 4, 6, 7; Grand Central Terminal/42nd Street

Created by Raymond Hood, who with it established his credentials as the father of New York skyscraper architecture, the 1930 Daily News Building (now called the News Building) is a landmark, a no-frills structure of thrusting verticality. Inside the largely original lobby, a frieze recounts the rise and rise (though its immediate prospects are in question) of the New York newspaper that became a legend for its punchy headlines and salacious stories. An immense revolving globe sits at the center of displays on meteorological themes. If the building seems familiar, you may be remembering the 1980s *Superman* movies, in which it starred as the offices of the *Daily Planet*.

COLUMBIA UNIVERSITY RIOTS

By 1968, the student activism that had begun a few years earlier with the Free Speech Movement at the University of California at Berkeley had escalated into nationwide campus demonstrations protesting against US involvement in Vietnam and inept academic administrations. In April, Columbia University saw marches, sit-ins and the taking of five university officials hostage for 26 hours. The besieged university president eventually asked city police to clear the campus, in the course of which they arrested 698 students and injured 100—and united the student body and university staff in allegations of police brutality.

95

PETER COOPER

The fortunes of inventor and philanthropist Peter Cooper, grandfather of museum founders Sarah, Amy and Eleanor Hewitt, were built on glue and iron. The Cooper foundry, in New Jersey, was where the tracks of the US's first great railroads were forged. Recognizing that his riches stemmed from the "cooperation of the masses," Cooper founded the first free college, the Cooper Union, which still stands in what is today the East Village (see pages 98–99).

THE DAKOTA IN MOVIES AND BOOKS

Plenty of the Dakota's residents have had leading roles in movies. So, too, has the building. With its turrets, towers and gables, the Dakota provided a suitably unsettling location for Roman Polanski's 1968 story of demonic possession, *Rosemary's Baby*. It also played a part in the 1970 time-travel novel, *Time and Again*, by Jack Finney.

The Dakota Apartments: home of the stars, and a screen star itself

▶ Dakota Apartments

1 West 72nd Street
Subway: 1, 2, 3; 72nd Street

Wealthy New York house owners of the 1880s had yet to be convinced that apartment living was the lifestyle of the future when Edward S. Clark, heir to the Singer sewing machine fortunes, commissioned a luxury apartment house in what is now the Upper West Side but was then wild, open land dotted by shanty dwellings and not even linked to the city's power supplies.

So far out was the site that critics suggested it might as well be in the Dakota territories—which is how the building got its name and the ears of corn, arrowheads and the Native American head that decorate its entrance.

As the city spread northward and Midtown Manhattan house prices rocketed, there were suddenly lots of enthusiastic takers for the Dakota's marble floors and oak- and mahogany-paneled dwellings. The building quickly became—and continues to be—a prestigious address, with a roll call of rich and famous residents that has included Leonard Bernstein, Lauren Bacall, Judy Garland and John Lennon—who was murdered while entering the building in 1980.

More inspired by Manhattan's celebrity-filled soirées than by its art museums, Andy Warhol might be the one world-famous artist New York can call its own.

Born Andrew Warhola to Czech immigrant parents in Pittsburgh, Andy Warhol moved to New York in 1949 and within seven years was among the city's most sought-after commercial artists, much of his work appearing in high-society magazines.

Fame in a soup can Warhol loved the party-going life of New York but found his own fame, and artistic vocation, after a trip to a supermarket in 1962. As pop artists created collages of consumerist images, Warhol began painting soup cans, according the gravity of serious portraiture to each one.

He then went onto depictions of dollar bills, electric chairs and Brillo boxes, relishing the publicity that his work aroused. A reviewer wrote that Warhol's silk-screened images of Marilyn Monroe were "as sentimental as Fords coming off the production line." In reply, Warhol declared, "I want to be a machine" and named his studio the Factory.

In the mid-1960s, Warhol's Factory became a magnet for oddball characters in New York, many of whom starred in the underground movies that the artist began making, including *Chelsea Girls*, described by one critic as "an image of the total degeneration of American society."

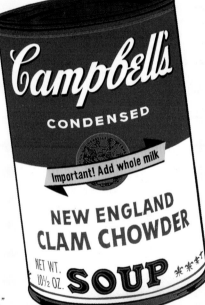

Getting rich The Factory's excesses ended in 1968, when Warhol narrowly survived an assassination attempt and found his financial affairs under scrutiny. Feeling that he should be earning more money, the guru of pop art became a society portrait painter, charging $25,000 a time, while his revamped *Interview* magazine began providing lucrative advertising alongside its celebrity gossip.

Warhol's wealth and fame became greater than his creativity. Moving to an expensive Upper East Side house in 1975, he spent a great deal of time and money on several ill-fated projects and appeared happiest during his daily shopping expeditions.

Shortly before his death in 1987, Warhol commented, "Getting rich isn't as much fun as it used to be."

ANDY WARHOL SAID
"In the future, everybody will be famous for 15 minutes."
"I don't think my art has any lasting value."
"I never wanted to be a painter. I wanted to be a tap dancer."

New York

LITTLE UKRAINE

In an area of the East Village around Second Avenue, between 4th and 14th streets is New York's Little Ukraine. Ukrainians began settling here in the late 1800s and, though their numbers have been greatly depleted, are still much in evidence among the neighborhood's many Slavic restaurants and stores selling traditional Ukrainian crafts—such as painted Easter eggs. The Ukrainian Museum, 203 Second Avenue (planning to move to East 6th Street), has changing exhibitions on past and present Ukrainian life in New York and in the homeland.

▶ The East Village *IFCC3*

In the 1950s, rising rents in Greenwich Village began pushing New York's more radical artists and writers across Broadway into the East Village. Here they took cheap apartments in tenement buildings otherwise inhabited by hard-up Eastern European immigrants, many of them from the Ukraine.

The heart of New York hippiedom in the 1960s and the epicenter of its 1970s punk rock scene, the East Village was regularly at the vanguard of alternative culture. Despite increasing signs of gentrification, expect to see at least one person dressed head-to-toe in leather and sporting bright green hair. Bizarre one-of-a-kind stores, ethnic eateries and a vibrant street scene are the things the East Village does best, although a handful of historical sights are also worthy of attention.

Astor Place carries the name of John Jacob Astor, one of early 19th-century New York's wealthiest men. Like the similarly extremely affluent Cornelius Vanderbilt, Astor owned one of the series of marble-fronted houses that became known as **Colonnade Row**. Once the grandest residences in New York, those that have managed to survive, now looking rather shabby, are on Lafayette Street (numbers 428 to 434).

Across Lafayette Street, Astor financed the city's first free public library in a brownstone building which, since the 1960s, has been the **Public Theater** (originally known as the Joseph Papp Public Theater), a venue for varied theatrical, cinematic and other arts events.

Another 19th-century remnant is the **Cooper Union Building**, which is just south of Astor Place. Founded in 1859 by the millionaire railroad tycoon Peter Cooper to provide free education for all, the college was the first of its kind in the US and also became an airing place for a range of political views: Abraham Lincoln was one of the famous orators who spoke here.

East of Astor Place is St. Mark's Place, where the unprepossessing building at number 77 was home to Anglo-American poet W. H. Auden from 1953. This was where, four decades earlier in the basement, Leon Trotsky had plotted the Russian Revolution. Nearby, the church of **St. Mark's-in-the-Bowery** (tel: 674-6377; *Open* for events only) arose on the estate of New York's Dutch governor, Peter Stuyvesant, in 1799. Its original body was later topped by a spire and fronted by a cast-iron portico. The church serves its congregation with Episcopal services, poetry readings and performance art. On the church's eastern side, Stuyvesant and six generations of his descendants lie buried.

St. Mark's-in-the-Bowery carries on the area's cultural tradition by staging poetry readings

The East Village stores and sights

This walk touches historical sites and also highlights the contemporary flavor of the East Village.

Begin at the 1799 church of **St. Mark's-in-the-Bowery** and continue along Stuyvesant Street to the **Cooper Union Building** (1859), the US's first free college.

In Astor Place is the huge Bernard Rosenthal **Alamo** cube sculpture which spins on a point when pushed. Turn onto St. Mark's Place, once the center of the punk rock movement, now a touristy collection of piercing shops, cafés and T-shirt kiosks. You can eat cheaply at **La Palapa** (77 St. Mark's Place) or at **Café Mogodor** (101 St. Mark's Place).

Unusual shop in the East Village

Turn on Avenue A to 7th Street and walk west to Second Avenue for funky vintage shops, such as **Tokio 7** (64 East 7th Street). Stop for a beer at **McSorley's** (15 East 7th Street), a local landmark since 1854.

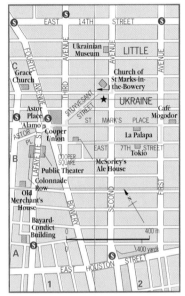

THE WALL OF HONOR
Running around the edge of Ellis Island close to the ferry dock, the American Immigrant Wall of Honor records 200,000 names—just a small percentage of those who became American citizens here. Ellis Island arrivals you may have heard of include Isaac Asimov, Irving Berlin, Bela Lugosi, Golda Meir, Edward G. Robinson and Rudolph Valentino.

Ellis Island: The future of many a would-be American was determined in these buildings. Museum displays now bring to life the hopes, fears, and disappointments of those newly arrived immigrants

▶▶▶ Ellis Island 48C2

Latest information tel: 269-5755; www.nps.gov/ellis
Approximately 100 million present-day Americans have ancestors who passed through Ellis Island, a modest speck of land in the shadow of the Statue of Liberty in New York's Upper Bay. From 1892 to 1924 this was the country's busiest immigration center.

Later serving as an army hospital and as an enemy alien detention center, Ellis Island was closed in 1954 and suffered total neglect until a $160-million restoration project reopened its major building as the Ellis Island Immigration Museum in 1990.

Those who arrived at Ellis Island hoping to become Americans were drawn from Europe's underclasses (immigrants of means were processed elsewhere and allowed immediate entry into the US). The elation they experienced on seeing the Statue of Liberty was usually quickly dissipated as they reached the place nicknamed the "Island of Tears" and faced the bureaucracy that stood between them and American citizenship.

These would-be Americans were screened for signs of insanity and contagious diseases and questioned about their relatives and their work skills. Any sign of sickness, or giving the wrong answers, could mean being detained and perhaps deported.

Some also got their first taste of American corruption at Ellis Island: Among the many scams were bribes for immigration officers and overpriced train tickets for onward travel in the US.

From statistics projecting the country's future ethnic make-up to trunks and string bags that carried treasured possessions from overseas, the museum has many eye-opening exhibits. However, it is the taped oral histories of former arrivals that do most to suggest the hopes, the fears and the sheer sense of bewilderment that most of the would-be immigrants experienced as they stepped into this building.

▶▶▶ Empire State Building 151B2

34th Street at Fifth Avenue (tel: 736-3100; www.esbnyc.com)
Open: daily 9.30–midnight, last lift 11.30pm.
Admission: moderate
Subway: B, D, F, N, R; 34th Street
The Statue of Liberty may be a more potent national symbol, but New York's most enduring emblem is the Empire State Building, rising above Midtown Manhattan with a gracious, ageless aplomb. As construction mania

EMPIRE STATE BUILDING FACTS

Height: 1,472 ft (449m)
Weight: 365,000 tons.
Number of bricks: 10 million.
Budget: $60 million.
Actual cost: $40,948,900.
Tallest visitor: King Kong, 1933.
Greatest tragedy: plane crashing into the 79th story in 1945, killing 14.

The lobby of the Empire State Building

NEW YORK SKYRIDE

If the views from the observation levels of the Empire State Building fail to satisfy, get an aerial view of the city on the New York Skyride—a flight simulator tour of the city at dizzying speed. The Skyride is on the Empire State Building's third floor. *Open* daily 10–11pm; tel: 1-888 SKYRIDE.

swept through New York during the booming 1920s, the Empire State Building was the winner in the financiers' race to create the world's tallest building, snatching the title in 1931 from the Chrysler Building and holding it until the first World Trade Center tower was finished in 1973.

The building rose to 1,250ft/380m (gaining an extra 222ft (70m) with a TV mast in 1951), and was constructed in only two years. The zoning laws (see page 24) of the time resulted in the tiered design that tempers the

At Federal Hall National Memorial, the statue of George Washington commemorates his inauguration as president, which took place in an earlier building on the site

SKYSCRAPER MUSEUM
With plenty of gist on what its name suggests, the museum sits at the southern tip of Battery Park (39 Battery Park Place; tel: 968-1961. *Open* Wed–Sun 12–6. *Admission: inexpensive*) and makes a fitting stop amid the Financial Districts forest of high rises.

THE ORIGINAL FEDERAL HALL
The historic significance of the present Federal Hall is eclipsed by that of its predecessor, which housed the first US government and which was where, in April 1789, George Washington was sworn in as the country's first president.
Despite its role in US history, the original building reached such a dilapidated state that it was sold for scrap in 1812.

impact of the structure's bulk and contributes to its elegant profile.

Conceived in an economic boom, the building was completed amid the gloom of the Depression, the Wall Street crash occurring as the 2-acre (0.8-ha) site—which held the original Waldorf-Astoria Hotel—was being cleared. Consequently, much of the office space remained unrented for years, and most of the building's early income was from tourists visiting for the views.

Once you have admired the art deco fittings of the lobby, descend to the concourse for a ticket and ride the express elevator to the 86th-floor observation level. On a clear day you can see for 80 miles (130km). The enclosed 102nd-floor level has been closed to the public due to long lines.

▶ **Federal Hall National Memorial**   *104B2*
Wall and Nassau streets (tel: 825-6888; www.nps.gov/feha)
Open: daily 9–5, closed Sat and Sun during winter.
Admission: free. Subway: 2, 3, 4, 5; Wall Street
Its finely proportioned steps and Doric columns impose themselves grandly in the heart of the Financial District, but a sense of history is disappointingly missing from the echoey interior of the 19th-century Federal Hall. Built as the first US Custom House, it later served as a bank before being declared a national memorial in 1939.

If you are exploring the Financial District, Federal Hall ought to be on your itinerary, but do not expect anything spectacular. Inside, only a short film and a rather tame collection of exhibits record events that took place on the site: A glass-encased section of balcony railing, on which Washington leaned when addressing the crowds after his inauguration, and a pair of the great man's belt-buckles form the highlights.

▶ **Film Center Building**   *151C1*
Ninth Avenue, between 44th and 45th streets
Open: business hours (lobby only)
Subway: A, C, E; 42nd Street
You may not want to visit any of the film companies that have offices here, but the Film Center Building justifies a visit to view one of the city's most stunning art deco interiors: Its foyer, cloakroom and entrance hall are all the work of Ely Jacques Kahn. Already an outstanding modernist architect, by the late 1920s Kahn had also built up a reputation for his distinctive interior decoration which was based on interlinked geometric forms—employed here to wonderful effect.

▶▶ **Financial District**   *IFCA2*
The nation's monetary institutions took root in Lower Manhattan from the early 1800s, and as the city grew, so did its Financial District, quickly becoming a global center of trade and commerce. Side by side in this compact area stand grandiose neo-classical buildings, whose form signified their status as repositories of wealth, and the high-rise glass and steel blocks that are the contemporary towers of mammon.

The exuberant 1980s saw Wall Street (just one of several thoroughfares, but internationally synonymous with the highest of high finance) yield millions and give birth to the yuppie. But the party was over by the end of the decade, when a succession of scandals put the greedy behind bars and heralded the economic uncertainties of the 1990s.

Facing Wall Street from Broadway, the striking neo-Gothic form of **Trinity Church** (tel: 602-0800; www.trinitywallstreet.org) has, since the 1840s, been reminding the Financial District's power brokers of a force greater than money. Note the bronze doors and the reredos, and continue into the small church museum to look at drawings showing a Manhattan skyline dominated by church spires rather than high-rise towers. In the 17th-century graveyard (*Open:* daily 7–5) lies Alexander Hamilton, the first US treasurer.

Predating Trinity Church by almost a century is **St. Paul's Chapel** (tel: 233-4164, www.saintpaulschapel.org; *Open:* Mon–Sat 10–6, Sun 10–4), Manhattan's only surviving prerevolutionary church. Laid out in a Georgian style with a surprisingly bright interior, the chapel was regularly visited by George Washington, and dutifully maintains the Washington Pew, where the first president sat during the service marking his inauguration in 1789.

WALL STREET'S NAME
An oaken barricade erected by Dutch governor Peter Stuyvesant in 1653 to mark the northern boundary of New Amsterdam and deter British invaders was the "wall" that gave the world-famous street its name. The wall never quite fulfilled its promise, because its planks were steadily removed to build and repair the wooden homes of settlers. In 1699 its remains were finally demolished by the then well-entrenched British.

Now dwarfed by skyscrapers several times as high, Trinity Church began life as the city's tallest building, at 264ft (80m) high

103

THE FEDERAL RESERVE
Many Financial District buildings house major financial corporations where every day millions of dollars are traded and transferred in paper and electronic transactions. One of the few that actually holds money—in the form of gold—is the Manhattan branch of the Federal Reserve (33 Liberty Street; tel: 720-6130, www.ny.frb.org), formally known as the Federal Reserve Bank of New York. Nationally, the Federal Reserve acts as banker to major banks and to the US government, regulates monetary policy and sets interest rates. The high security of the fortresslike building can be lawfully penetrated on free guided tours, but tickets must be acquired well in advance. *Open* Mon–Fri 9–5; tours at 10.30, 11.30, 1.30 and 2.30.

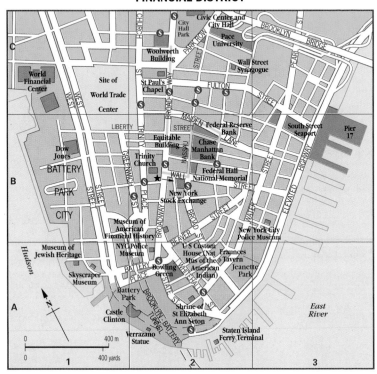

FINANCIAL DISTRICT

Walk

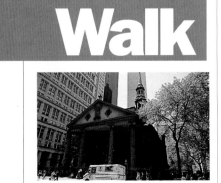

Financial District architecture

Encompassing historic churches and financial and architectural landmarks, this walk is an excellent way to explore the varied facets of the Financial District.

Begin at **Trinity Church** (page 103) and continue along Wall Street, stop-

ping at **Federal Hall** and detouring along Broad Street for the **Stock Exchange** (page 182).

Continue along Nassau Street for **Chase Manhattan Bank**, the first international-style structure in Lower Manhattan. Across Maiden Lane, you can gaze at over 11,000 tons of gold—the wealth of many nations—stored below ground at the **Federal Reserve Bank** (advance reservations essential, tel: 720-6130). Otherwise, examine the richly decorative ironwork of the enormous building's facade.

On the corner of Broadway, the much-detested 1915 **Equitable Building** rises for 40 stories; this was New York's first ever high-rise office building and the first to plunge its neighboring buildings—and much of the street below—into relative darkness. Continue along Broadway for **St. Paul's Chapel** (page 103); aim to arrive for a free lunchtime concert, and finish in the ornately decorated lobby of the Woolworth Building (page 192).

Tussles during the 19th century among Eastern Europe's Slavic peoples—Poles, Ukrainians and Russians—and the totalitarian suppression of more recent times helped create two of New York's most stridently nationalistic communities: the Poles and the Ukrainians, who now coexist peaceably alongside their former foes, the Russians.

Polish-Americans Struggles against colonial oppression in their own country made New York's Poles natural allies of the Americans in the revolutionary battles with the British. Not much later, New York offered refuge to those who had led an unsuccessful Polish republican uprising in 1830. The 234 immigrants who arrived were among Poland's finest minds, and were to give New York its first Polish cultural institutions.

Later Polish arrivals found factory jobs in the Greenpoint area of Brooklyn, though some opened the stores and bookstores that would become community focal points. Soviet control of postwar Poland brought exiled intellectuals, while the collapse of Communism in the 1990s led to more arrivals.

The Ukrainians Enforced military service in the czar's army caused many Ukrainians to flee their Russian-dominated homeland during the 1800s. Arriving in New York with their families, they turned a section of what is now the East Village into the world's largest urban Ukrainian community by 1919.

Russian immigrants The bulk of Russian immigrants were Jewish refugees who had fled persecution under the tsar (see page 139). More symbolic of the effect of European political upheavals, though, were the Russian aristocrats who arrived in New York as Leon Trotsky (here since the abortive 1905 revolution) left for Moscow to help the Bolsheviks seize power. Another arrival was groundbreaking choreographer George Balanchine. These newly arrived Russians quickly became integrated into New York society—a far cry from the former Soviet Russians who later settled in Brighton Beach (see page 75).

THE PULASKI AND KOSCIUSZKO BRIDGES
Two of the bridges—the Pulaski and the Kosciuszko—linking Brooklyn and Queens bear the names of Poles who aided the American cause in the Revolutionary War. Cavalry expert Casimar Pulaski was noted for his bravery in battle (he died in an attack on the British); the engineering skills of Thaddeus Kosciuszko were crucial in preparing the anti-British fortifications at West Point and Saratoga.

105

The first taste of America for European immigrants: Ellis Island

New York

The Flatiron Building—an unmistakable Fifth Avenue landmark

23 SKIDOO

A story goes that in the days when well-dressed ladies had skirts to their ankles, high winds would find voyeurs lingering outside the Flatiron Building on 23rd Street hoping to spot female legs exposed by the breeze. The shouts of the police when moving the gentlemen on are thought to be the origin of the term "23 skidoo."

DANIEL H. BURNHAM

The architect of the Flatiron Building, Daniel H. Burnham, made his name in Chicago in the 1880s, where, in partnership with John Root, he pioneered the modern skyscraper by making the first use of a steel frame to support a high-rise structure. Burnham's design ideas became a fundamental element in the highly influential "Chicago School" of architecture. Burnham's Chicago work was made possible partly because of a devastating fire that required the entire downtown area to be rebuilt. He also played an important role in the reshaping of San Francisco, wrecked by the earthquake of 1906, for which he planned a new Civic Center.

▶ **Flatiron Building**   *151A2*

Broadway and Fifth Avenue at 23rd Street
Subway: N, R; 23rd Street

Architect Daniel H. Burnham solved the problem of fitting a building into the triangular plot of land where Broadway crosses Fifth Avenue with the most logical solution: a triangular building. It was the world's tallest (285ft/87m) on its completion in 1902 and was one of the first to be erected around a steel frame—the basic support of every subsequent skyscraper.

Nowadays, it is not height or building techniques that make the Flatiron Building one of New York's most-loved structures but its pretty French Renaissance features and the fact that its limestone body tapers to an impossibly slender 6-ft (2-m) wide corner curve on 23rd Street. In recent years, the building has provided a convenient sobriquet for the immediate area, now known locally as the "Flatiron District."

▶ The Forbes Galleries   113C2

Fifth Avenue, between 12th and 13th streets (tel: 206-5548)
Open: Tue, Wed, Fri, Sat 10–4. Admission: free
Subway: L, N, R 4, 6; 14th Street/Union Square

Even in New York, few magazine publishers have broken the speed record for ballooning across the country or have hurtled along Fifth Avenue on a motorcycle. Malcolm S. Forbes did both of those things, and more, in a career that began by accident and left him with wealth estimated, at his death in 1990, to be in excess of $700 million.

Born in 1919, two years after his father had founded *Forbes*, a ground-breaking magazine of investigative financial journalism, Forbes had turned the ailing title into a thriving concern by the time he took it over in 1964. One of the secrets of his success was a genius for garnering maximum publicity for himself and the magazine. Through the 1970s the media doted on Forbes and his colorful activities, which ranged from lavish parties to his off-beat collecting interests.

The Forbes Galleries bear the fruits of Forbes' quirky collecting passion. They occupy the first floor of the Forbes Magazine building. Among the displays are 500 model boats and submarines (some of them in bathtubs) viewed to the accompaniment of what purports to be the sound of the Battle of Jutland. Some 12,000 model soldiers are arranged in battle-ready poses, and there is an amazing room of trophies awarded for achievements such as having the best pure-bred bull of 1878 and the best 5 acres (2ha) of turnips grown with Bradburn's manure.

The Presidential Papers room holds less eccentric material, drawn from the Forbes collection of 3,000 historical documents, while another special room displays scores of objets d'art made by master jeweler–goldsmith Peter Carl Fabergé for the last two czars of Russia, though some of the gem-encrusted Easter eggs once here have been sold.

▶▶ Fraunces Tavern   104A2

54 Pearl Street (tel: 425-1778; www.frauncestavernmuseum.org)
Open: Tue–Fri 10–5, Thu 10–7, Sat 11–7. Admission: free
Subway: 1, 4, 9; Bowling Green, South Ferry or Broad Street

This Federal-style brick building, which looks like a dollhouse beneath the glass-and-steel high-rises of the Financial District, stands on the site of the original Fraunces Tavern, a hotbed of subversion during the 18th century, when its customers included George Washington and his fellow revolutionaries. At the successful completion of the Revolutionary War, Washington made a famously emotional farewell to his officers here after a meal in the Long Room. The revolutionary era is commemorated by the Tavern with displays of period furniture, paintings and other objects of interest.

It may seem strange today, but the tavern became the unofficial seat of several government bodies during the earliest days of nationhood and spent three years as the recognized base of the Department of Foreign Affairs, the War Department and the Treasury, before being unceremoniously sold to a Brooklyn butcher.

If you visit the tavern around lunchtime, the atmosphere is enhanced by the smell of food wafting up from the renovated restaurant.

THE SALMAGUNDI CLUB
At 47 Fifth Avenue, opposite the Forbes Magazine Galleries, an 1853 Italianate brownstone mansion built for a coral magnate provides a home for the Salmagundi Club. Founded in 1871 (but moving here in 1917), the Salmagundi Club is the oldest artists' club in the United States and numbered Stanford White and Louis Comfort Tiffany among its early members. Occasional exhibitions provide a chance to peek at the building's extravagantly appointed interior.

The word "salmagundi" describes a mixed salad dish popular in the 18th century, but was presumably adopted from a series of pamphlets, the *Salmagundi Papers*, written and published in the early 1800s by author Washington Irving and friends. The *Salmagundi Papers* satirized New York life and, among other things, first coined the word Gotham as an alternative name for the city.

A BOMB AT THE FRAUNCES TAVERN
George Washington was not the last revolutionary to make a point at Fraunces Tavern. In January 1975, the building was rocked by a bomb that killed four Wall Street businessmen and left 55 people injured. Responsibility was claimed by an underground group called the FALN, in revenge for the US Government's resistance to Puerto Rican independence.

For those with money·and a well-known face (or name), New York is the ultimate playground. What follows is a very selective Manhattan list for the well-heeled person about town. For visitors who need to budget carefully, a peek inside one or two of these establishments offers a glance at the luxurious end of New York's wide spectrum of lifestyles.

Daniel (60 East 65th Street, between Madison and Park avenues, tel: 288-0033). One of the reasons Daniel Boulud decided to relocate his gastronomic temple was that he couldn't accommodate all of the power players and food lovers clamoring for reservations. Some $15 million and 40 additional seats later, you still have to reserve a table four weeks in advance. The restaurant is a formal affair, an elegant combination of contemporary style and stateliness. Think ethereal soups, whole-roasted fish, succulent braised meats and a seasonality and freshness of ingredients unsurpassed by any of the city's great restaurants. Café Boulud in the Surrey Hotel (20 East 76th Street) approximates the flagship's fare and flair at slightly reduced prices.

Jean Georges (Trump International Hotel, 1 Central Park West at Columbus Circle, tel: 299-3900). Like superstar chef Jean-Georges Vongerichten himself, this four-star restaurant is smart and elegant. During the day it is flooded with sunlight, at night the glow radiates from the beautiful crowd. In keeping with the stylish environment, the food is conceptual and artfully presented: for example seared sea scallops with raisin caper sauce. Equal emphasis is placed on service, and the tableside show is like a fine ballet. Don't miss the extravagant tea service and the homemade marshmallows in a variety of flavors, paraded around the room in glass apothecary jars and snipped ceremonially onto your plate. A seasonal prix fixe menu is set at $85.

GETTING AROUND NEW YORK
When a special occasion takes priority over money spent, you can see the city from a Rolls-Royce, Hummer, Ferrari Testarossa or another eye-catching make and model to suit your speed. Prices are from $350 to $1,000 for a three-hour minimum rental. Silver Star Limousine (tel:914/476-3311 or 914/476-9448; www.silverstarlimo.com) are among the operators awaiting your call.

Four Seasons (99 East 52nd Street, between Park and Lexington avenues, tel: 754-9494). The serious trade here is power-lunching corporate executives—plus a sprinkling of lawyers, politicians and publishers. On the ground floor of Mies van der Rohe's landmark Seagram Building, this Philip Johnson-designed restaurant features a large Picasso tapestry and other noted modern pieces. The lunch menu is designed to be good but simple, so it does not detract from the deals being struck across the tables. At dinner, the chef presents ably prepared contemporary American creations, some of which are finished at your table. A full dinner here is liable to cost $100 per person; lunch should be around $40.

The "21" Club (21 West 52nd Street, between Fifth and Sixth avenues, tel: 582-7200). A row of cast-iron model

Luxurious restaurants

jockeys stand to attention along the facade of the "21" Club, which opened on New Year's Eve 1929 and was just one of scores of speakeasies lining 52nd Street. Despite a complete refurbishment in the 1980s, the "21" Club's dark, wood-paneled walls, deep-pile carpets and jacket-and-tie requirements offer a picture of old-style luxury rarely found in New York today. Although appearances suggest otherwise, it is not an exclusive club, but there would be no point in showing up without a reservation. Many regulars come here to confirm their place in the New York social pecking order as much as to dine on Erik Blauberg's reworked American classics. Try the famous "21 Burger," or the pretheater prix fixe dinner as a way to sample the goods without going broke.

Alain Ducasse New York (Essex House, 155 West 58th Street, tel: 265-7200). A once-in-a-lifetime meal here requires a reservation, a jacket and tie and an unflinching approach to credit card use. Yet it might be argued that chef Ducasse's artful French fare is worth every penny. A seasonal, prix fixe menu might include confit of duck foie gras, apricot gelée, spring green peas with crayfish, filet of black sea bass, clear Osetra caviar, champagne sabayon, sautéed rack of milk-fed veal and lightly creamed morels. The menu is set at—take a deep breath—$225, but then here culinary classics become new sensory sensations. Antiques, contemporary photographs and works of art from Alain Ducasse's private collection furnish the lovely central space.

SIGHTSEEING BY HELICOPTER

One way to beat the crowds at the Empire State Building is to view it, and the rest of Manhattan, from a helicopter. Sightseeing helicopter flights are operated day and night by Island Helicopter Sightseeing (tel: 683-4575) and Liberty Helicopter Tours (tel: 800/542-9933 or 967-6464).

SPECIALITY GROCERS

Manhattan's avid food lovers are willing to pay high prices for superior quality and variety at fancy food emporiums such as **Citarella** (Sixth Avenue at 9th Street) in Greenwich Village, with exquisite produce, meat, fish and pastries, and the huge SoHo trendsetter **Dean & Deluca** (560 Broadway at Prince Street) where food is displayed like art. On the Upper West Side, there's **Zabar's** (2245 Broadway at 80th Street), which sells fine foods on the street level and kitchenware upstairs. On the Upper East Side are the **Vinegar Factory** and **Eli's**, also owned by the Zabar's clan. The **Chelsea Market** (88 Tenth Avenue) is a block-long food mall with good independent purveyors, and the new **Whole Foods** (Columbus Circle at Central Park southwest) is the most magestic of the city's branches, which all have a superior selection of organic produce, meat and dairy products.

The luxurious Plaza Hotel: evocative of Old World elegance

Having made his fortune in Pittsburgh, industrialist Henry Clay Frick moved to New York, where he had this elaborate mansion built to house his superb collection of European art

MOVING PICTURES
Each summer, Henry Frick had his fantastic art collection packed into crates and transported in a special railway car so he could enjoy it while staying at his estate in Massachusetts. Asked if he was worried about losing the priceless canvases through an accident in transit, Frick allegedly replied, "No, they're insured."

▶▶ Frick Collection   151D2

70th Street at Fifth Avenue (tel: 288-0700; www.frick.org)
Open: Tue–Thu, Fri 10–9, Sat 10–6 and Sun 1–6.
Admission: moderate
Subway: 6; 68th Street

Henry Clay Frick made a fortune through coke and steel, and was little loved in his day for his mean-spirited business practices. Ironically, the Frick Collection of 14th- to 19th-century European art, housed on the first floor of the French-style mansion in which Frick spent the last five years of his life (he died in 1919), is perhaps the most loved of New York's many art collections.

The absence of ropes, descriptive texts and other museum trappings is intended to make seeing the collection akin to visiting a private house. The collection is a triumph of quality over quantity, and there is not one painting that does not deserve its wall space.

Highlights are many and naturally vary according to individual taste. Few could fail to be impressed, however, by Gainsborough's *The Mall in St James's Park*, a refined vision of privileged promenaders that stands out in a dining room lined by 18th-century English portraiture.

The living hall has two particularly potent canvases: Titian's *Portrait of a Man in a Red Cap* and El Greco's *St. Jerome*. But the cream of the collection is hung in the west gallery: Two of Turner's studies of northern European ports resonate on facing walls, close to Rembrandt's 1658 *Portrait of a Young Artist—Self-Portrait* and his much debated (its authenticity is disputed) *Polish Rider*.

After leaving the final room, take a break in the garden court before starting through the collections once again, this time concentrating on the outstanding sculptures, tapestries and decorative arts exhibits.

▶ Garment District   IFCD1

On and around Seventh Avenue between 30th and 40th streets, the Garment District is the heart of New York's renown fashion industry, its warehouses and factories packed with the latest work of designers whose creations are displayed in showrooms. Many local stores specialize in rag trade items such as fabrics, ribbons, buttons, trimmings and lace. The sharp contrast between fashion's glitzy public face and the reality of low-paid workers who stitch and sew has long stained the area, although the divisions are receding as the district's warehouse-to-office conversions attract more diverse professions. Designers such as Ralph Lauren and Calvin Klein are among those honored with bronze and granite plaques embedded in Seventh Avenue, locally titled "Fashion Avenue."

▶ General Grant Memorial   IBCB2

Riverside Drive at 122nd Street (tel: 666-1640; www.nps.gov/gegr) Open: daily 9–5. Admission: free
Subway: 1; 116th Street

The largest mausoleum in the US, its gray granite form rising 150ft (46m) beside the Hudson and its entrance fronted by six Doric columns, the General Grant Memorial (commonly known as Grant's Tomb) holds the remains—in 9-ton marble sarcophagi—of Ulysses S. Grant and his wife Julia. As commander-in-chief of the Union forces in the Civil War, Grant achieved enormous fame: An estimated million people lined the route of his funeral procession in 1885. Inside, a chilled atmosphere prevails, and your footsteps echo as you walk around reading the accounts of Grant's distinguished military service and his less successful eight-year tenure as 18th US president. The decorated benches outside result from a community arts project.

▶ Gracie Mansion 187C2

East End Avenue at 88th Street (tel: 570-0985; www.ntc. gov/html/om/html/gracie.html)
Guided tours: Apr–Oct, Wed 10, 11, 1, 2. Admission: moderate
Subway: 4, 6; 86th Street

The official residence of the mayor of New York since 1942, Gracie Mansion was built in 1799 as a country retreat for shipping magnate Archibald Gracie. After his business collapsed, Gracie sold the mansion, and it spent an ignominious period as a refreshment stand before being purchased by the city. Renovations have made the mansion a finer example of Federal architecture (the first architectural style considered distinctly American) than it was in its infancy. The house can be viewed only on guided tours.

GRANT'S MILITARY CAREER
Following an unremarkable graduation (21st in a class of 39) from West Point Academy, Ulysses S. Grant distinguished himself in service, but resigned from the army in 1854 while stationed in California. Grant failed as a farmer (his subsequent occupation), and was working as a clerk in his father's store in Illinois at the outbreak of the Civil War. His military experience led to his appointment as brigadier of the Illinois Volunteers. A series of battle successes followed, showing a strategic brilliance that culminated in Grant's capture of the Confederate stronghold of Vicksburg after a 47-day siege in 1863. The following year, Grant was made commander of all Union armies. As president, Grant faced the postwar Reconstruction period and difficulties that would have tested the skills of the most experienced politician—his battle planning skills proved no match for the chicanery of Washington DC.

HENDERSON PLACE
In a cul-de-sac on the north side of 86th Street, close to Gracie Mansion, stands the lovely row of 24 Queen Anne-style houses that constitute the Henderson Place Historic District. The houses were commissioned during the 1880s by fur-hat manufacturer John C. Henderson to provide homes for "persons of moderate means."

The grandiose mausoleum of Civil War general Ulysses S. Grant was inspired by Napoleon's tomb in Paris

Greenwich Village secondhand stores may not offer such good bargains as less fashionable areas of the city, but they are hard to beat for sheer variety

GRACE CHURCH
One of the few things in Greenwich Village likely to bring to mind the European Middle Ages is the 1846 Grace Church, on Broadway, between 10th and 11th streets. The church's finely proportioned Gothic Revival design—among the earliest examples of the style in the US—helped its architect, James Renwick, win the commission for the larger, grander St. Patrick's Cathedral in Midtown Manhattan. Set on Broadway's first curve, the church's spire could originally be seen from as far south as what is now Battery Park.

▶ ▶ ▶ Greenwich Village   IFCC2

No place in New York has a greater cultural aura than Greenwich Village. For almost 100 years this has been a breeding ground and rallying point for the nation's most inventive and imaginative minds.

From its earliest days, Greenwich Village has kept its distance from mainstream New York life. Its first homes were built to enable the wealthy to escape the outbreaks of disease that were common in the 1790s, pushing back the boundaries of the city that, until then, had been contained within present-day Lower Manhattan.

By the late 1800s, the rich were moving north again, and their Greenwich Village town houses were being converted into stores, factories and boarding houses for immigrants. By the turn of the 20th century, Greenwich Village's diverse ethnic mix had fostered an atmosphere of tolerance that, coupled with low rents, attracted the unconventional elements that gave birth to the country's first, and its most celebrated, enclave of non-conformity.

Over three decades, writers and artists from Walt Whitman to Edward Hopper were to turn American culture upside down from their Greenwich Village bases. During the 1950s, the earliest Beat writers began taking Greenwich Village still further away from the materialist values of middle America, but rents were soon on the rise as new transit links made Greenwich Village the target of moneyed professionals in search of a well-placed neighborhood full of character.

Living in Greenwich Village today certainly requires financial security, but the lawyers and investment bankers who have flocked here have certainly not dampened the community spirit or Greenwich Village's rebellious streak. A Bohemian mood still percolates through its innumerable Italian cafés and restaurants, even though today most Greenwich Village visitors are on shopping or nightlife expeditions rather than seeking creativity's cutting edge.

(Continued on page 116)

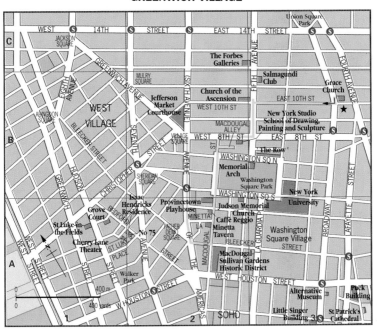

GREENWICH VILLAGE

113

Walk

The heart of Greenwich Village

From Grace Church in the east, this walk goes through the heart of Greenwich Village, ending at the foot of Christopher Street.

Leaving Grace Church, walk along 10th Street to the 1840 **Church of the Ascension**, by English architect Richard Upjohn, also known for Trinity Church in the Financial District.

Eighth Street holds many stores and the New York Studio School of Drawing, Painting and Sculpture, first home of the Whitney Museum. This was founded in 1931 by Gertrude Vanderbilt Whitney; her own studio was a converted stable at 17½ MacDougal Alley (a private street).

In business since 1785, **Caffè Reggio** is the oldest of many cafés lining MacDougal Street; its dark

interior has been seen in movies such as *Godfather II* and *Serpico*.

On Sixth Avenue, Village Square is dominated by the gables, turrets and towers of the 1877 **Jefferson Market Courthouse**, now a library. Across Sixth Avenue is **Balducci's**, a long-established purveyor of groceries and very fine foods.

Washington Square Park

Like delis and subway stations, bars are among the stock images of New York life. From rough-and-ready Bohemian hangouts to elegant hotel cocktail lounges, New York bars come in all sizes and forms. Don't miss this quintessential experience. (For guidance on bar-going etiquette, see pages 224–225.)

WINE BARS

In New York nowadays any restaurant that wants to be taken seriously offers several decent wines by the glass. But a proliferation of wine bars offering hundreds of wines has upped the ante. Wines are sold either as single servings or in tasting "flights" (wines grouped by region, style, vintage or other characteristics). Check out Divine Bar (244 East 51st Street), Le Bateau Ivre (230 East 51st Street), Enoteca i Trulli (122 East 27th Street) and Punch & Judy (26 Clinton Street).

NEW YORK'S OLDEST BAR

In business since 1854, McSorley's Old Ale House (15 East 7th Street) is justified in its claim to be New York's oldest surviving bar. For years a men-only establishment patronized by career drinkers from the Bowery's Skid Row, McSorley's began admitting women in 1970 and now attracts a young, mainly student crowd.

Writers, artists and bars Greenwich Village is littered with bars where major names of art and literature have gathered to eat, drink and (not infrequently) be carried home very much the worse for wear.

On his New York stays, Welsh poet Dylan Thomas held court at the **White Horse Tavern** (567 Hudson Street). One night in 1953, a drunken Thomas spluttered, "I've had my 18th whisky, and I think that's the record." Within a few days he was dead. The literary associations might seem all but buried beneath the throng of customers, but cuttings on the wall remind drinkers at **Pete's Tavern** (129 East 18th Street) that this was once a lair of O. Henry, the pen name of William Sydney Porter, short-story writer and a trenchant New York observer in the early 1900s. To sample the East Village's Bohemian ambience, slip into something black and then into **d b a** (41 First Avenue), a popular local hangout with a minimalist style and a good variety of beers and single malts.

No longer in its original location, the **Cedar Tavern** (82 University Place) was a meeting place for the painters of what became the New York School of Abstract Expressionism. As Jackson Pollock and others loudly lamented the state of art, Beat writers such as the late Allen Ginsberg and William Burroughs eavesdropped from neighboring tables.

Bars for beer-drinkers Beer connoisseurs will welcome the 200 imported varieties sold at the **Peculier Pub** (145 Bleecker Street). The wooden bench tables here often overflow with New York University students. Detailed menu descriptions will help you choose from the 50 or so beers served at **The Blind Tiger** (518 Hudson Street). There's no such help at **The Ginger Man** (11 East 36th Street), but the selection of beers and single malt scotches is even larger. **Heartland Brewery** (135 Union Square West) offers microbrewed beer. What would you expect from a bar called **Brewsky's** (41 East Seventh Street)? Yes, beer, but this wood-floored, no-frills East Villager serves a whopping 700 varieties, probably including your hometown's ale.

Bars with a view In Midtown Manhattan, try the 39th-floor **Top of the Sixes** (666 Fifth Avenue), or the **Top of the Tower** at the Beekham Tower Hotel (3 Mitchell Place, off 49th Street) for a splendid view across the East River. The **Pen Top Bar** housed in the Peninsula Hotel (700 Fifth Avenue) offers its drinks from a rooftop terrace.

Bars for the beautiful people The resurgence of Chelsea has given a boost to the nightlife potential of the venerable Chelsea Hotel (222 West 23rd Street; see page 85). where **Serena** has deep-drop sofas and a crowd mulling cocktails and the meaning life, love and celebrity. The minimalist Philippe Starck-designed **Hudson Bar** (256 West 58th Street) in the Hudson Hotel is a white-on-white fantasy of minimal design. Though actually a restaurant, **The Park** (118 Tenth Avenue) attracts a discerning crowd for nightly quaffs and nibbles; opened by the man behind B-Bar, expect a who's who crowd. Even the most fashionable New Yorker tends to get overshadowed by the design of **SX 137** (137 Essex Street), a bar-cum-nightclub, complete with black-rubber bar and serving one-of-a-kind cocktails, once drunk never forgotten.

Hotel bars Many are favored by well-heeled and socially aspirant locals for their elegant surroundings, celebrity clientele and lack of loud music. The **King Cole Bar** at the St. Regis Hotel (2 East 55th Street) serves drinks in front of an impressive Maxfield Parrish mural. For a private tryst, try **Fifty Seven Fifty Seven** at the Four Seasons Hotel (57 East 57th Street), which draws publishing and media bigwigs. The scene at Mercer Hotel's **Merc Bar** (99 Prince Street) in SoHo is white hot, and the **Grand Bar** at the SoHo Grand Hotel (310 West Broadway) attracts the fashionable every night.

MARIE'S CRISIS CAFÉ

Few places symbolize changing New York better than Marie's Crisis Café (59 Grove Street). Nowadays, do not be surprised to find this lively bar packed by gay men singing hit songs from famous Broadway shows. Two centuries ago it was a home of Thomas Paine, whose publication, *Crisis*, helped fuel the American Revolution.

The photos and flags that adorn the walls of McSorley's Old Ale House suggest a time when New York bars provided informal employment centers and enabled many new immigrants to land their first jobs in the United States

115

Washington Square Memorial Arch

INSIDE THE MEMORIAL ARCH
In 1916, maverick artist Marcel Duchamp and friends forced their way through the locked door of Washington Square Park's Memorial Arch and climbed the 110 steps to the top. Once there, they hung balloons, Chinese lanterns and banners proclaiming Greenwich Village as the independent republic of New Bohemia. After having a picnic, Duchamp and company were forced down by militiamen.

With somewhat less of a spectacle, a man is thought to have lived in the arch for seven months during World War II. He was noticed only when he hung his washing out to dry.

(Continued from page 112)

There is no better place to begin exploring Greenwich Village than **Washington Square Park**▶▶▶ where jugglers, actors, unicyclists and chess-players put on a show for the families, visitors and the street-wise kids who promenade along the park's pathways.

On the park's northern side, the triumphal **Washington Memorial Arch**▶▶ stands at the foot of Fifth Avenue, 11ft (23m) high and erected by Stanford White in 1892 on a spot where he had earlier raised a wooden marker to celebrate the centenary of Washington's inauguration.

What the white marble arch does not commemorate, however, are the 22,000 people who were buried beneath the park when it served as a mass cemetery during epidemics. There is also no reminder of the fact that during the early 1800s some of the park's trees were, in fact, used for public hangings.

Besides ending hangings and covering over the burial ground, the creation of the park in 1827 greatly increased the social cachet of the immediate area. Fashionable town houses rose around it, the only survivors being **The Row**▶▶ on the north side: Note their porticoes, shuttered windows and elongated stoops—emphasizing the distinction between the owner's entrance and the servants' entrance at ground level.

To the park's south and east are a few of the buildings of New York University. With 14 separate schools scattered throughout Greenwich Village, the university is one of the city's major landowners.

(Continued on page 118)

New York City is home to one of the most vibrant gay and lesbian communities in the U.S.A., centered around Chelsea and Greenwich Village. The contributions of its members help to make New York what it is in publishing, art and design, theater, dance, restaurants, law, business and other fields.

The census of 1880 found five men in prison for "unspeakable crimes against nature"—a euphemism of the time for homosexual activity. By the 1930s, a small network of gay rendezvous points had spread across Manhattan; places where discretion was uppermost and which remained invisible to the heterosexual world.

In the period following World War II, when the values of family life were extolled to the hilt, gays and lesbians increasingly felt the backlash. Sexual minorities were pilloried in the press, and the police were urged to clamp down on behavior that was feared and perceived as a menace to society.

Gay Pride In 1969, the two days of rioting that followed a police raid on Greenwich Village's Stonewall Inn became a turning point in gay history: For the first time, the community had risen up to defend itself against the authorities, and its newfound solidarity led to the founding of the Gay Pride movement.

The movement's many achievements are celebrated annually by the Gay Pride Parade along Fifth Avenue and through Greenwich Village (see page 27).

Gays have steadily become established and largely accepted throughout the city. Gay issues are now widely debated throughout mainstream media, while legal breakthroughs include the formal recognition of gay couples in 1993. In the last few years gays have also featured prominently in the rejuvenation and gentrification of the Chelsea neighborhood.

INFORMATION
Given the high integration of gays and lesbians into New York life, details of events, clubs and other aspects of particular gay and lesbian interest are widely covered by the mainstream media. For answers to more specific questions, try the Gay and Lesbian Community Center, One Little West Twelfth Street (tel: 620-7310; www. gaycenter.org).

117

Greenwich Village is home to a substantial gay and lesbian community

STROLL: GREENWICH VILLAGE

The maze of side streets off Christopher Street holds some of Greenwich Village's quietest and prettiest corners. Take time to admire the lovely row of brick and brownstone Italianate houses on St. Luke's Place and venture into Bedford Street for the Isaacs-Hendricks Residence (see page 130) and the 9-ft (3-m) wide house at number 75½. Its dainty dimensions did not deter actor John Barrymore, poet Edna St. Vincent Millay, or screen star Cary Grant from living in it at various times.

Street cafés line Bleecker Street in Greenwich Village, a home for Beat writers in the 1950s and 1960s

(Continued from page 116)

Not content with his Memorial Arch, Stanford White also erected the **Judson Memorial Church▶**, on the park's south side, in largely Romanesque style. More noteworthy than the architecture are the church's stained-glass windows, the work of Hudson River artist John LaFarge.

A block away, on MacDougal Street, the unremarkable exterior of the **Provincetown Playhouse** does nothing to suggest that the group based here forged new ground in American drama in the 1910s, helped in no small measure by the talents of Eugene O'Neill.

Just south, on the corner of Minetta Lane, the **Minetta Tavern▶** displays photos and mementos from Greenwich Village's earliest days as a center for the arts.

Running across MacDougal Street, **Bleecker Street▶▶▶** holds the best of Greenwich Village's bars and clubs, though nothing these days matches the stirrings of the early 1960s when local folk clubs spawned talents such as Bob Dylan, Judy Collins and Arlo Guthrie.

A decade earlier, the cafés in Bleecker Street had reverberated to the performance poetry and drunken debates of embryonic Beat writers: Gregory Corso, Jack Kerouac, Allen Ginsberg and William Burroughs (see page 119).

More restaurants, bakeries and cafés line Bleecker Street as it continues westward across Sixth Avenue into the West Village, the main artery of which, Christopher Street, cuts westward from Village Square and the extraordinary **Jefferson Market Courthouse** (see page 113), toward the Hudson River; on Sixth Avenue is Balducci's (see page 113).

At 53 Christopher Street was the **Stonewall Inn**. It gave its name to the "Stonewall Riots," which united the local gay community in 1969 and led to the founding of Gay Pride (see page 117), which was to spawn a number of similar organizations in many parts of the world.

A small group of characters frequenting the bars around Columbia University and Greenwich Village in the 1940s evolved into what became the Beat Generation, the USA's first postwar subculture and one that used drugs, jazz and Eastern religion to inspire the new forms of writing that, for a brief time in the 1950s, seemed set to tear US society to pieces.

If the Beat Generation had a starting point, it was the West End Café (on Broadway, between 113th and 114th streets) in the mid-1940s. Here teenaged student Allen Ginsberg, 30-year-old William Burroughs and 22-year-old Jack Kerouac swapped ideas, later adjourning to an apartment at 421 West 118th Street to hold lively discussions to the sound of the newly emerged bebop jazz.

Beat writing Ginsberg began writing "serious" poetry, Kerouac worked on his breathless prose style, and Burroughs steadily assembled the pieces that would evolve into his novels. By the end of the 1940s, the chief hangouts were the San Remo (189 Bleecker Street) and the Cedar Tavern (then at 24 University Place).

Success and notoriety Ginsberg was living in San Francisco in 1956 when, besides working for an advertising agency and studying Buddhism, he wrote his epic poem, *Howl*, describing characters and ideas from the past few years. The poem was published to enthusiastic reviews—and an obscenity trial that greatly increased the notoriety of "the Beats," as did *On the Road*, Kerouac's novel published the next year.

When Ginsberg and Kerouac returned to New York, the *Village Voice* proclaimed "Witless Madcaps Come Home to Roost," and the events of a decade earlier quickly became, and continue to be, a source of legend.

WHY "BEAT GENERATION"?
Ginsberg and another writer, John Clellon Holmes, conceived the term "Beat Generation," partly from the "Lost Generation" of the 1920s and partly from a Times Square junkie who always described himself as "beat." When Holmes's novel *Go* was published in 1952, the New York Times reviewer seized on the handy phrase, but this did not help Ginsberg, Burroughs, or Kerouac find publishers for their work.

119

The late Allen Ginsberg (left) listens to a speaker at a 1960s anti-Vietnam War rally near Tompkins Square Park

For every major religious edifice such as St. Patrick's Cathedral or the Cathedral Church of St. John the Divine, New York has dozens more that seldom receive a visit from passing travelers. Many of these are mentioned in the A–Z section of this book, but those described below are especially notable for illustrating the city's many forms of ecclesiastical architecture or for highlighting the city's endless diversity.

SAME CHURCH, DIFFERENT RELIGION
Indicative of the changing ethnic make-up of the Lower East Side, the 1895 Russian Orthodox Cathedral at 4th Street, between Avenues C and D is now San Isidro y San Leandro Orthodox Catholic Church of the Hispanic Rite, which is serving the Lower East Side's now predominantly Puerto Rican population.

The statue of Shinran-Shonin outside the New York Buddhist Church

Greek Orthodox New York's earliest Greek church, **St. Nicholas Greek Orthodox Church**, was buried by the collapse of the World Trade Center in 2001. The Greek community's religious focal point had already moved north, however, to the icon-rich **Greek Orthodox Cathedral of the Holy Trinity** (74th Street near First Avenue; tel: 288-5876), which opened in 1931.

Episcopal Dating from 1929 and from the drawing board of Hardie Philip, who also worked on Temple Emanu-El (see page 187), the **Church of the Heavenly Rest** (corner of Fifth Avenue and 90th Street; tel: 289-3400) features a stripped Gothic exterior while art deco angels and English stained glass enliven the interior. After a lengthy walk around the Upper East Side or Central Park, this church can indeed provide a heavenly rest.

Jewish Also in what is now the Financial District, New York's first Jewish residents established the city's earliest synagogue some 300 years ago on what became William Street. A replica of the 20-seat shrine can be seen on the fifth floor of the **Wall Street Synagogue** (47 Beekman Street; tel: 227-7800). Completed in 1887, **Eldridge Street Synagogue** (12 Eldridge Street, between Canal and Division streets, tel: 219-0888; *Open:* Sun 11–4, Tue and Thu at 11.30 and 2.30. *Admission: inexpensive*) is also deeply rooted in New York history, being the first synagogue raised by eastern European Jews. The past is documented within its museum.

Roman Catholic In 1918, just north of the Central Synagogue, architect Bertram Goodhue produced an accomplished and imposing facade for the **Church of St. Vincent Ferrer** (Lexington Avenue at 66th Street; tel: 744-2080), but he saved his best touches for the expansive interior. Note the reredos and Charles Connick's exceptional stained-glass windows.

Russian Orthodox The seat of the Russian Orthodox Church in North America is on New York's Upper East Side, where the **St. Nicholas Orthodox Cathedral** (97th Street near Fifth Avenue; tel: 996-6638) was erected at the turn of the century, financed by donations collected across the czarist Russian empire. The cathedral's

AN EMBARRASSED ARCHITECT
With Grace Church (see page 112) and St. Patrick's Cathedral (page 150), church architect James Renwick made his name. Among his less acclaimed works, however, was the 1846 **Calvary Church** (Park Avenue at 21st Street; tel: 281-2192). The church still stands but without its steeples.

121

splendidly ornate style—red brick patterned with blue and yellow tiles and five bulging onion domes—is based on the church architecture of 17th-century Moscow.

Muslim The design of St. Nicholas is strikingly different from the drab buildings around it, as is that of the **Mosque of the Islamic Culture Center** (Third Avenue at 96th Street), which also deviates from the usual grid-style alignment of Manhattan buildings by being pointed toward Mecca. The first permanent place of worship for New York Muslims, the $12-million mosque was largely financed by the government of Kuwait.

Buddhist On the other side of Central Park, you might easily go right past the **New York Buddhist Church** (Riverside Drive, between 105th and 106th streets; tel: 678-0305) without realizing the fact—were it not for the unmistakable bronze statue of Shinran-Shonin, the 13th-century founder of a Buddhist sect, that stands outside.

Armenian Apostolic Built to resemble the 4th-century Cathedral of Holy Etchmiadzin in Armenia, the mighty **St. Vartan Cathedral of the Armenian Orthodox Church** (630 Second Avenue; tel: 686 0710), its entrance raised 5ft (1.5m) above street level, arose in the 1960s. The interior features include 15th-century stone crosses from Armenia.

From the imposing Temple Emanu-EL (above left) to the Episcopalian St. Mark's in-the-Bowery (above): New York's places of worship mirror its diverse ethnic make-up

GUGGENHEIMS AROUND THE WORLD

A 1998 exhibition, the Art of the Motorcycle, sponsored by BMW, and a subsequent fashion-magazine-sponsored retrospective of the work of clothes designer Giorgio Armani, caused the Guggenheim to upset art purists as many questioned the increased role of business in the museum's displays. Nonetheless, the exhibitions gave the museum some of its best-ever attendance figures and provided further impetus for its global expansion plans. These include branches in Berlin, Las Vegas and Venice, with another due in Rio de Janeiro. These follow the continuing success of the architecturally stunning Bilbao Guggenheim. The latter's architect, Frank Gehry, is also behind the new Manhattan Guggenheim, planned for the East River at the foot of South Street.

►►► Guggenheim Museum 187C1

Fifth Avenue, between 88th and 89th streets (tel: 423-3500; www.guggenheim.org)
Open: Sat–Wed 9–6, Fri 10–8. Admission: moderate
Subway: 86th Street

A member of an ultrawealthy New York family whose fortunes were founded on copper and silver mines, Solomon R. Guggenheim followed the usual track of an Upper East Side millionaire with more money than he knew what to do with by dabbling in art. Guggenheim's first purchases were unremarkable Old Masters, but his tastes were changed radically in 1927 when he met Baroness Hilla Rebay von Ehrenwiesen, an outspoken and energetic enthusiast of European abstract art.

Through the baroness, Guggenheim met artists such as Robert Delaunay, Fernand Léger and Albert Gleizes and quickly amassed a superb stock of their work and works by other contemporary artists, particularly Wassily Kandinsky, hanging them on the walls of the rooms he occupied with his wife at New York's Plaza Hotel. At the suggestion of the baroness, Guggenheim commissioned architect Frank Lloyd Wright to design and build a museum to be called (with an ideological correctness insisted on by the baroness) the Museum of Non-Objective Painting.

Guggenheim had been dead for 10 years by the time Wright's extraordinary achievement opened in 1959, its name changed to the Solomon R. Guggenheim Museum. It proved to be the architect's only New York building, and he referred to it as his "Pantheon." By this time, Guggenheim's initial collection of abstracts had been enlarged and greatly broadened in scope by purchases and bequests, particularly the Thannhauser Collection of impressionist and post-impressionist paintings that were bequeathed by a prominent dealer and collector.

The best way to see the collection is to take the elevator to the top level and slowly work your way down the museum's remarkable spiral ramp. In this way you can study the exhibits, look over the parapet to the lobby below and finish up where you began without ever getting lost.

Precisely what will be on show when you visit has been scheduled years in advance; the museum stages several special exhibitions each year, often focusing on the work of an individual artist. What you can be fairly certain of seeing is the permanently displayed Thannhauser Collection, hung in comparatively orthodox fashion in several galleries reached off the second level of the ramp.

Highlights of the Guggenheim's permanent collections include works by Kandinsky, Modigliani, Klee, Mondrian, Braque, Chagall, Gleizes and Malevich.

Among these, Van Gogh's painting entitled *Mountains at Saint-Rémy* is outstanding, its vibrant swirls of color painted in 1899 as the artist recovered from one of his bouts of mental illness.

Works by Cézanne include *Still Life: Flask, Glass and Jug* and *Bibémus*, a shimmering pre-abstract landscape, and the slightly mystifying *Man With Crossed Arms*, described as a "proto-Cubist" piece, whose figure has been thought to embody the spirit of quiet resignation that the artist possessed during the last years of his life.

A couple of paintings by the enigmatic artist Henri Rousseau (also known as "Le Douanier"—the Customs Man) are amusing and defiantly odd. In *The Football Players*, five handlebar-moustached and ludicrously attired figures strike up absurd poses while frolicking with a ball in a forest; similarly handlebar-moustached but more correctly attired soldiers make up the core of *The Artillery Men*.

The earliest of several canvases by Picasso, *Le Moulin de Galette*, was painted in 1900 when the artist was only 19 years of age and was inspired by his first visit to Paris. The gloomy but angular figure of 1904's *Woman Ironing* is a product of the latter stages of what is known as Picasso's Blue Period; from a year or two later, *Fernand with a Black Fortilla* marks a change of style—and perhaps the first step toward Cubism.

The most striking piece in the Thannhauser Collection is also the earliest: *The Hermitage at Pontoise*, an 1867 landscape by Camille Pissarro. The artist later became a leading impressionist (Gauguin and Cézanne were among Pissarro's students and associates) but here uses a realist style that goes hard against the grain of traditional French landscape painting—and seems to make the idyllic rural scene radiate from the canvas.

RAYMOND HOOD
Architecture buffs impressed by his subsequent Daily News Building and Rockefeller Center's RCA Building (as the GE Building used to be known) may care to cast an eye over Raymond Hood's 1928 apartment block at 3 East 84th Street, bearing many of the features—such as pressed-metal spandrels—that later appeared in a refined form on his more well-known works.

The vertiginous interior of the Guggenheim

It has been called a doughnut, a snail and an insult to art, but Frank Lloyd Wright's Guggenheim Museum is one of the outstanding contributions to New York architecture—even though it often steals the show from the art that it exhibits. Wright inserted the inscription "let every man practice the art he knows" in bronze on the entrance floor—intended perhaps as a lasting riposte to the building's critics.

THE GUGGENHEIM ADDITIONS

In 1993, the completion of Gwathmey/Siegel's 11-story tower, welded to the rotunda, provided much-needed extra office and exhibition space despite being widely criticized for its failure to blend with Wright's original building. Meanwhile, plans are underway for a third Guggenheim, intended to rise on piers in the East River.

More than 40 years after it opened, the Guggenheim remains a unique feature of the New York landscape

Organic architecture The originator of the "Prairie style," Wright in his best architecture blended buildings into the organic, natural forms around them. The Guggenheim's predominantly curving exterior is totally out of step with the vertical lines of the neighboring Upper East Side apartment houses but has a great deal in common with the trees and shrubbery of Central Park, directly across Fifth Avenue.

With the Guggenheim Museum, his only major New York commission, Wright also made a radical departure from the traditional room-by-room gallery style. The exhibits here occupy partitioned spaces off a quarter-mile (400-m) long spiral walkway that rises six stories high, steadily growing wider as it climbs.

Controversy The architect persistently battled with the city authorities and disagreed with the museum's director over the structure's supposed failure to meet the practical needs of an art museum. All this contributed to delays, and 16 years elapsed between Wright's finished plans and the Guggenheim's opening in 1959, the year of his death. The aesthetic debate has raged ever since, though the museum is now very much part of the Upper East Side landscape.

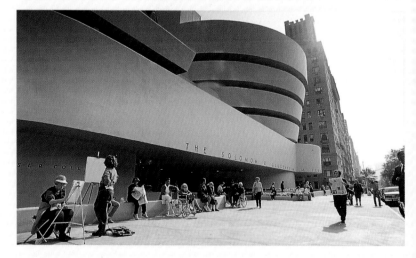

► Harlem
IBCC2

Increasingly a part of the city's tourist circuit and long a vital and distinct component in New York's character, Harlem begins north of Central Park at 110th Street and splits into two sections.

Above the Upper West Side, West Harlem (or Harlem proper) is the longest-established home of the city's African-American population. Above the Upper East Side is East Harlem—or **El Barrio** ("the Neighborhood") —which has become New York's largest Spanish-speaking enclave. The majority of East Harlem residents have Puerto Rican origins.

During the 1890s, eager to repeat the success they had had on the Upper West Side, property speculators covered West Harlem with brownstones and apartment blocks. The anticipated buyers never materialized, however, and Harlem's homes were rented out largely to black tenants. Rents were inflated because of housing pressure—thousands of African-Americans were arriving in New York, and the competition was great. Tens of thousands of the nation's blacks fled the Deep South for Harlem, seen at the time as a promised land. By the 1920s, the Harlem Renaissance was in full swing: a flowering of African-American culture through art and literature as jazz and blues percolated through Harlem nightclubs such as the **Cotton Club** and **Smalls' Paradise**.

On the main commercial strip, West 125th Street, stands the **Apollo Theater** (at number 253), legendary for its

FIDEL CASTRO IN HARLEM
Arriving to address the United Nations in 1960, Cuban leader Fidel Castro and his entourage spent several nights in a Midtown Manhattan hotel, reputedly running up a $10,000 bill for damage before being asked to leave. No other hotel was eager for Castro's patronage, but Harlem's Teresa Hotel (272 West 125th Street), long known as a radicals' meeting place, filled the breach. During its week-long stay, the Cuban contingent was cheered by locals and was visited by Soviet leader Khrushchev. In 1971, the Teresa was converted into an office building.

125

Not many people visit Harlem for its architecture, but the buildings can be just as lively as the atmosphere

MARCUS GARVEY IN HARLEM

Arriving in Harlem from Jamaica in 1914, Marcus Garvey predated the Black Panthers in the 1960s in encouraging black pride and assertiveness. Winning many followers through his brilliant powers of oration, Garvey founded the Universal Negro Improvement Foundation, published the *Negro World* newspaper and purchased two ocean liners to carry out his promised repatriation of America's blacks to Africa.

Eventually, Garvey was arrested on trumped-up charges and deported. He died in London in 1940. Garvey's doctrines became crucial elements in Rastafarianism, and in 1973 the Harlem park that straddles Fifth Avenue, between 120th and 124th streets was renamed in his honor.

Unfortunately, the park, which holds a curious fire-watch tower dating from 1856, is a drug-users' hangout and is best left unvisited.

Harlem gospel choir

amateur talent nights and for showcasing every African-American jazz, blues and soul act, from Billie Holliday in the 1930s to James Brown in the 1960s. Brown's *Live at the Apollo* album was recorded here in 1962 and captures some of the venue's raw excitement. You will also find the temporary exhibitions and photographic archive of the **Studio Museum in Harlem** (144 West 125th Street; tel: 864-4500, www.studiomuseuminharlem.org; *Open*: Wed–Sat 12–6, Sun 10–6. *Admission: inexpensive*) and more soul-food restaurants than anyone could wish for.

Rare books, documents, art and artifacts pertaining to African-American history make up some of five million items housed at the **Schomburg Center for Research in Black Culture** (515 Malcolm X Boulevard; tel 491 2200, www.nypl.org/research/sc/sc/html). It also hosts drama, concerts and temporary exhibitions.

For the best of early Harlem architecture, explore the **St. Nicholas Historic District** on 139th Street. The stylish 1890s town houses between Seventh and Eighth avenues were occupied by successful blacks from 1919 and hence earned their lasting nickname "Striver's Row."

Upbeat Sunday gospel services have become one of the major points of visitor interest in Harlem, although the tour group numbers at some churches have led to complaints that the local congregations are being ignored. One of Harlem's most celebrated churches for its outstanding choir and history of community involvement, is the **Abyssinian Baptist Church** (see page 60).

Shabbier than its westerly counterpart, **East Harlem** was first settled by working-class Italian and Irish families but, from the 1920s on, it steadily evolved into the city's major Puerto Rican neighborhood. The **Museum of the City of New York** and **El Museo del Barrio** (see pages 156–157) stand on its fringes, but the place to visit is **La Marqueta**, found under the Park Avenue viaduct, where salsa music resounds among the market stalls and food stands.

▶ **Hispanic Society of America**　　　　*IBCD2*
Broadway at 155th Street (tel: 926-2234; www.hispanicsociety.org) Open: Tue–Sat 10–4.30, Sun 1–4. Admission free
Subway: 1; 157th Street
Paintings by Velázquez, El Greco, and Goya are among the most prized possessions of the Hispanic Society of America, founded in 1904 by Archer M. Huntington, son of magnate Collis P. Huntington. However, this collection of Spanish and Portuguese art, archeology, tilework, and tomb decorations is overall less impressive than its setting: a sumptuous two-story Spanish Renaissance interior, decorated with ruby-red terra-cotta.

As their country is a self-governing common-wealth territory of the US, Puerto Ricans are automatically US citizens. The right to settle freely led to Puerto Ricans forming the biggest Spanish-speaking community in New York.

Early 19th-century New York drew Puerto Ricans active in the sugar and coffee trade. Others, who were inspired by the American Revolution, came here hoping to use the city as a base to plot the overthrow of their Spanish colonial masters.

The US in Puerto Rico In 1898, Puerto Rico was deeded by Spain to the United States, which established a military government on the Caribbean island and allowed American interests to rule its economy. In return, Puerto Ricans were granted United States citizenship (although not until 1917) and so were able to settle freely in the United States.

The profiteering of American companies encouraged Puerto Rican migration and, by 1930, around 45,000 Puerto Ricans had settled in New York. Many were employed in jobs formerly held by upwardly mobile Jews and Italians; others worked in their traditional trades such as cigar-making.

El Barrio Although there were a number of Puerto Rican neighborhoods across Manhattan, the area around the low-rent apartments of East Harlem became *El Barrio*, base of Puerto Rican cultural institutions and Spanish-language movie theaters and publications. Over a period of time, Fiorello La Guardia (who took office in 1933) recognized the political power of the Puerto Ricans by encouraging them to register to vote.

In the 1950s, when inexpensive flights began operating between New York and San Juan—the Puerto Rican capital—the Puerto Rican population in New York soared to 600,000, some spilling from El Barrio into the Bronx. The majority of the new arrivals had been rural-dwelling farm laborers, who subsequently found it difficult to adjust to big-city life.

Americans of Puerto Rican descent are now a major part of the city's ethnic jigsaw puzzle. While the area is celebrated among trendy New Yorkers for its spicy foods and for its salsa music, El Barrio unfortunately continues to struggle with every contemporary inner-city problem.

SAN JUAN HILL
When Yankee Stadium was completed in 1923, it was dubbed "the House that Ruth built," after baseball's most famous player. One might well call Lincoln Center "the House that Bernstein built." The great irony is that the construction of the new home of Leonard Bernstein's New York Symphony Orchestra required the utter destruction of the neighborhood that was the setting for his most famous work, *West Side Story*. More than 1,500 families in the area then known as San Juan Hill—most of them black and/or Puerto Rican—were displaced.

127

At an exhibition in Los Angeles in 1956, the phrase "the New York School" was first coined, referring to the group of artists who, in New York a decade or so earlier, had spearheaded abstract expressionism, the country's first modern art movement, thus creating a worldwide audience for American art.

THE CEDAR TAVERN
Rare is the major art movement that was not influenced to some degree by drunken debate. Abstract expressionism was no exception. The favored gathering place of many of the artists who became the New York School was the Cedar Tavern, then at 24 University Place. Here, discussions would rage into the night and sometimes culminate in an inebriated rearrangement of the furniture.

Fans of abstract expressionism who also like a drink may be pleased to know that the Cedar Tavern still exists (though it has moved to 82 University Place). These days, however, it is plain and rather uninteresting.

The Armory Show of 1913 (see page 149) not only brought modern European art to the US for the first time, but also made it plain that the country had no modern style to call its own. Dadaist Marcel Duchamp summed up America's contribution to world art as "her plumbing and her bridges."

Even if they viewed it only as a stop on the way to Paris, however, New York was still a magnet for young American artists. They arrived to escape humdrum rural towns, to take classes at the city's Art Students League, and to paint in spacious light-filled loft studios available for cheap rents.

European influences As Europe moved toward war, many of the continent's most innovative and influential artistic minds fled across the Atlantic. When the Nazis marched down the Champs-Elysées, New York eclipsed Paris as the nerve center of international art.

In the late 1940s, as the conclusion of the war seemed to present a world free of the shackles of traditionalism and filled with new possibilities, a new group of abstract expressionists emerged.

Jackson Pollock A farmer's son from Wyoming, Jackson Pollock had arrived in New York in the 1920s and was later employed for a short time at the embryonic Guggenheim Museum.

In 1947, Pollock seized one of his paintings from its easel, fixed it to the floor, and started applying paint directly from the can in great sweeping arcs across the canvas. Soon after, Pollock dispensed with easels and brushes entirely, pouring paint onto the flat canvas and manipulating it with "sticks, trowels or knives."

As the final product depended entirely on the act of Pollock dripping and throwing paint (compared to a western cowboy's lasso skills), the technique gave rise to the term "action painting" (also called "gestural painting").

De Kooning, Gottlieb, and Rothko Another key abstract expressionist was Willem de Kooning. While de Kooning used figures much more than Pollock—often formed by white contours on black—he was every inch the action painter, attacking his canvas with an energy that sent specks of paint flying in every direction.

A major influence on the abstract expressionists was the *Pictographs*, a series of paintings by Adolph Gottlieb, each of which was divided into compartments holding a mythological figure or symbol.

The abstract expressionists sought to transmit primal emotional states through their work—a goal that went beyond what was possible within traditional painting and which the horrors of the war had helped awaken.

Mark Rothko, an associate of Gottlieb's, became the foremost figure of what was termed the "color field" branch of abstract expressionism. As the full terrors of the Nazi concentration camps emerged, there was a special poignancy when Rothko, the Latvian-born son of Russian Jewish émigrés, asserted that "human incommunicability" had rendered figurative painting obsolete. Rothko's work evolved into floating rectangles of color, which, he said, provided "a spiritual basis for communion."

Barnett Newman and after Barnett Newman likened the color field artists' work to that of "primitive" cultures, keen to reach a "metaphysical understanding." In the late 1940s, Newman produced the first of his "zip paintings," their flat field of color split by a narrow vertical line.

Ironically, it was a misinterpretation of Newman's work that influenced later artists such as Jasper Johns. These later artists paved the way for the break away from the mentally wrought canvases of abstract expressionism to the re-casting of familiar images practiced by the 1960s pop art movement.

Perhaps in keeping with the anguished soul-searching of their work, the lives of abstract expressionism's two major figures both ended prematurely: Jackson Pollock died after driving his car into a tree in 1956 and Mark Rothko committed suicide in 1970.

ABSTRACT EXPRESSIONISM ON DISPLAY
The Museum of Modern Art (see pages 158–160) has an excellent collection of abstract expressionist works and, besides those mentioned on these pages, also features work by other highly influential members of the movement such as Robert Motherwell, Franz Kline and Arshile Gorky.

The Guggenheim Museum (pages 122–124) has a fair number of abstract expressionist canvases in its possession (sometimes on display in temporary exhibitions), and important works by Pollock, de Kooning and Rothko can be seen at the Whitney Museum (page 191).

One, a huge canvas of 1950 by Jackson Pollock, now in MoMA

Great ocean liners such as the *Queen Mary* and the *USS United States* would berth at the piers at the western ends of 48th, 50th and 52nd streets (just north of the Intrepid Sea-Air-Space Museum) in the days before air travel made them uneconomic. To make the docking area as luxurious as the ships, the swanky New York Passenger Ship Terminal was completed in 1976. Unfortunately, most scheduled services had been abolished by that time, although modern luxury cruise ships can sometimes be seen docked here.

PHOTOGRAPHY HOUSE
One of the most handsome neo-Georgian mansions on the Upper East Side is home to a branch of the International Center of Photography. The four-story red-brick building was completed in 1914 by the firm of Delano & Aldrich for Willard Straight, a wealthy ex-diplomat who founded the influential *New Republic* magazine.

▶▶ International Center of Photography   *187D1*

1133 Sixth Avenue at 43rd Street (tel: 857-0000; www.icp.org) Open: Tue–Thu 10–5, Fri 10–8, Sat and Sun 10–6. Admission: inexpensive. Subway: B, D, Q; 42nd Street

The International Center of Photography (ICP) is one of the world's few museums entirely devoted to photography. It has several galleries mounting changing exhibitions of both internationally established names and lesser-knowns.

One gallery is usually filled with selections from the Center's permanent collection, which holds prints by almost every notable photographer you can think of: Henri Cartier-Bresson, Ernst Haas, Weegee and Robert Capa to name a few.

▶ Intrepid Sea-Air-Space Museum   *151C1*

West end of 46th Street (tel: 245-0072; www.intrepidmuseum. org) Open: Mon–Fri 10–5, Sat and Sun 10–6. Admission: expensive. Subway: A, C, E; 42nd Street

The flight deck of the *Intrepid*, a Navy aircraft carrier, is the core of this militaristic museum. Permanently moored on the Hudson River, the *Intrepid* saw action in the Pacific during World War II and served in an antisubmarine role during the Vietnam War.

The vessel is stuffed with exhibits from its own wartime adventures—its aircraft shot down 650 enemy planes and destroyed 289 ships—and from its peacetime role of retrieving Mercury and Gemini space capsules. On its deck sits an A-12 Blackbird, the highest, fastest spy plane ever built.

Other maritime vessels on show include the *Edson* destroyer, which saw 30 years of service, and the *Growler*, a strategic missile-carrying submarine built in 1958. A tour of its innards includes the missile command center and brings the sobering realization that World War Three could have started at this very console. Also displayed are a variety of American, British and French fighter aircraft and a former British Airways concorde. An additional fee (inexpensive) brings the chance to fly a simulated mission at the controls of an F-18 fighter.

▶ Isaacs-Hendricks Residence   *113A2*

77 Bedford Street, Greenwich Village Subway: 1; Christopher Street

You could be forgiven for walking right past the Isaacs-Hendricks Residence without noticing it. Alterations in 1836 and 1928 have detracted from its Federal style, of which it is one of the earliest surviving examples, having been erected in 1799. The clapboard wall on the side that backs onto Commerce Street is the main clue to the house's architectural pedigree.

▶ Jan Hus Presbyterian Church   *187B2*

74th Street, between First and Second avenues Subway: 6; 77th Street

Named after the Czech martyr of the Reformation, the Jan Hus Presbyterian Church was founded in 1914 to serve Czech settlers in an area that was known as Little Bohemia into the 1930s. The church, with a bell tower modeled on the Powder Tower in Prague, is more popular for its secular activities than for its services. Musical and dramatic events are staged at the church's hall.

Only a small fraction of New York's Czech-American population now lives in Little Bohemia and, besides the church, there are only a couple of notable reminders of the Czech presence, such as the run-down Bohemian National Hall, on 73rd Street, between First and Second avenues, raised in 1895.

▶ Jewish Museum   *187D1*

Fifth Avenue at 92nd Street (tel: 423-3200; www.jewishmuseum.org) Open: Sun–Wed 11–5.45, Thu 11–8, Fri 11–3. Admission: moderate. Subway: 6; 96th Street

An imitation French Gothic château might seem a strange home for the largest stock of Judaic ceremonial art and historical objects in the US, but the fine collections of New York's Jewish Museum have been housed in just such a place since 1944. It was then that the premises were bequeathed to the museum by the widow of their original owner, banker Felix M. Warburg.

Some of the tremendous stash of coins, household objects and religious pieces date back to Roman times; much more is representative of Jewish life from medieval times into the present century. One exemplary feature is the re-created turn-of-the-century café in which visitors can select oral histories of Jewish lives in various European cities of the time, and of early Jewish arrivals to the United States.

The Jewish Museum also stages lively and sometimes provocative temporary exhibitions that are designed to explore the Jewish experience from new and challenging perspectives. There is also a Childrens' Activity Center that offers arts and crafts projects related to Jewish culture and traditions.

CZECHS IN NEW YORK
The first significant group of Czechs in New York arrived in 1848 to practice the free thinking denied them by the ruling Hapsburg Empire. Nicknamed the "48ers" they founded many of the institutions that were to provide assistance to the second wave of Czech immigrants who arrived in the 1870s.

The Nazi invasion, the Soviet coup and the failure of the 1968 Prague Spring also brought fresh waves of Czech migration, most of the newcomers becoming quietly assimilated into suburban American life.

131

The Intrepid Sea-Air-Space Museum

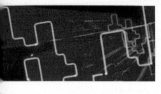

Informed to the point of overload, New Yorkers enjoy TV spanning national networks and public access channels, countless radio stations and newspapers that range from venerable nationals to neighborhood free newspapers.

Television Alongside the networks with their mixture of national and local programming, the Time-Warner-owned NY1 brings a lively blend of news, weather, sports and entertainment gossip focused solely on New York. While all hotel rooms have televisions, budget-priced rooms may lack extra cable channels, and even medium-priced options tend to be skimpy on the selections available. Therefore, one perk of more costly hotels is a fuller range of viewing options, sometimes including Manhattan's public-access channels on which people—ranging from astrologers to self-styled sex therapists—pay to make a half-hour show. New York's daily newspapers carry full listings of TV programs. A full week's listings are also included as a separate magazine with the Sunday *New York Times*.

Radio New York has many radio stations. FM frequencies offer a wide choice of stations, each with its own specialty, from round-the-clock hip-hop, soul, funk, jazz, country, heavy rock or classical sounds. Stations on the AM wavebands are primarily spoken word, and include phone-ins of the kind that should, at the very least, quickly acquaint visitors with the New York accent.

The cast of hit TV series "Law and Order," which is set in New York

Newspapers Of New York City's daily newspapers, *The New York Times* is unmatched for in-depth coverage of international and national affairs, while its Metro section delivers the New York news that matters. The special features of the *Times* provide intriguing insights into city life, and the Friday edition is invaluable for its listings of weekend events and activities. The Sunday edition, particularly as the Christmas-shopping season begins to advance, becomes, literally, a heavyweight as its pages fill with ever more tempting advertisements. While the city

132

once had several flourishing dailies, there has been a general falling off in newspaper readership that has left the *New York Times* as a virtual monopoly when it comes to the serious-minded reader.

While the *Times* is regarded as politically liberal, the tabloid *New York Post* is the home of conservative reaction, despite having some sharp columnists. The Page Six gossip column (which may not be on page 6) is avidly read. New Yorkers who hate the *Post*'s politics but love tabloid headlines turn instead to the *Daily News*. The *Daily News* has built its reputation on well-written racy stories which match its famously racy headlines. It can be relied upon to reveal the most heinous of crimes and the juiciest of scandals.

The weekly *Village Voice* began in the mid-1950s as an alternative paper (author Norman Mailer was one of its cofounders) and is now as much a part of the city as the Empire State Building. It explores city politics and fringe issues with relish and carries comprehensive arts and entertainment listings. However, the *Voice* faces competition from other weeklies such as the entertaining, easier-to-read and better presented *New York Press*, the smaller *Time Out New York*, with comprehensive listings and sharp, compact reviews, and the *New York Observer* with its engaging news, features and arts reviews.

Magazines Appearing in weekly editions, the *New York* magazine is a glossy celebration of the New York lifestyle and has an extensive events-listing section. The *New Yorker*, also published weekly, is noted for long, detailed articles written by literary heavyweights. The *New Yorker* is hardly light reading, although there are many who buy it solely for its thoughtful film reviews, its cartoons and its humor columns.

Free publications Many free publications are found in New York's shops, restaurants, bars and hotel lobbies, and in special bins around the city. Some specialize in particular areas, such as pet care, advancing your career, or the beliefs of the New Age; others are neighborhood publications such as *The Villager, Resident* and *Tribeca Trib* and well worth reading for gossip and local news. *New York Blade* is a free weekly with news and features of interest to the gay community.

A sense of occasion is never lacking at the Metropolitan Opera House: The crystal chandeliers above the auditorium are sucked into the gold-leafed ceiling before a performance

GUIDED TOURS OF LINCOLN CENTER
Hour-long guided tours depart from the concourse level four times daily on weekdays. The anecdote-packed tours weave through the major buildings (except the Metropolitan Opera House; see below), visiting backstage areas and often catching rehearsals in progress (tel: 875-5350). Tours of the Metropolitan Opera House leave from the entrance foyer of the Met, Mon–Fri at 3.45pm and on Sat at 10am (tel: 769-7020).

▶ Lincoln Center for the Performing Arts   *151D1*
62nd to 66th streets, between Columbus and Amsterdam avenues (www.lincolncenter.org)
Subway: 1; 66th Street/Lincoln Center

Parts of the Lincoln Center for the Performing Arts may reflect the less enduring aspects of 1960s design, however, the music and drama staged there is rarely considered unimpressive.

The complex arose in the 1960s as part of a Utopian plan to give New York a single cultural rendezvous point. One element in Lincoln Center's genesis was the decision of the New York Philharmonic, faced with what seemed likely to be the imminent destruction of Carnegie Hall, to seek a home of its own. Philharmonic Hall was completed here in 1962, changing its name in 1973 to Avery Fisher Hall in honor of the man who parted with $10 million to improve its atrocious acoustics (not completely brought up to scratch until the 1980s).

The Philharmonic's search for new premises coincided with that of the Metropolitan Opera; the 10-story **Metropolitan Opera House** (tel: 362-6000) now rises boldly above the plaza, two enormous Marc Chagall murals visible through its windows.

Home of the New York State City Opera and New York City Ballet, the **New York State Theater** (tel: 870-5570), designed by Philip Johnston, was successfully remodeled in the 1980s. Two of the better 1960s contributions are Eero Saarinen's **Vivian Beaumont Theater** (tel: 239-6200), and the neighboring **New York Public Library for the Performing Arts** (tel: 876-1630), from the firm of Skidmore, Owings and Merrill. The library holds 50,000 tomes and has three galleries for temporary exhibitions.

On the north side of the complex is the world-famous Juilliard School, which lists violinist Itzhak Perlman and actor William Hurt among its alumni. Beside the school, **Alice Tully Hall** (tel: 875-5050) provides an intimate and acoustically brilliant home for the Lincoln Center Chamber Music Society—and for free concerts given by students (usually Wednesday lunchtimes).

▶▶ Little Italy 87B2

Both Italian and not very large, Little Italy has had its boundaries steadily eroded by the expansion of Chinatown and by the drift of its original inhabitants to Italian enclaves in the Outer Boroughs. Between 1890 and 1924, however, 145,000 immigrants from Sicily and southern mainland Italy settled here, in an area between Houston and Canal streets.

After years of decline the area is now showing signs of gentrification with stores and restaurants spreading from SoHo and the East Village into its northern edge, now dubbed **NoLiTa** (north Little Italy). Many of the few thousand Italians remaining in the neighborhood are employed in the restaurants, cafés and bakeries along Grand and Mulberry streets. The food is good but far from cheap, and the cost-wise way to take in Little Italy's atmosphere is with a cappuccino at an outdoor table.

The closest the district comes to a genuine Italian landmark is **Umberto's Clam House** (129 Mulberry Street), which acquired fame for all the wrong reasons in 1972, when, in settlement of a gangland feud, "Crazy" Joe Gallo was shot while dining on a seafood supper.

The local Irish, who predated the Italians, had their spiritual needs fulfilled by what is now **"Old" St. Patrick's Cathedral** (263 Mulberry Street; tel: 226-8075; *Open:* daily 7–8.45). The city's earliest Gothic-style building, it lost its original facade in an 1866 fire and was demoted to a parish church when a new St. Patrick's Cathedral was consecrated in Midtown Manhattan in 1879.

Take a look at the **Old Police Headquarters** at 240 Centre Street. This Renaissance palace, topped by a green dome, was an immeasurably imposing symbol of law and order when it arose in the midst of one of the city's most crime-ridden districts in 1909.

Walk on to the **Puck Building** at 295–307 Lafayette Street. This was completed in 1886 to house the *Puck* satirical magazine and, with its deliriously complex red brickwork, was instantly revered as a prime example of New York commercial design.

FESTIVAL OF ST. GENNARO

Each September, Little Italy's Mulberry Street is lined by makeshift stalls selling homemade sausage, calzone and other Italian specialties (plus an increasing number of Chinese ones) and jumps to the sound of marching bands in a two-week celebration of the Feast of St. Gennaro. The religious aspect of the festival, honoring the patron saint of Naples, is evident as a likeness of the saint is carried along the streets and showered with dollar bills. In 1995, the festival was almost cancelled following allegations that most of the estimated $10 million raised by the event went to one of New York's Italian crime families. Mayor Giuliani refused to licence stallholders until guarantees were made that the proceeds would reach charities.

The tenements of Little Italy. Many of them have a restaurant or a café at street level—worth a stop at any time for a cappuccino, ice cream or a pizza

Italians first arrived in large numbers in New York during the 1880s. Through a combination of hard work, traditional values and business acumen, the Italian community had become sufficiently prosperous to take the helm of the city by the 1940s.

A refuge for Italian liberals and revolutionaries through the 19th century, New York's first Italian neighborhood was on Bleecker Street during the 1860s. Its population was chiefly made up of sophisticated northerners. By contrast, the grinding poverty of rural southern Italy triggered the massive influx of the late 1800s, and 145,000 people were soon packed into the tenements of what became, and still is, Little Italy.

Exploitation of immigrants

Speaking little or no English, these new arrivals were exploited, not least by their fellow countrymen who had been in the US long enough to learn the language yet who still knew enough about traditional Italian values to overwork and underpay the immigrants.

Little Italy's men built New York's sewers and subways and its women worked in garment industry sweatshops. Any spare money was sent home to their villages. Many Italians had escaped Little Italy for East Harlem by the 1910s, and by the 1940s had become wealthy enough to move to suburban areas in the Outer Boroughs.

Rising fortunes
It was from East Harlem that Fiorello La Guardia emerged. This Protestant Italian son of a Jewish mother was destined to be remembered as the best mayor the city of New York ever had. La Guardia's rise was a symbol of the assimilation of Italian-Americans into city politics, a sphere where they replaced the Irish as the dominant ethnic group.

With descendants of the first Italian-Americans excelling in every walk of New York life, a new wave of immigrants appeared almost unnoticed during the prosperous 1980s. In contrast to the Italian arrivals of a century or more earlier, these Italians were affluent and stylish. They moved into the Upper East Side and opened the up-market boutiques and critically acclaimed Italian restaurants that won the hearts and wallets of New Yorkers who could afford to shop and eat in them.

Many Italians work in the restaurant industry, providing New Yorkers and visitors alike with pasta, pizza and other universally popular specialties

136

▶▶▶ Lower East Side

IFCB3

Don't come to the Lower East Side expecting epoch-making architecture, fashionable faces, glamourous boutiques or expense-account restaurants. While new bars and boutiques are making in-roads, this is still downbeat New York with few pretensions. It is traditionally the first stop for newly arrived immigrants from around the world whose priority is to work hard and earn enough money to move on.

The first to arrive in the Lower East Side were the Irish, fleeing their homeland's famine in the mid-1800s. They were followed by successive waves of German and Eastern European immigrants, including the two million Jews who turned the Lower East Side into the world's largest Jewish community.

Living in windowless rooms in overcrowded tenements and often working in sweatshops for breadline wages, the immigrants nonetheless founded cultural institutions and places of worship and established the educational organizations that were to make their children's lives easier than their own.

The 1924 tightening of immigration laws slowed the European influx into the Lower East Side, although by then its more successful inhabitants had moved on and established ethnic pockets elsewhere, and it was to these districts that new arrivals headed.

With land here yet to become valuable, many Lower East Side tenements remain, as do the delis, garment and jewelry stores on which the first locals made their money. Nowadays, the owners are likely to be Indian or Korean, representing the latest waves of immigration.

Less immediately obvious to outsiders are the Lower East Side's Caribbean immigrants, including the many Puerto Ricans who dominate a broad area east of Essex Street and spill north across Houston Street into Alphabet City (see page 60).

It is the stores and their heavily discounted prices that bring most visitors to the Lower East Side. The area is at its busiest on Sundays when bargain-hunting New Yorkers descend on the narrow streets off Delancey Street

TENEMENT LIFE: THE ANNUAL MOVE
Few Lower East Siders ever stayed in a particular tenement for longer than they had to, and the offer of a free month's rent in return for a year's tenancy was usually sufficient inducement for tenement dwellers to up stakes and move every 12 months. It also became common for entire families to move back and forth across the same street, often moving in and out of the same tenements many times at yearly intervals.

137

For vast stocks of cut-price clothing, the stores and stalls of Orchard Street, at the heart of Jewish New York on the Lower East Side, are hard to beat

HOW THE OTHER HALF LIVED

Photographs and text by Jacob Riis, published as *How the Other Half Lives* in 1894, focused attention on the grim realities of everyday life in the Lower East Side and were instrumental in bringing about laws improving housing and working conditions. Nonetheless, for most Lower East Side residents, the only real escape was to save enough money for a move to Brooklyn, the Bronx or Queens.

WALKING TOURS

The Lower East Side Tenement Museum organizes various walking tours, each concentrating on a specific facet of Lower East Side life— such as ethnic heritage, the lives of women, tenement architecture and the exploits of New York's earliest street gangs. The walks are not cheap but they are enjoyable and informative. For details and reservations, tel: 431-0233.

Typical Lower East Side tenements on Delancey Street. Buildings like these sprang up in the 19th century to house newly arrived immigrants—often in very overcrowded and unhealthy conditions

for some of the biggest clothing discounts to be found in the city. The crush is fiercest outside the garment stores lining **Orchard Street▶**. If the crowds get overwhelming, explore the marginally less busy neighboring streets such as Allen, Grand and Essex. The tumult of Sundays is not repeated during the week, when the streets are much quieter—and actually rather dull. An exception to this is the **Essex Street Market▶**, where Lower East Siders buy their fresh meat, vegetables and fruit.

The current ethnic mix of the area is evident in the conversations carried out here in Yiddish, Spanish and Chinese—and in the plantains and bean sprouts sitting alongside the Jewish staples. The market is closed on Sundays. If you plan a weekend visit, it is useful to bear in mind also that many stores are closed on Saturdays in observance of the Jewish Sabbath.

When you're done with shopping and sampled fresh-made knishes (doughy pastries filled with meat or potatoes) from one of several dozen Jewish bakeries, make sure to visit the **Lower East Side Tenement Museum▶▶▶** (97 Orchard Street; tel: 431-0233, www.tenement.org; *Open:* guided tours only Tue–Fri every 40 minutes from 1.20–4.45, Sat and Sun every half-hour 11.15–4.45. *Admission: inexpensive*), which is situated in a six-story tenement that was built in 1863 and housed 11,000 people over a 70-year period.

The museum provides a fascinating background to Lower East Side life and reveals countless illuminating facts about the deprivations of tenement living, at least for those tenement dwellers of an earlier age. The upper floors have been re-created to show the conditions that the house's tenants endured.

Since 1654, when 23 Sephardic Jews deported from Brazil landed in New York and resisted the Dutch governor's attempts to remove them, the Jewish community has shaped the character of New York life. The city's Jewish population has given the world everything from bagels to Irving Berlin.

Established and respected in the commercial life of colonial America, the Sephardic community—which traces its origins back to Moorish Spain—continued to flourish after the American Revolution.

In the 1830s, arrivals from Germany, the Ashkenazy—who had a different set of Jewish traditions—began looking for new opportunities in the city.

Germans and Russians Assisted by mutual aid societies, the Germans settled in the Lower East Side and were soon establishing the area's jewelry and garment industries. Such businesses employed other Ashkenazy: Russian Jews who arrived during the late 1800s, fleeing the pogroms of Czar Alexander III. For the most part, these Russians shunned the charity offered by the German Jewish aid societies and formed their own self-help organizations. In the garment industry sweatshops, the Russians formed powerful labor unions.

The Ashkenazy immigrants also brought a rich cultural life to the Lower East Side, particularly with the Yiddish theaters in an area which became known as the "Yiddish Rialto." Although the Yiddish theater began with vaudeville and farce, the arrival of Jacob Gordin, a leading Russian playwright, helped it develop serious drama and stage works by the likes of Norwegian playwright Henrik Ibsen and Russian playwright Maxim Gorky. Future stars such as Walter Matthau and Edward G. Robinson cut their teeth before the lively Yiddish theater audiences. At the same time, the smoke-filled Lower East Side cafés became centers of political and literary debate, as well as the venues for closely fought chess matches.

Some anti-Semitism was encountered, but New York immigrants never suffered the hostilities that had been their fate in Europe, and Jewish culture soon became deeply embedded in New York life.

Later arrivals The Lower East Side was still the first area of settlement for poor Sephardic arrivals from Turkey, Greece and Syria during the Balkan Wars of the 1910s. By the 1930s, however, Europeans fleeing the rise of Nazism were able to move directly into comfortable Jewish enclaves established in the Upper West Side and the Outer Boroughs.

In the 1970s, Soviet Jews began settling in Brooklyn's Brighton Beach. Today, the most conspicuous aspects of New York's Jewish community are seen in areas dominated by ultra-orthodox sects, such as the Satmarers and Lubavitchers.

139

Black hats (fur trimming denotes a rabbi) and matching long coats make men belonging to the rigidly orthodox Satmar Sect instantly recognizable

Many visitors come to New York for no reason other than to shop. Once the flagship designer boutiques and the big-name department stores drew the crowds, however, the attention of serious shoppers is turning to the city's flea markets and secondhand shops—where the quest for that elusive item at a giveaway price can bring sheer pleasure to many.

FASHION CONSCIOUS

Both a do-gooder fundraising event and a fashion free-for-all is the annual POSH Sale, organized by Lighthouse International (110 East 60th Street, between Lexington and Park avenues; tel: 821-9200, www.lighthouse.org), a non-profit organization that benifits the vision-impaired. New York City clothing designers and well-to-do women donate their samples and barely used couture to the sale, usually held in late spring, which the Lighthouse organization passes onto the shopper at bargain prices. There are three tiers of admission—starting at $100 on the first day of the sale and dropping to $10 on the last ones.

Flea markets Wherever the New York sidewalk is wide enough you are likely to find an impromptu flea market. The merchandise will probably range from out-and-out junk to stolen goods (often with fake designer labels). Resist temptation and instead visit one of the city's four main official flea markets, where better fare turns up.

Every weekend the **Annex Antiques Fair and Flea Market** (Sixth Avenue at 26th Street) features a varied stash of bric-a-brac, clothing and jewelry. The quality is highly variable, but a browse can be worthwhile. Nearby is the **Chelsea Antiques Building** (110 West 25th Street, between Sixth and Seventh avenues), where vendors sell everything from exquisite jewels to collectibles.

Prices are higher at the Saturday **Greenwich Village Flea Market** (Greenwich Street at Charles Street), although this small market merits a visit if you are exploring the neighborhood.

On Sunday, the **Green Flea Indoor/Outdoor Market** (Columbus Avenue, between 76th and 77th streets) is a larger and somewhat more commercial affair with clothing, jewelry, ornaments and furniture. On Saturday, the same market can be found at West 84th Street, between Columbus and Amsterdam avenues.

Books Not only do they love bargains, New Yorkers also love to read. Spend a whole day browsing in the **Strand Book Store** (Broadway at 12th Street) and you will barely make an impression on its 8 miles (13km) of shelves; the stocks range from dog-eared paperback best-sellers to discarded review copies of pristine hardbacks—all sold for a fraction of their original price.

This second-floor shop is a bit out of the way but **Archivia Books** (1063 Madison Avenue, between East 80th and East 81st streets) stocks new, used and out-of-print titles that span the arts. **Argosy Bookstore** in Midtown (116 East 59th Street, between Park and Lexington avenues) sells scholarly books, maps and prints that have been gently used.

Clothing The city's more affluent elements may shop for clothes among the designer-name stores that proliferate in Midtown Manhattan, but the sartorially adventurous—and those in search of a bargain—target the array of vintage clothing stores downtown in Greenwich Village, SoHo, on the Lower East Side and the East Village.

The enormous stocks of **Antique Boutique** (712–714 Broadway) have plenty to keep the vintage-clothes fanatic

ANNUAL FAIRS
There are several annual neighborhood fairs that allow residents and retail establishments the opportunity to peddle their wares or get rid of old junk, as the case may be. The Atlantic Antic, on Atlantic Avenue in Brooklyn each September, is one the best. Also noteworthy is the Stuyvesant Town Fair each May.

Left: you will find plenty of junk (and, just possibly, a bargain or two) on sale in Canal Street

engaged, although dedicated bargain-hunters might be better served by a search through the racks at **Cheap Jack's** (Broadway, between 13th and 14th streets).

In the East Village, **Filthmart** (531 East 13th Street, between Avenues A and B) hawks black concert T-shirts emblazoned with the rock bands of the 60s to the 80s, lots of denim and leather accessories. Taking its cue from the Fifth Avenue shops, **Screaming Mimi's** (382 Lafayette Street at Great Georges Street) always has inspired window displays and gorgeous getups from the 50s to the 70s in a well-lit and organized Nolita space. On the Lower East Side, you'll find cool and dressy pieces from the 70s and 80s at **Marmalade** (172 Ludlow, between Houston and Stanton streets). The fashionable ladies at **Foley & Corinna** (108 Stanton, between Essex and Ludlow streets) stocks vintage and used but stylish contemporary pieces. Another happy hunting-ground is **Alice Underground** (Broadway, between Broome and Grand streets). Resale shops such as **Ina** (101 Thompson Street and 21 Prince Street) and **Ina Men** (262 Mott Street) sell used haute couture like Prada and Gucci at a fraction of the original price.

CDs and Records New York has a massive audience for all kinds of music, but predominant on the secondhand racks are indie rock and classical rarities. **St. Mark's Sounds** (16 and 20 St. Mark's Place) has two branches: One sells jazz, the other new rock. **Footlight Records** (113 East Twelfth Street) is the city's prime source of show music, big band records and movie soundtracks, and also has a strong jazz selection. Classical music fans should explore the used records of **Academy Records & CDs** (12 West 18th Street) and seek out the costly rarities at **Gryphon Records** (233 West 72nd Street).

It is hard not to be overwhelmed by the sheer volume of print at the Strand Book Store, which claims to be the world's largest second-hand bookstore

The Met's imposing neo-classical entrance

THE ORIGINAL BUILDING

Few New York facades are as overwhelming in their grandeur as that of the Metropolitan Museum of Art, even though the exuberant neo-classical features that greet visitors to the Met's Fifth Avenue entrance are but one of many additions made to the museum's original body. In 1880, in an effort to blend the planned museum into its setting on the edge of Central Park, its original architects Jacob Wrey Mould and Calvert Vaux (one of the park's co-designers) devised a High Gothic form for the main facade, which then faced the park.

As its collections grew, so too did the museum building. In 1902 it gained the Fifth Avenue entrance that remains in place today. Only a segment of Mould and Vaux's work can still be seen, inside the much more recent Robert Lehman Wing.

▶▶▶ **Metropolitan Museum of Art**   *187C1*

Fifth Avenue and 82nd Street (tel: 535-7710)
Open: Sun, Tue–Thu 9.30–5.15, Fri and Sat 9.30–9.
Admission: moderate donation. Subway: 4, 6; 86th Street

Founded in 1870, the Metropolitan Museum of Art is now among the world's most important museums. Over the years, the collection itself has been greatly swelled by donations from some of America's richest people.

The Met will exhaust you long before you exhaust it. The best way is to think of it as a dozen or so separate museums. Plan your visit bearing in mind that some galleries close in rotation. Schedules are available from the desk. If you cannot decide where to begin, aim first for the European paintings on the second floor.

The Dutch galleries include almost a whole room of Rembrandts and five of Vermeer's 40 extant paintings.

Among the Spanish contributions, focus on El Greco's *View of Toledo*, a striking depiction of the 16th-century religious center below menacing clouds and Velázquez's *Juan de Pareja*, a portrait of his assistant, painted in the 1640s during his second trip to Italy.

Moving on, the French rooms reveal choice works that span three centuries. Among many striking pieces, George de la Tour's *The Penitent Magdalen* has a rare ability to draw the viewer into its dark corners, and Rousseau's *The Forest in Winter at Sunset* seems to resonate with the primeval forces of nature.

After the changing displays of drawing and photography you reach the 19th-century European painting and sculpture. The galleries of French impressionists and post-impressionists include contributions from Manet, Monet, Cézanne, Gauguin and Renoir, but winning the day are the canvases of Van Gogh, among them *Self-Portrait with a Straw Hat* and the stunning *Cypresses*.

(Continued on page 144)

Detailed explanatory labels are an essential aid to comprehending the Met's Egyptian collections, an otherwise overwhelming stash of 40,000 objects that stretch from pre-dynastic times to the arrival of the Romans.

You don't need to be a scholar to enjoy the collections or the lasting impression they provide of one of the world's greatest civilizations. Some of this colossal stock of treasures were donated by individuals but many come from the Met's own 40-year excavation program. The single biggest exhibit, the Temple of Dendur (see panel), was a gift from the government of Egypt to the United States in the 1960s.

Although the walk-through Tomb of Perneb—a structure that draws attention as soon as you enter the Egyptian galleries—is a reconstruction, most of the objects on display are originals in such excellent states of preservation that they seem far younger than they really are; their imagery, and their often extravagant use of color are surprisingly forceful.

The trappings of death The most powerful examples are the numerous brightly decorated coffins, that of the 12th-dynasty (1897–1843 BC) Khnumnakht being particularly notable for its painted eyes—intended to allow the dead to look into the land of the living.

The smaller items, too, can be striking. From the Ptolemaic period (332–30 BC) are a sculptured Anubis, the jackal-headed god of embalming who watched over the dead, and the erect and disconcertingly alert bronze likeness of a cat, used as a coffin for the animal regarded by some ancient Egyptians as sacred. Look also for the detailed 11th-century (2009–1998 BC) house and garden models from the tomb of Mekutra, used to show the layout of the deceased's property.

THE TEMPLE OF DENDUR
Destined to be submerged following the construction of the Aswan Dam, this 2,000-year-old temple was packed up and transported to the museum from its original site on the banks of the Nile. The sandstone temple, a monument to Isis and two Egyptian brothers who drowned in the Nile, was constructed around 15 BC in an effort by the Roman emperor Augustus to win the hearts of the conquered locals. It manages to be both spectacular and disappointing, overwhelmed by the modern gallery that was built to contain it and overlooked, through a vast glass wall, by the trees of Central Park and the penthouses of Fifth Avenue.

143

The Temple of Dendur stands in its own huge gallery

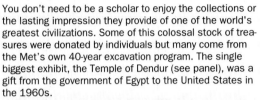

(Continued from page 142)

The American Wing holds an outstanding collection, defining the development of art and design in the US as European traditions were by stages mimicked, absorbed and finally submerged, as American styles developed.

Foremost among the paintings are the finely detailed landscapes of the Hudson River artists, many of which captured the continent's natural breadth and diversity as white settlers steadily forged westwards. A series of period rooms shows the progress of the decorative arts, from Queen Anne armchairs and Philadelphia Chippendale chests of drawers to the unique art nouveau glasswork of Louis Comfort Tiffany, who worked in Long Island, and a large living room that brilliantly expresses the vision of Frank Lloyd Wright's Prairie-style architecture, intended to replicate the wide open spaces of the American heartland in a domestic setting.

Compared with their American counterparts, the European period rooms seem vulgarly stuffed with finery—they include Venetian bedrooms, English interiors by Robert Adam and a Louis XIV state bedchamber. The phenomenal collection of clocks, mirrors and objets d'art lining the adjacent passageways is enough to bring tears to the eyes of any passing antique dealer.

Just steps away, a flamboyantly decorated 16th-century Spanish patio leads to the stairwell and the main entrance to the museum's cache of medieval art. Should medieval art be your abiding interest, make this your first call. Only with a clear head are the 4,000-odd exhibits—from the fall of Rome to the dawn of the Renaissance and from a tiny 3rd-century Alexandrian medallion to a three-story-high wrought-iron choir screen from 17th-century Spain—likely to fall into a comprehensible pattern.

(Continued on page 146)

MORE MEDIEVAL ART
After a thorough rummage through the Met's main collections, true medievalists might consider forsaking the remainder of the museum for New York's second batch of medieval treasures, displayed at the Met's Cloisters wing (see pages 92–93). Admission tickets are valid at both locations on their day of issue.

One of the less well-known and more restful corners of the labyrinthine Met: the Petrie Sculpture Court

144

After a bright introductory room describing the founding of Islam by Muhammad in 622 and the religion's steady outward spread from Mecca, the sides of the initial galleries are lined with dozens of well-stocked display cases, each holding a wonderful assortment of gold and silver pieces such as beads, pendants and plaques from the craftsmen of Egypt, Iran and Syria during the 9th, 10th and 11th centuries.

A side room is even more copiously stocked, holding the enormous collection of ceramics unearthed during the Met's own excavations in Nishapur during the 1930s and 1940s. The Iranian town was a 10th-century center of Islamic creativity.

Calligraphy and ceramics Flanked by exquisite mosque lamps and perfume sprinklers, another gallery holds a series of leaves from the Koran, demonstrating the development of calligraphy from angular kufic scripts on parchment from 9th-century Egypt to the final refinement of cursive scripts achieved by the oblique cutting of the pen nib in 13th-century Iraq. In the same room stands a 14th-century prayer niche (Mihrab), each of its tiny ceramic tiles individually fired to maximize the glaze and heighten the floral decoration. Since it showed the direction of Mecca, the Mihrab was (and still is) the most important item in a Muslim place of worship.

Small is beautiful Many exquisite examples of 14th-century miniature painting, used in text illustration and characterized by pure and harmonious colors and a strong sense of pattern-ing, are displayed in rotation. The influence of miniature artwork was car-ried over into Islamic carpet design in later years, and carpets and prayer rugs are the prize exhibits of subsequent galleries. Look especially for the lavish textiles—some decorated with gold leaf—with which Mogul emperors lined their tents. Finally, peer into the Nur ad-Din Room, a reassembled winter reception room typical of a wealthy Syrian home of the early 1700s: Heavily decorated wood-paneled walls rise from a patterned marble floor and reach up to stained-glass windows and a sumptuous beamed ceiling.

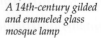

A 14th-century gilded and enameled glass mosque lamp

PRINTS AND PHOTOGRAPHS

As comprehensive and as engrossing as any other section of the museum, the Met's collections of prints and photography include everything from Rembrandt etchings to Russian constructivist photography. Every print-maker and shutter-clicker that you have ever heard of—and many less familiar—are represented.

(Continued from page 144)

Unlike the tightly packed rooms of the main museum, the newer Lila Acheson Wallace Wing holds spacious, light-soaked galleries and makes an excellent setting for the museum's 20th-century art.

Picasso's portrait of Gertrude Stein is a piece that stands out, though the bulk of the collection is provided by Americans—de Kooning, Lichtenstein, Pollock and O'Keeffe among them. This is not the greatest collection of modern art in New York (for that, see the Museum of Modern Art, pages 158–160), but the side room holding selections from the Berggruen collection of Paul Klee drawings is a definite plus. So, too, is the rooftop sculpture garden, reached by an elevator. Its views across Central Park tend to draw your attention away from the sculpture,

Changing exhibitions of sculpture and sweeping views over Central Park are two good reasons to visit the Met's rooftop

which is taken from the permanent stock in the museum and exhibited on a rotating basis.

The Michael C. Rockefeller Wing, named after the collector who disappeared (presumed drowned) on a trip to Papua New Guinea in 1961, houses the art of Africa, Oceania and the Americas. Of a large, wide-ranging and constantly intriguing assemblage, items from the Asmat tribe of Irian Jaya (the region of Indonesia adjoining Papua New Guinea) are perhaps the most absorbing.

The **Greek and Roman art** collections include Cypriot, Greek and Roman sculpture, painted Greek vases, Roman portrait busts, one of the few surviving Etruscan chariots, and some remarkable wall paintings from a villa at Boscoreale, buried by the AD 79 eruption of Mt Vesuvius. Another engaging piece is the diminutive *Seated Harp Player*, a marble Cycladic sculpture.

Since the early 1970s, the museum has developed its **Asian Art** holdings into one of the world's best. The collection of early Chinese art includes major Buddhist sculptures, ceramics and jade.

(Continued on page 148)

Bequeathed by a millionaire banker who allegedly spent his youth roaming Europe tracking down masterpieces and telegramming his father for the money to buy his discoveries, the Robert Lehman Collection provides a relaxing interlude from the museum's more popular galleries.

The Lehman Collection's more important paintings, chiefly 14th- and 15th-century Italian works, are all on display on the second floor in reassembled period rooms from the Lehman house at West 54th Street. The various other paintings vie for attention with the temporary exhibitions of drawings at the lower level, including work by Dürer and Rembrandt.

Botticelli Modest in size but immense in its importance, the highlight of the collection is perhaps Botticelli's *Annunciation*, revealing the achievements of late 15th-century Florentine art in the use of perspective. The painting sets a row of classical pillars between a resonant Virgin and the Archangel Gabriel. God's message arrives as light through a doorway, the rays cutting a diagonal path, splitting the painting's horizontal and vertical lines and linking the two figures.

Venetian painters The Bellini family is represented with a Madonna and Child by Jacopo Bellini and an early work by his more famous son, Giovanni, placed at around 1460 and depicting the Madonna and Child in intense poses before an eerily still landscape. From a few years later, another Venetian, Jacometto Veneziano, contributes two portraits: *Alvise Contarini* and *Nun of San Secondo*, intriguing works prefiguring the Venetian portrait style that came to prominence during the 1500s.

Giovanni da Paolo Among a strong complement of Sienese works, da Paolo's *Expulsion from Paradise* stands out, not least for its lively use of color. The painting shows God soaring above an intensely vibrant constellation, pointing a finger at a barren Earth—the destination for a spindly Adam and Eve who are being shooed out of Eden by a nervous angel.

Another interesting Sienese contribution in the Lehman pavilion is the painting, *Temptation of Saint Anthony Abbot*, credited to the Osservanza Master.

FRENCH WORKS
The collection's 19th-century French paintings are less inspired despite bearing famous names: Monet's unusually airy *Landscape near Zaandam* is worth a look, as are *Promenade among the Olive Trees* (above) by Matisse, and Cézanne's *House behind the Trees on the Road to Tholonet* and *Girl Bathing*.

147

Jacopo Bellini's Madonna and Child

New York

EATING AND DRINKING AT THE MET

A thorough exploration of the Met calls for great stamina, and even if you have consumed a hearty breakfast before arriving, you will be in need of further nourishment well before it is time to leave.

On the museum's first floor, near the entrance to the Michael C. Rockefeller Wing, a spacious atrium holds a self-service cafeteria, with a choice of hot and cold dishes at reasonable prices, and a slightly more expensive waiter-service restaurant.

If you are only pretending to visit the museum—or its size simply becomes too much to bear—you could while away the day over a glass or two of something deliciously tempting at the atrium's bar.

Figures and figurative art: visitors and exhibits at the Metropolitan Museum of Art

(Continued from page 146)

Astor Court, a re-creation of a Ming-era scholar's garden in Soochow built by craftsmen from that city, is a center for traditional garden architecture.

The Japanese collections span thousands of years but their strongest pieces are undoubtedly the wonderful screen paintings of the Edo period, when years of peace and stability enabled great blossoming of artistic talent: Ogata Korin's *Waves* is just one eye-catching example.

The Met has a couple of off-beat departments that—though not designed for the purpose—might well come as a godsend if you have young minds to keep occupied.

The Musical Instruments galleries house 4,000 weird, wonderful, and sometimes priceless tune-making devices. Among the displays, look for the remarkably unattractive legs of the world's oldest existing piano—dated 1720 and a product of the workshops of Bartolommeo Cristofori—and a Stradivari violin made in 1691 which has been restored to its original appearance.

Strange instruments are plentiful, such as the 19th-century Indian mayuri, a kind of bowed sitar in the shape of a peacock, and a Native American shaman rattle, its carved animal emblem intended to symbolize the transfer of magical power from the spirits to the shaman.

Though it gets comparatively scant attention from the public, the Met's Arms and Armor collection is among the best of its kind to be found. Close study of the massed rows of suits of armor, from the 15th century onwards, reveals the high level of artistic flair and craftsmanship that went into the creation of battle apparel.

In temporary exhibitions, the **Costume Institute** displays selected parts of its enormous wardrobe of 60,000 items—from every corner of the world—of clothing and accessories, spanning everything from 19th-century Parisian ballgowns and Mary Quant mini-skirts to Korean bridal gowns and African tribal wear. Items from the US include 1940s clothing and 1920s "flapper" attire.

▶▶▶ Midtown Manhattan   IFCD2

Midtown Manhattan is the New York of popular imagination: A place where battalions of office-workers march along packed sidewalks to the sounds of wailing police sirens and bumper-to-bumper traffic, as street vendors dispense hot dogs and pretzels in the shadows of the high-rise buildings. It is here that many of New York's main attractions are found—the Empire State Building, the United Nations complex, Rockefeller Center, St Patrick's Cathedral, the Chrysler Building, the Museum of Modern Art, Grand Central Terminal, Times Square and the Broadway theater district, plus a number of major department stores such as Macy's and Bloomingdale's—all of which are detailed elsewhere in this book.

▶ Mount Vernon Hotel Museum   151D3

61st Street at York Avenue (tel: 838-6878; www.mvhm.org)
Open: Tue–Sun 11–4; Jun and Jul until 9 on Tue.
Admission: inexpensive. Subway: N, R, 4, 6; 59th Street
On land purchased in 1795 by William Stephen Smith, an aide to George Washington, arose this Ashlar stone building that became the Mount Vernon Hotel, its gardens a popular day trip for wealthy New Yorkers until 1833. Eight rooms display colonial-era furniture and exhibitions on early 19th-century New York.

▶▶▶ Murray Hill, Gramercy and Flatiron   IFCD3

Murray Hill and neighboring Gramercy, north of 14th Street and east of Fifth Avenue, retain much of the refined ambience that made them fashionable addresses for the well-to-do of the late 1800s. Spared the relentless bustle of much of Manhattan, a wealthy mood remains despite many of the orginal brownstones being replaced by comfortable apartment buildings. Just across Fifth Avenue from Gramercy is the trendier, resurgent Flatiron District, while **Union Square▶** (see page 183) can be found on the area's southern fringe.

(Continued on page 152)

Stroll through the vast skyscapers of Midtown and past the famous Macy's department store

149

THE ARMORY SHOW

The 69th Regiment Armory, on Lexington Avenue, between 25th and 26th streets, is not the only National Guard barracks to be modeled on a medieval fortress, but it is the only one to have staged the legendary Armory Show of 1913, the first exhibition of modern European art in a country then still obsessed with traditional landscapes and portraiture. The work of Marcel Duchamp and others shocked critics and public alike and the Armory Show's effect on American art was profound. A small plaque on the Armory's facade notes the historic event.

Midtown Manhattan landmarks

Beginning at the Empire State Building and finishing at the United Nations complex, this walk passes seven decades' worth of landmark New York architecture.

After visiting the **Empire State Building** (pages 100–102), continue north along Fifth Avenue to the **New York Public Library** (page 168), its entrance set back from the street and guarded by sculptured lions. Behind the library is the restored **Bryant Park**, landscaped in 1934. Walk east along 42nd Street to Grand Central Terminal (pages 166–167) and the **Philip Morris Headquarters**, on Park Avenue, a modern building with a gallery holding exhibits from the Whitney Museum of American Art.

Further east on 42nd Street, pass through the cast bronze doors of the 1923 **Bowery Savings Bank** (now the Home Savings Bank of America) to see the lavish Romanesque interior. Close by, note the stunning art deco bas-reliefs by Edward Trumbull on the exterior of the **Chanin Building**. Ahead are the unmistakable **Chrysler Building** (page 89) and **Daily News Building** (page 95), while turning north on First Avenue reveals the **United Nations** complex (page 184).

View of St. Patrick's Cathedral and the Olympic Tower

Midtown churches and museums

Beginning and ending at Rockefeller Center, this walk includes several Midtown churches, the **Museum of Modern Art** (pages 158–160), and the **American Craft Museum** (page 62).

Facing **Rockefeller Center** (pages 173–174) across Fifth Avenue, the twin-spired **St. Patrick's Cathedral** was completed in 1878 in rich, carved Gothic form. Inside, the chapels and shrines glow with candlelight.

On East 50th Street, the art deco **Waldorf-Astoria Hotel** has accommodated royalty and every US president since its opening in 1931. Inside, admire the art deco interior and the lobby stores that cater to every whim of the well-heeled traveler. Nearby, the slim octagonal brick tower of the **General Electric Building** is another art deco landmark. Byzantine-style **St. Bartholomew's Church** boasts a splendid triple-arched entrance portal and a mighty dome that adds to the interior's sense of airyness. Back on Fifth Avenue, a single corner tower gives **St. Thomas' Episcopal Church** a disjointed look, but don't miss the striking reredos inside. The architect, Bertram Goodhue, also designed St. Bartholomew's and had a hand in several other noted Manhattan churches.

MIDTOWN MANHATTAN

UPPER WEST SIDE

UPPER EAST SIDE

WEST 72ND STREET

EAST 72ND STREET

Dakota Apartments

St James Episcopal Church

Asia Society

Strawberry Fields

Frick Collection

Central Park

The Mall

Museum of American Folk Art

Temple Emanu-El

Church of St Vincent Ferrer

Rockefeller University

American Federation of the Arts

EAST 64TH ST

Lincoln Center for the Performing Arts

American Bible Society

Dairy

Wollman Memorial Rink

Zoo

Museum of American Illustration

Mount Vernon Hotel Museum

QUEENSBORO BRIDGE

COLUMBUS CIRCLE

N Y Coliseum

CENTRAL PARK SOUTH

Bloomingdale's

EAST 57TH ST

Carnegie Hall

Trump Tower

Newseum

WEST 57TH STREET

New York Convention & Visitors Bureau

Museum of Modern Art

Sony Wonder Technology Lab

Central Synagogue

WEST 53RD ST

St Thomas Episcopal Church

EAST 53RD STREET

De Witt Clinton Park

Museum of American Design

Museum of TV & Radio

St Bartholomew's Church

General Electric Bldg

WEST 49TH STREET

Radio City Music Hall

St Patrick's Cathedral

EAST 50TH ST

Waldorf Astoria Hotel

Rockefeller Center

THEATER DISTRICT

EAST 47TH ST

Times Square Visitors Center

Met Life (former Pan Am) Building

United Nations

Intrepid Sea-Air Space Museum

WEST 45TH STREET

Film Center Building

Times Square

Grand Central Terminal

Chrysler Building

WEST 42ND STREET

Philip Morris

E 42ND ST

Port Authority Bus Terminal

Bryant Park

HQ

Chanin Building

Daily News Building

MIDTOWN TUNNEL

WEST 39TH STREET

New York Public Library

Bowery Savings Bank

Pierpont Morgan Library

EAST 37TH STREET

LINCOLN TUNNEL

WEST 37TH STREET

GARMENT DISTRICT

Macy's Store

MURRAY HILL

Jacob Javits Convention Center

WEST 34TH STREET

Madison Square Garden

EAST 34TH STREET

Heliport

General Post Office

Empire State Building

NYU Medical Center

WEST 30TH STREET

Penn Station

Little Church Around the Corner

Tin Pan Alley

EAST 28TH STREET

Chelsea Park

Bellevue Hospital Center

WEST 26TH STREET

CHELSEA

Madison Square Park

Metropolitan Life Building

EAST 23RD STREET

WEST 23RD STREET

General Theological Seminary

Flatiron Building

National Arts Club

GRAMERCY

Gramercy Park

WEST 20TH STREET

EAST 20TH STREET

WEST 18TH STREET

Theodore Roosevelt Birthplace

Players Club

STUYVESANT TOWN

Stuyvesant Square

FLATIRON

800 m

800 yards

WEST 14TH STREET

EAST 14TH STREET

Hudson

WEST END AVENUE

AMSTERDAM AVE

BROADWAY

CENTRAL PARK WEST

COLUMBUS AVE

FIFTH AVENUE

MADISON AVE

PARK AVENUE

LEXINGTON AVE

THIRD AVE

SECOND AVE

FIRST AVE

YORK AVE

ROOSEVELT DRIVE

East River

QUEENS

FRANKLIN

HIGHWAY

MILLER

TWELFTH AVENUE

ELEVENTH AVENUE

TENTH AVENUE

NINTH AVENUE

EIGHTH AVENUE

SEVENTH AVENUE

AVENUE OF THE AMERICAS

151

Madison Square Park: The square holds several tributes to notable figures in US history

(Continued from page 149)

It was from the mid-1800s that the city's élite began to relocate from Greenwich Village into the new areas of Murray Hill and Gramercy. Particularly prominent citizens favored elegent brownstones overlooking **Gramercy Park**▶▶. Between 20th and 21st streets, the park was the center-piece of a town plan modeled on the great, aristocratic squares of London. Still the city's only private park, local residents are given a key in return for an annual fee towards its upkeep. Amid the park's luxuriant foliage, and visible through its iron railings, are several statues including that of actor Edwin Booth in the role of Hamlet.

It was Booth, one of the leading tragic actors of his time (and brother of John Wilkes Booth, assassin of Abraham Lincoln), who founded the influential **Players Club**▶ at 16 Gramercy Park South. Designed by noted architect Stanford White, the building is easily spotted by the ornamental theatrical masks decorating its entrance.

The co-designer of Central Park, Calvert Vaux, added the Ruskin-influenced Gothic features to the building next door, now the **National Arts Club** but earlier occupied by Samuel Tilden, governor of New York from 1874. Tilden's stand against corruption in New York public life did not alleviate his fears of public insurrection: He had a secret passageway set under the house to hasten his escape if angry mobs attacked the entrance, and rolling steel barriers set behind the windows.

Theatrical connections continue north into **Murray Hill**▶. When asked to provide a funeral for an actor in 1870, one Murray Hill church representative said "we don't accept actors but there's a little church around the corner that does." From then on, the 1849 Church of the Transfiguration, on 29th Street just off Fifth Avenue, became better known as the **Little Church Around the Corner**▶▶, serving New York thespians in spiritual need.

BASEBALL'S BIRTHPLACE
Baseball was introduced to the US in 1842, but not until 1845 did a group of enthusiasts – who had been playing the game regularly at what later became Madison Square Park – band together to create a fixed set of rules and the first baseball club, the Knickerbocker Club. As baseball spread in popularity across the country, it was known at first as the "New York Game".

A picturesque garden fronts the church, and the intimate interior holds several memorials to actors.

Stylish hotels and a smattering of elegant restaurants tucked into quiet residential streets characterize the bulk of Murray Hill, where a rare surviving brownstone is the grand home and library of financier J. Pierpont Morgan (see page 169).

To the west of Murray Hill at the foot of Madison Avenue, **Madison Square Park▶** is dotted with 19th-century statuary and overlooked by the unmistakeable 1909 clocktower of the Metropolitan Life Insurance Building. The park was the original site of Madison Square Garden, a venue for entertainment and sports events up until the 1920s. Its much larger namesake now looms between Seventh and Eighth avenues.

Near the park, the Flatiron Building (see page 106) gives its name to the surrounding Flatiron District. This area was dubbed "Silicon Alley" during the 1990s when it gained many of the city's internet and multi-media companies, along with some up and coming publishers and advertising companies. These, along with a batch of new restaurants and stores, have helped turn a once nondescript neighbourhood into one of Manhattan's most fashionable few blocks.

Cheek-by-jowl Midtown skyscrapers—with a view!

153

It was an Irishman, Thomas Dongan, who gave his name to the charter of 1686 that created New York's modern system of administration. As governor of a British colony, however, Dongan probably never expected that in years to come his countrymen would flock to New York to free themselves of British oppression and take a controlling grip on New York life.

THE UNWELCOME IRISH
Most of the large numbers of penniless Irish that arrived in the city during the 1800s were forced to occupy the worst areas, and some turned to petty crime in order to make a living. In so doing, they incurred the wrath of many long-established New Yorkers. Some turned against Irish immigrants as a whole. The auctioneer and one-time city mayor Philip Hone wrote of New York's Irish population: "They increase our taxes, eat our bread and encumber our streets, and not one in twenty is competent to keep himself."

Under British rule, Protestant and Catholic Irish were established in professional life in New York, but—mindful of British treatment of the Irish at home—both groups embraced the American Revolution and saw their chance to build a truly democratic, self-governing society.

Fall and rise The potato famines brought tens of thousands of Irish into New York during the 1800s. They arrived on the "Irish berths": cramped, airless sections of ships where disease was rife, and once ashore, the penniless Irish—faced with residents' growing anti-Catholic feeling—were forced to occupy crowded rooms, often in atrocious conditions.

By 1860, Irish Catholics made up a quarter of the city's population and were the backbone of the police force, fire-fighting teams and building trades. Irish organizational skills created powerful unions and paved the way for Irish domination of New York's entire administrative machine from the 1870s to the 1940s.

Church and tavern One symbol of the Irish Catholic ascendancy in New York was the building of St. Patrick's Cathedral in 1878. But while the church was important in Irish immigrant life, so too was the tavern. A first stop for new arrivals, taverns were informal clearing-houses for jobs. Some served free lunches to Irish workmen.

Irish-Americans are still strongly represented in New York public office. New York's last outpost of authentic Irish culture is Bainbridge, in the Bronx. First settled in the 1840s by Irishmen who saw its enticing greenery while working on the Harlem Railroad, Bainbridge's bars are the genuine article, without an ornamental leprechaun or bottle of green beer in sight.

St Patrick's Day (17 March) sees the city's biggest street parade, along Fifth Avenue

▶▶ Museum of Art and Design   *151C2*

53rd Street, between Fifth and Sixth avenues (tel: 956-3535;
www.americancraftmuseum.com)
Open: Tue, Wed and Fri–Sun 10–6, Thu 10–8.
Admission: inexpensive. Subway: E, F; Fifth Avenue
Pottery, textiles, furnishings, sculpture and more feature
at the Museum of Art and Design (MAD). Compiled from
loaned pieces and selections from the permanent holdings, exhibitions usually last several months. Due to
relocate to larger premises at 2 Columbus Circle.

▶ Museum of American Financial History   *104B2*

Broadway at Bowling Green (tel: 908-4519;
www.financialhistory.org) Open: Tue–Sat 10–4.
Admission: free. Subway: 4; Bowling Green
This one-room collection need not detain you long,
but it is an appropriate stop when touring the Financial

Woven hangings at the
Museum of American
Folk Art—a showcase for
the talents of craftspeople
from all over the Americas

155

District. Inside the former Standard Oil Building, once
presided over by multimillionaire John D. Rockefeller, the
changing exhibitions explore diverse historical avenues
in the US economy.

▶▶ Museum of American Folk Art   *151D1*

45 West 53rd Street (tel: 265-1040; www.folkartmuseum.org)
Open: Wed–Sun 10.30–5.30, Fri 10.30–7.30.
Admission: moderate. Subway: E, F; Fifth Avenue
From toys and weather vanes to carved walking sticks and
gravestone rubbings, the collections of the Museum of
American Folk Art are drawn from the output of artists
and craftspeople—many of them revered figures within
their own communities—from all over the Americas. Be it
Mexican wooden animal figures or Navajo blankets, the
work on display is frequently of an exceptionally high
standard and decorated with symbolic detail that only
becomes apparent with close inspection.
   In a city that often seems focused on honoring the art of
Europe, these exhibitions of indigenous American culture
are very welcome, and they are now housed in one of
New York's most striking contemporary buildings.

The Museum of the City of New York, whose dignified grand entrance on Fifth Avenue is the gateway to a mixed collection charting aspects of the Big Apple through the ages

THE NEW YORK ACADEMY OF MEDICINE

A short walk from the Museum of the City of New York is the New York Academy of Medicine (2 East 103rd Street; tel: 822-7300), which occupies a 1926 building raised with Byzantine, Italian and Romanesque features. Inside, the academy's library is open to the public. One reason to drop in might be to view the collection of 4,000 cookbooks (many of them rare), donated by a physician who believed that the key to good health was a nutritious diet. *Open Mon–Fri 9–5.*

SPECIAL EVENTS

The Museum of the City of New York organizes numerous special events, including puppet shows for children and classical concerts and lectures for adults. During the spring and fall, the museum also runs four-hour guided walking tours through different sections of the city. For details on any or all of these events, tel: 534-1672.

▶ Museum of the City of New York   *IBCA3*

Fifth Avenue at 103rd Street (tel: 534-1672)
Open: Tue, Wed and Fri–Sun 12–6, Thu 12–8.
Admission: moderate. Subway: 6; 96th Street

Chronicling the rise and rise of one of the world's most diverse and colorful cities is no easy task, and while the Museum of the City of New York has its share of interesting bits and pieces from the early years of the great metropolis, it struggles to bring them together with any cohesion. Many of the museum's exhibits seem lost in the spacious innards of this neo-Georgian building.

The devoted history buff will find plenty here to mull over, however. Chronologically, things begin on the third floor with staid dioramas of Native American life in the years leading up to European discovery. Far more intriguing are the earliest maps of the New York area and drawings and paintings from the mid-1600s, thought to be the earliest depictions of what was then the Dutch trading post of Nieuw Amsterdam.

Six undistinguished period interiors give a very general impression of the furnishings – from simple Dutch tables to ornate English colonial cabinets – that stood in New York drawing rooms from the 17th to the early 20th century. Close by, several cases hold a glittering array of New York-made silver tea caddies, tankards and cutlery that graced the kitchens of the city's most illustrious residents from the late 1700s.

A few figureheads and many model ships and boats are the principal pieces in a forgettable room intended to document the city's growth into a major seaport. Take care, though, to look at the paintings—such as Alonzo Chappel's simple but expressive *Bowery on a Rainy Day*, painted in 1849, and another that shows ice-skaters in Central Park during 1865—that hang on nearby walls and do more to evoke the New York of their period than many of the more valuable exhibits around them.

The museum enjoys its finest moment on the third floor, where a glorious collection of toys (some dating to the mid-1700s) includes a room filled by elaborate three- and four-story dolls' houses. The dolls, too, are as impressive as the houses and include a specimen of almost every type produced in the US from the late 18th to the mid-19th centuries. The oldest doll is a French-made import dating from 1724.

The Rockefeller Rooms on the museum's fifth floor comprise the master bedroom and dressing room from the mansion purchased in 1884 by John D. Rockefeller at West 54th Street—a site which is now consumed by the garden of the Museum of Modern Art. A wealth of intricately carved woodwork with mother-of-pearl inlays inspired by English designer Charles Eastlake, the rooms were the height of fashion in Victorian New York. What is not on view here is the mansion's wonderful Moorish room, which is now to be found in the Brooklyn Museum (see page 79).

Temporary exhibitions fill the first-floor rooms, while the museum's basement is occupied by poorly arranged memorabilia from New York's earliest fire-fighters. The centrepiece is a well-maintained hose-carriage of 1865, but smaller and more revealing pieces fill the surrounding display cases. Among the helmets, lamps, model fire-appliances and press clippings detailing New York's most famous fires and the men who put them out, look for the fire-fighters' ear trumpet—a device intended to improve communication in blazing buildings. When plugged at one end, it also served as a beer-drinking vessel and a handy weapon for when the "fire laddies" (as they were known) gathered for an evening in a tavern.

EL MUSEO DEL BARRIO
A few strides across 104th Street from the Museum of the City of New York, El Museo del Barrio (tel: 831-7272, www.elmuseo.org; *Open* Wed–Sun 11–5, Thu until 8. *Admission: inexpensive*) is very much a product of its East Harlem environment, evolving from a local school classroom into a museum devoted to the cultures of Latin America, particularly that of Puerto Rico. The small permanent collection of pre-Columbian objects is regularly eclipsed by temporary exhibitions that span paintings, sculpture, video and more, reflecting diverse aspects of Latin American life, past and present.

157

Times change: one of the museum's dioramas shows what New York's East River waterfront looked like in the 1850s

Queuing for a special MoMA exhibition

THE MOMA BUILDING
In 1939, MoMA acquired not only its current home but also what would, on completion, be one of the first international-style buildings in the US. Architects Philip Goodwin and Edward Durrell Stone interrupted the row of brownstones on West 53rd Street's with a facade of marble, tile and glass. The very term "international style" had been coined at a MoMA exhibition in 1932 by Philip Johnson, who was later to oversee several additions to the building, most notably the Sculpture Garden.

Van Gogh's Starry Night

▶▶▶ Museum of Modern Art   151C2
53rd Street, between Fifth and Sixth avenues (tel: 708-9400, www.mona.org) Open: Sat–Mon and Thu 10–5, Fri 10–7.45 Admission: moderate. Subway: E, F; Fifth Avenue

Nowhere else in the world will you find a museum so well stocked, so aptly designed to illustrate art's principal movements and trends, or showing so many of the major works of the last 160 years of artistic achievement.

Be it Picasso, Mondrian, Matisse or any number of others whose names are writ large in the history of art, the Museum of Modern Art (MoMA) not only has them but often has some of their most influential works too, including Van Gogh's *Starry Night*, Picasso's *Les Demoiselles d'Avignon* and Pollock's immense and mesmerizing *One*.

Since World War II, MoMA has played a pivotal role in defining the way art is assessed, understood and displayed. As New York eclipsed Paris as the center of the art world, MoMA was uniquely placed to play a leading role. As European artists arrived in New York (destined to have a great impact on the new generation of American artists who helped make the city the dynamic heart of contemporary creative art from the 1940s to the 1960s) so too did their art, not least Picasso's *Guernica* held by the museum on extended loan throughout the Franco dictatorship before it returned to Spain in 1981.

In the late-1990s, however, MoMA began to dramatically change its thinking and, in a major departure from its long-held adherence to a linear, chronological approach to arranging its collections (so large that only around 12 percent could find space in the museum's airy and well-lit galleries), began undertaking a daring new approach.

The new millennium was marked by the museum with a series of temporary shows collectively titled MoMA 2000. In this, the accent was on thematic exhibitions which mixed artists from different times and cultures and work spanning painting, photography, design, video and multi-media, and room-sized installations. The series was to divide both the critics and the public alike, but seemed to show the museum's future direction, emboldened by a major expansion and renovation project completed in 2004.

As defensive as the museum was of its new approach, by the time of the unveiling of the new look museum future prospects seemed to be a return, if only partially, to a chronological arrangement, not least because the bulk of MoMA's many visitors expect nothing else.

However, the museum's apparently radical approach might be seen as entirely in keeping with the ground-breaking early days of the museum, founded in 1929 to "help people enjoy, understand and use the visual arts of our time."

Hard to believe it may be but when MoMA staged its first exhibition, the artists featured—Cézanne, Gauguin, Seurat and Van Gogh—were not represented in any other New York museum. Even the otherwise all-emcompassing Metropolitan Museum of Art considered such

THE SCULPTURE GARDEN

Directly opposite the lobby, and a great place to pass an hour on a sunny afternoon after viewing the interior exhibits, is MoMA's Abby Aldrich Rockefeller Sculpture Garden, filled with an excellent and diverse collection of sculpture. Highlights include Henry Moore's *Family Group*, Picasso's *She Goat*—and Rodin's striking *Memorial to Balzac*, a towering bronze that was rejected by its Parisian commissioning committee in the 1890s.

159

names to be too avant-garde. Nonetheless, 47,000 people visited the MoMA exhibition in a single month.

A decade later, MoMA acquired its present site (a gift of the Rockefeller family, one of whom was among the museum's founders) and through the energy of its young director, Alfred H. Barr Jr, and the benevolence of a host of millionaire benefactors, steadily became the world's primary repository for many of modern art's most important works, gaining a prestige that few rivals can match.

Acquiring the site of the Dorset Hotel and two townhouses adjacent to the present museum in 1995, MoMA began its building expansion project. Architect Yoshio Taniguchi promised "to transform the Museum of Modern Art into a bold new museum while maintaining its historical, cultural and social context." Among other benefits, the new-look museum has doubled its existing gallery space. While building was in progress, exhibitions continued at MoMA's 53rd Street base until 2002, at which point they were moved to a temporary home in Queens (known as MoMA QNS; map reference 48D3), where they stayed until the new museum opened.

Inside MoMA's 53rd Street building – New York's earliest piece of architecture in the international style and a fitting home for some of the most famous paintings and sculptures of the 20th century. Clever design, using plenty of natural light and with space to stand back and relax, allows unhurried appreciation of the exhibits

The highlights of MoMA's collection provide a changing but unfailingly impressive gathering of seminal items that provide a thumbnail sketch of modern art's major twists and turns.

WHAT'S ON AT MOMA
Changing shows can be great news for art-loving New Yorkers but less so for visitors who may have traveled to New York only to find that their favorite artworks are in storage or away on loan. To find out what exhibitions will be on during your stay, visit visit the museum's web site, www.moma.org, or tel: 708-9480.

Europeans Key European works include Van Gogh's much eulogised *Starry Night*, the intense swirls of color indicative of his painting at Arles in the late 1880s; one of Monet's *Water Lilies* paintings, a study of the subtleties of light and shadow on water where the colors appear to undulate before your eyes; and an example of Matisse's *The Dance*, one of the series of large murals created by the French artist in the early 1930s. Picasso's *Three Women at the Spring* and Braque's *Man With A Guitar* and *Woman with a Mandolin* are formative Cubist statements, while Mondrian's *Broadway Boogie-Woogie* reveals the impact of New York, its jazz rhythms and grid-style streets, on the Dutch artist. Among MoMA's surrealist holdings are Magritte's *The False Mirror* and Dali's *The Persistence of Memory*, painted in 1931—a landmark in itself as it denoted the first appearance of the soft watches that became Dali's most original and celebrated images.

The Americans The first American modern art movement, abstract expressionism (see pages 128–129) and the so-called New York School is well represented with works by Pollock, particularly *One*, the mightiest of his drip canvases; Rothko's shimmering blocks of color; and pieces by the Dutch-born De Kooning. As a prime example of gesturism, look for Motherwell's *Elegy to the Spanish Republic*. Partly as a reaction to abstract expressionism came noted works such as Johns' *Flag* and *Target* series, Rausechenburg's bold collages depicting an excessively consumerist sociey, and the comic-strip blow-ups of Lichtenstein.

Allow yourself time whilst you are in the museum to appreciate the works

▶▶ Museum of Television and Radio 151C2

25 West 52nd Street (tel: 621-6800 for daily events, 621-6600 for general information; www.mtr.org)
Open: Tue–Sun 12–6 (Thu until 8), theaters open later.
Admission: inexpensive. Subway: E, F; Fifth Avenue

For serious media students and couch-potatoes alike, the Museum of Television and Radio is the stuff that dreams are made of. For almost anyone else, a visit will be a highly entertaining experience—and a perfect antidote to the more run-of-the-mill forms of sightseeing. More than 40,000 American television and radio broadcasts from the 1920s to the present are stored here, all of them available to the public at little more than a flick of a switch. Several thousand new programmes are added every year.

A number of small screening rooms show selections from the museum's televisual archive (schedules are available from the lobby, or tel: 621-6800), while the headphones in the cozy radio listening room can be switched to one of five separate channels, each exploring a different area of broadcasting history—from a landmark Metropolitan Opera broadcast to a wartime comedy

A TV addict's dream come true—the Museum of Television and Radio offers your own choice of viewing at one of around 100 individual video consoles

show. If you have a special interest you can riffle through the library's computerized cataloguing system and make your own selections from the entire collection. Not only listing television programme titles, the database also carries details of the personnel involved in each production—a handy resource if you have forgotten who played Thing in *The Addams Family* or want to discover the real-life identity of your favorite *Batman* villain.

Once you have made your choice (restricted to two hours of viewing time), leave the library for the viewing room, where your selection will be made ready for you almost immediately (though there may be a three-day wait for particularly obscure items) for private watching at one of the video consoles.

Commercials—of which the museum has 10,000 in stock —feature among the daily screenings. Also on view are television shows from other countries, from heavyweight documentaries to vintage episodes of *Monty Python's Flying Circus*.

THE MUSEUM BUILDING
You may be too eager to renew your acquaintance-ship with Perry Mason or Lou Grant to notice, but the building that houses the Museum of Television and Radio is a curious blend of classical and modern styles by architects Philip Johnson and John Burgee. With its 16-story limestone-clad tower, the structure has been described as the world's first vertical museum.

The advent of art deco coincided with the skyscraper boom that gripped New York during the 1920s, and the new decorative style was seen as the natural accompaniment to the world's most adventurous architecture. Walk around the city and you will find the art deco influence everywhere, from world-famous buildings to fine details of decoration.

ZONING LAWS

In 1915, when the Financial District's Equitable Building rose straight up in the air, robbing adjacent streets and buildings of their sunlight and breezes, the city authorities responded with the US's first set of building regulations—or zoning laws. The Zoning Law of 1916 divided New York into commercial and residential plots; high-rise buildings had to recede as they rose above the street. This greatly affected the architecture of the city for the next 50 years.

Art deco sculpture in Rockefeller Center

Art deco first emerged in 1925 at the Paris Exposition Internationale des Arts Décoratifs, a show intended to highlight the fine skills of French craftsmen at a time when the German Bauhaus was revolutionizing the world of the decorative arts.

New York was already aware of the art deco style, however, as the Metropolitan Museum of Art had amassed a collection of the finest European work and inadvertently aided the creation of an American art deco style dubbed "moderne." With the emphasis on overall effect rather than individual craftsmanship, art moderne was tailor-made to the needs of the American market. Mass-produced terra-cotta and bronze friezes covered with geometric designs and floral patterns, available by mail order, soon began appearing on buildings all over the country.

This new style began to affect interiors, too. Some of New York's finest art deco entranceways and lobbies, such as the Film Center Building (see page 102), are the work of the talented architect Ely Jacques Kahn.

One of the city's earliest art deco buildings was the **New York Telephone Company** (also called the

Barclay-Vesey Building, 140 West Street), described by one critic as "Mayan art deco." To get around the constraints imposed by the narrow street, designer Ralph Walker gave the building a series of pedestrian arcades decorated by a cast-concrete frieze cluttered with depictions of bunches of grapes, rabbits, elephant heads, bells and much more.

Chrysler Building The single most spectacular and lastingly impressive art deco building in New York, the Chrysler Building (see page 89) was one of the first buildings to use exposed metal. It rises in a series of cutbacks with each new level marked by a different type of decoration—a brickwork frieze of car wheels and immense winged radiator caps. Its most distinctive feature, however, is the seven-story dome, which takes the form of a tiered arch with triangular dormer windows encased in chrome steel.

Empire State Building The Chrysler Building's status as the world's tallest building was soon eclipsed by the Empire State Building. Built purely for commercial renting, every inch of the Empire State Building was critical, and consequently the decoration was kept to an absolute minimum – allowing the structure to emerge as a fine specimen of skyscraper art deco at its most restrained and dignified.

Chanin Building Sculptor René Chambellan's facade for the Chanin Building (122 East 42nd Street), which draws the eye away from the nearby Chrysler Building, depicts swooping birds on a bronze band that winds around the building below a terra-cotta frieze of geometric animal forms. Inside the bronze- and marble-dominated lobby, further bas-reliefs depict the "City of Opportunity" – or New York as it was for the building's owner, Irwin Chanin, a property developer who struck it lucky.

Raymond Hood Destined to become one of the leading architects of Rockefeller Center, Hood used black brick and gold terra-cotta to emphasize the upright form of the **American Radiator Building** (40th Street between Fifth and Sixth avenues). He later developed this idea with vertical columns of windows and spandrels for the **Daily News Building** (see page 95).
   In the former **McGraw-Hill Building** (42nd Street, between Eighth and Ninth avenues), with its green and gold terra-cotta, Hood continued his move towards the International Style, but the building's lobby retains its impressive art deco interior.
   With **Rockefeller Center** (pages 173–174), New York art deco had its greatest day. Raymond Hood had a large hand in the centre's showpiece RCA (now GE) Building. At the foot of the building, Paul Manship's golden *Prometheus* sculpture is the first of scores of art deco items decorating the entire complex. Meanwhile, Rockefeller Center's **Radio City Music Hall** takes art deco into another dimension. Its vast and extraordinarily theatrical interior is intended to be just as much a part of the evening's entertainment as the performers appearing on the stage.

The Chrysler Building, resplendent with eagle gargoyles

164

▶ National Academy of Design 187C1

*Fifth Avenue at 89th Street (tel: 369-4880; www.
nationalacademy.org) Open: Wed and Thu 12–5, Fri, Sat and
Sun 11–6. Admission: inexpensive. Subway: 4, 6; 86th Street*
Founded in 1825 by a group of accomplished artists,
architects, sculptors and engravers—including Samuel
Morse, the artist/inventor, and the creator of Washington
Square's handsome town houses, Ithiel Town—the
National Academy of Design was established with the
intention of becoming an artist-run school and museum.
Selections from the permanent collections are shown in
the upstairs galleries, but one piece you can be certain of
seeing is the sculptured figure of Diana by Anna Hyatt
Huntington, which pivots at the foot of an elegant staircase leading up to the Academy's galleries.

▶▶ National Museum of the American Indian 104A2

*US Custom House, Bowling Green (tel: 514-3700;
www.nmai.si.edu) Open: daily 10–5. Admission: free.
Subway: 4; Bowling Green*
Exhibits inside the architecturally distinguished US
Custom House (see page 190) are drawn from the many
diverse native cultures of North, South and Central
America. The presentations explain something of the
beliefs and lifestyles of the peoples. While many important items have been returned to the tribes that previously
owned them, the museum retains a hugh quantity of bas-
kets, quilts, pottery and more, including some of the
infamous treaties that paved the way for European colonization of traditionally Native American lands.

*A focal point at the
National Academy of
Design: Anna Hyatt
Huntington's statue
of Diana*

▶ New York City Fire Museum　　　　　IFCB2

278 Spring Street, SoHo (tel: 691-1303;
www.nycfiremuseum.org) Open: Tue–Sat 10–5, Sun 10–4.
Admission: inexpensive donation. Subway: 6; Spring Street

It may not be at the top of every New York visitor's
itinerary, but the New York City Fire Museum fills
three floors with the buckets, hand-pumps, and horse-
drawn fire-appliances that saved the city from near-total
destruction on more than one occasion. The antiquated carriages are exhibited alongside an impressive collection of
hose-pipe nozzles, ladders, axes, tools, fire alarms, extin-
guishers, uniforms and helmets.

▶ New York City Police Museum　　　　104A2

100 Old Slip (tel: 480-3100; www.nycpolicemuseum.org)
Open: Tue–Sat 10–5. Admission: inexpensive donation.
Subway: 4, 5; Bowling Green, 1, 2; Wall Street, N, R;
Whilehall, South Ferry

Gathered in the grand setting of the 1925 Cunard Building,
where passengers of great ocean liners once bought their
tickets, are guns, knives, truncheons and mugshots of public enemies that prove that policing the city's streets has
rarely been an entirely peaceful affair. Among many gruesome artifacts is the machine gun used by Al Capone's
gang to eliminate a rival.

▶▶ New-York Historical Society　　　　IFCF2

Central Park West at 77th Street (tel: 873-3400; www.
nyhistory.org) Open: Wed–Sun 10–6. Admission: inexpensive.
Subway: 1; 79th Street

Predating all the city's other museums, the New-York
Historical Society was founded in 1804 (dating its hyphen)
and was uniquely placed to receive the bequests of
wealthy New Yorkers. The society has a substantial
collection of works, from early portraits of significant New
Yorkers to important canvases from the country's first
home-grown art movement, the Hudson River School. The
society also holds a sizeable Tiffany collection and all
extant watercolors in Audubon's *Birds of America* series.

**THE GREAT FIRE
OF 1835**
The temperature in New
York City on 16 and 17
December 1835, was well
below freezing, but that
did not stop one of the
most destructive fires in
the city's history from
razing 674 buildings on a
13-acre (5.25-ha) site in
and around the Financial
District. Crowds arriving
from the notorious Five
Points slums looted the
burned-out buildings and
helped the flames engulf
many more. With
insurance companies
enduring the same losses
as many of their clients,
many of the city's banks
and financial institutions
were unable to reopen
and as a result New York
endured galloping inflation
for the next two years.

*Top: Early equipment at
the Fire Museum*

In the 1930s, passengers boarding the New York–Chicago early evening service from Grand Central Terminal were, quite literally, given the red carpet treatment. Few then would have thought that just a few decades later the terminal—an architectural tour de force that was dubbed "the gateway to the nation"—would be threatened by cheap air travel and by the rising value of the land on which it stands.

GRAND CENTRAL STATION?

Many people, including lifelong New Yorkers, often erroneously refer to Grand Central Terminal as "Grand Central Station." In fact, as trains can only begin or end their journeys there, "terminal" is the correct word to use. The confusion was not helped by an enormously popular radio drama series which began in 1937, set in New York and titled *Grand Central Station*, or by the fact that the local post office is, quite correctly, known as Grand Central Station.

Grand Central Terminal was completed in 1913 on a plot of land that then marked New York's northern edge. The land had been purchased by transport magnate Cornelius Vanderbilt (see page 37), who had gained control of all rail routes into New York. After a 10-year period of construction, the station was unveiled to wide public acclaim both as an engineering marvel and as a delight to the eye. It remains one of the world's great train stations: an enduring symbol of the city.

In the 1960s, the Penn Central Railroad (the company in charge of Grand Central Terminal and previously responsible for the demolition of the original and much-loved Pennsylvania Station) proposed to raise a 55-story office tower above the terminal, but these shortsighted plans were luckily thwarted by public pressure, and the building eventually became an official New York City landmark (in 1978), gaining lasting protection.

Architectural elegance The terminal's construction was a joint effort. The engineer William Wilgus and the architects Reed & Stem devised the innovative split-level design that allowed for a smooth flow of traffic—either train, subway or pedestrian—into and through the station; Whitney Warren focused on creating the terminal's graceful Beaux-Arts style. Since it was the arrival and departure point for millions of travelers (by 1939, as many people were passing through Grand Central Terminal each year as lived in the entire US), stores, hotels, restaurants and offices opened up in close proximity to the terminal, making the site a prime Midtown Manhattan plot. Many side entrances and maze-like tunnels link the terminal with its surrounding streets and adjacent office towers such as the former Pan Am Building, now the Metropolitan Life Building (see panel on page 183), just to the north.

On the terminal's southern facade you will first see Jules-Félix Coutan's 48-ft (15-m) high figures of Mercury, Hercules and Minerva, draping themselves around an American eagle. There is also a bronze likeness of Cornelius Vanderbilt—seemingly counting potential train passengers as they pass.

The interior Once inside, head for the terminal's second story and look upward. On the 150-ft (46-m) high vaulted

ceiling, French artist Paul Helleu used 2,500 electric lights to replicate the zodiacal constellations. The design is based on a medieval manuscript illustration, and the debate continues as to whether or not Helleu was aware that medieval illustrators commonly depicted the heavens reversed—giving God's view.

Look toward the northwest corner to spot the dark rectangle that provides an intentional reminder of the grime that had darkened the ceiling over 50 years and was removed (using a specially prepared organic soap) during the late 1990s. Another ceiling oddity is the segment that was cut out to accommodate the tip of a nuclear missile, part of a military display staged here in the 1960s.

The grandeur of the **Main Concourse** is often obliterated by the half a million commuters each day. Nonetheless, try to find a slow moment to descend the marble flight of steps onto its floor and contemplate its 75-ft (23-m) windows, its claim to be the world's largest room (it is 375ft/114m long and 120ft/37m wide), and the once serious suggestion to develop the concourse into three separate bowling alleys.

A pearl of a restaurant The terminal's balconies and lower level now hold a number of stores and restaurants, and a branch of the **New York Transit Museum** (tel: 878-0106; *Open:* Mon–Fri 8–8, Sat 10–6. *Admission: free*; see page 76). The restaurants include that of basketball superstar Michael Jordan and the **Oyster Bar**. The latter is known not only for its diverse selection of oysters and other seafood, but also for its low ceiling, covered by tan Guastavino tiles. In a vaulted area just outside the restaurant, a whisper into one corner can be distinctly heard in the other corner. However, the restaurant proper has no such magical acoustics—it's one of the noisiest eating spots in the city. Still, there are few better places in Manhattan for listening in on the lunchtime gossip of New York executives, although the suggestions that fortunes have been made on the Stock Exchange by inspired eavesdropping are apocryphal at best.

The huge scale and grand style of the Main Concourse (said to be the largest room in the world) affirm Grand Central Terminal as a monument to the halcyon days of train travel

GUIDED TOURS
For a more detailed exploration of Grand Central Terminal, join the free guided tour run by the Municipal Art Society (tel: 935-3960), which begins at 12.30pm each Wednesday from the Information desk on the Main Concourse.

The imposing New York Public Library on Fifth Avenue

THE LIBRARY'S TREASURES

The New York Public Library has an extraordinary stock of rare and valuable books and prints, some of which may be on display. These include a Gutenberg bible; a 1493 folio edition of a Christopher Columbus letter describing his American discoveries; the first full folio edition of Shakespeare, from 1623; the 1640 Bay Psalm Book (the first English book published in America); a handwritten copy of George Washington's farewell address; and an early draft of Jefferson's Declaration of Independence.

▶▶▶ New York Public Library   151B2

Fifth Avenue and 42nd Street (tel: 340-0830; www.nypl.org)
Open: Tue and Wed 11–7.30, Thu–Sat 10–6
Hours for special exhibitions vary. Guided tours: Wed 2.30
Subway: B, D, F; 42nd Street

You cannot actually borrow a book here, the Central Branch of the New York Public Library (the 3 million or so tomes are for reference only), but you can explore one of the city's finest expressions of architecture, a Beaux-Arts temple created by the legendary firm of Carrère & Hastings and opened in 1911. Its terrace and elegant steps are decorated by a pair of sculptured lions, fountains fronting statues symbolizing Truth and Beauty and bronze flagpole bases cast at Long Island. The triple-arched portico entrance leads into the exquisitely proportioned Astor Hall—named after John Jacob Astor, founder of the nation's first library (one of the three that combined to create the present library's original holdings)—and an information desk dispensing floor plans and marking the starting point for the tours.

Immediately ahead, Gottesman Hall stages some of the library's temporary exhibitions. Turn left for the De Witt Wallace Periodical Room at the end of the corridor. Publisher De Witt Wallace spent many hours in this room scanning periodicals and abridging their contents for his fledgling venture, the *Reader's Digest*. His profits financed the room's 1983 restoration: Its brass lamps and walnut chairs were joined by Richard Haas' murals of the offices of *New York* magazine and newspaper. Climb the marble stairs to the fourth floor, noting the original lamps and the drinking fountains on the way to the vaulted McGraw Rotunda, decorated in 1940 by Edward Laning's murals. This marks the entrance to the public catalog room, complete with computer databases. Beyond the catalog room lie the main reading rooms—the most beautiful part of the library. Across the corridor is the Edna Barnes Salomon Room, which displays the library's paintings and selections from its printed treasures.

▶▶▶ Pierpont Morgan Library 151B2

36th Street at Madison Avenue (tel: 685-0610; www. morganlibrary.org) Open: Tue–Thu 10.30–5, Fri 10.30–8, Sat 10.30–6, Sun 12–6; due to re-open 2006 following renovations. Admission: moderate. Subway: 6; 33rd Street

Born into wealth and educated in Europe, J. Pierpont Morgan had become one of New York's leading financiers by the closing decades of the 19th century. But, unlike his nouveau riche contemporaries, he trusted his own taste and judgment as he lavished a fortune on European cultural treasures, acquiring rare books, manuscripts and drawings that by 1890 had become one of the finest private collections in the country.

In 1902, Morgan commissioned the leading architect of the day, Charles F. McKim, to create the Renaissance-style Pierpont Morgan Library. The Palladian porch that marks the library's original entrance on 36th Street merits a special look, though the present entrance is on the Madison Avenue side and enters a 1928 annex on the site of Morgan's son's brownstone residence.

The temporary exhibitions could hold your attention for hours, but look first around the library itself, starting at the West Room, where Morgan's study is preserved as it was on the financier's death in 1913. Once described as "the most beautiful room in America," the study is lined with Italian Renaissance paintings and dominated by Morgan's immense wooden desk.

From the study, free-standing columns of green-veined marble mark the way to the imposing rotunda and the East Room. The East Room is one of the plushest reading rooms you are ever likely to see. Three tiers of bookcases, fashioned from bronze and inlaid walnut, rise to a ceiling covered by colorful murals of artists and scholars (and signs of the zodiac), while above the fireplace hangs a 16th-century Flemish tapestry. Sumptuous though it is, the East Room is never overbearing, and you could spend a long time here, poring over priceless letters and manuscripts.

THE PIERPONT MORGAN COLLECTIONS

The following are just a few items from the vast collections of the Pierpont Morgan Library: three Gutenberg bibles; a Shakespeare first folio; an autographed manuscript of Milton's *Paradise Lost;* manuscripts and early editions of Rudyard Kipling, Oscar Wilde and Gertrude Stein bearing the authors' doodles and changes; musical scores from the hands of Bach, Brahms and Beethoven; etchings and prints by Rembrandt, Rubens and Degas; and a huge selection of pre-19th century paintings and objets d'art.

Space for the studious: the reading room of New York Public Library. Choose your tome from the library's many miles of shelving and consult it here

STREET NUMBERING IN QUEENS

Anyone who has spent several days mastering the Manhattan street-numbering system will find the streets of Queens even more of a challenge. Part of the price for Queens affiliating itself to New York City in 1898 was the loss of its named streets for a numbering system imposed by the civic powers in Manhattan.

The system, it seems, is still having teething troubles. Usually streets and avenues run at right angles to each other, and an address such as 10–35 14th Street will be located on 14th Street near the intersection with 10th Avenue. This is not always the case, however, and most problems occur when neighborhoods run into each other at something other than a perfect right angle. If you get lost, the solution might be to ask a local. But then again it might not: Queens residents are often as baffled by the system as everyone else.

The interior of Bowne House, the oldest building in Queens

▶ Queens   48C3

Filling 119sq miles (308sq km) on the western end of Long Island, Queens is easily the biggest of the City's five boroughs. Sheer size renders its layout almost incomprehensible unless thought of in the way most of its residents do: as a patchwork of separate and self-contained communities, often with little in common with each other.

While most of Queens fits the house-with-two-car-garage stereotype of American suburbia, parts date back to colonial times and its population is a rich and diverse mixture echoing New York's immigration patterns. Large, yet comparatively recently arrived, communities of Chinese, Koreans, Indians and Japanese exist alongside areas long dominated by residents of Greek, Italian or Puerto Rican descent.

Even though you probably failed to realize it at the time, if your arrival point in New York was **La Guardia** or **JFK** airport, you have already had a brief taste of Queens. Both airports are sited in the borough. Planes into JFK swoop above the 20sq miles (52sq km) of marshlands comprising the **Jamaica Bay Wildlife Refuge** (tel: 718/338-3799), a place much more interesting to migrating birdlife than to all but the most ornithologically obsessed humans.

You will need a car and a very detailed map to explore all of Queens but the main points of interest—which will also give a broad flavor of the borough's ethnic mix—are slotted into a handful of key areas, easily reached by public transportation from Manhattan. Take the subway out of Manhattan to **Flushing**, for example, and you will see why the route is dubbed the "Orient Express." What Flushing's Japanese supermarkets, Korean restaurants and Chinese dim sum houses do not suggest, however, are the town's 17th-century links with Quakers.

At 137–16 Main Street, a Friends' Meeting House has stood since 1694 and, on a nearby corner, the 1661 **Bowne House▶▶** (tel: 718/359-0528, www.historichousetrust. org; *Open:* Tue, Sat and Sun 2.30–4.30. *Admission: inexpensive*), one of the city's oldest houses, has further connections with The Friends. The house's owner, John Bowne, was exiled for defying a ban on Quaker meetings. However, he persuaded the Dutch West India Company—who did not want to risk losing any would-be settlers—to insist that all religious groups would be tolerated in the new colony: A step toward the religious freedoms later enshrined in the Constitution.

The house holds some of Bowne's colonial furnishings, plus those of his descendants, who lived here until the 1940s. Tours of the small modest dwelling wend their way into the kitchen, where the clandestine Quaker meetings took place. A short walk from the Bowne House, the 1774 **Kingsland Homestead** (tel: 718/206-0545, www.preserve.org/queens/kingsland.htm; *Open:* Tue, Sat and Sun 2.30–4.30. *Admission: inexpensive*) is an example of the Dutch and English architectural mix that is typical of Long Island farmhouses of the period.

About a mile (2km) east of Flushing, **Flushing Meadows-Corona Park▶▶** (tel: 718/760-6565, www.nycparks.org) began life as a swamp and rubbish dump, but by 1939 it was drawing millions to the World's Fair that symbolized New York's emergence from the Depression. A few relics from the 1939–1940 fair remain, as do many from a second

The Unisphere in Flushing Meadows-Corona Park—a relic of the 1964–1965 World's Fair

THE UNITED NATIONS IN QUEENS
The City Building, which houses the Queens Museum in Flushing Meadows-Corona Park, was used by the United Nations as the organization awaited the completion of its site in Manhattan. Among the motions carried here was the one in 1947 that paved the way for the creation of the state of Israel.

171

World's Fair held in 1964–1965. Among these are Philip Johnson's **New York State Pavilion Building**—the architectural highlight of the 1960s show, but these days in a crumbled state—and the 140-ft (43-m) high **Unisphere**, intended to represent the Earth and its satellites.

Another 1960s survivor, the **New York Hall of Science▶** (tel: 718/699-0005, www.nyhallsci.org; *Open:* Jul and Aug, Mon 9.30–2, Tue–Fri 9.30–5; rest of the year Tue–Thu 9.30–2, Fri 9.30–5, Sat and Sun 10.30–6. *Admission: moderate*), is these days crammed with hands-on computer exhibits illustrating the rudiments of science to children.

More modest-sized memorabilia from both world fairs are displayed inside the **Queens Museum of Art▶** (tel: 718/592-9700, www.queensmuseum.org; *Open:* Wed–Fri 10–5, Sat and Sun 12–5. *Admission: inexpensive*) housed in a structure dating from the 1939–1940 fair. Most fascinating is the Panorama: a scale model of New York City covering 17,976sq ft (1,670sq m).

The park is also home to **Queens Zoo** (tel: 718/271-1500, www.wcs.org; *Open:* Apr–Oct, Mon–Fri 10–5, Sat and Sun 10–5.30, rest of year daily 10–4.30. *Admission: inexpensive*), as well as the **National Tennis Center**—which holds the annual US Open.

A busy street in Queens

Roosevelt Avenue, in the Jackson Heights neighborhood, known for its bakeries and restaurants

MUSEUM OF AFRICAN ART

Arts and crafts from sub-Saharan Africa form the core of the temporary exhibitions staged in this highly respected museum (3rd floor, 36-01 43rd Avenue, Long Island City; tel: 718/783-7700, www.africanart.org; *Open* Mon, Thu and Fri 10–5, Sat and Sun 11–6. *Admission: inexpensive).*

STEINWAY

Just east of Astoria is the town of Steinway, created by William Steinway in 1872 when he moved his piano factory here from Manhattan—partly to escape the power of unions. The factory still stands at 19th Avenue and 39th Street. Steinway himself, meanwhile, moved into a stonework Italianate villa overlooking the East River at 18–33 East 41st Street. The slightly spooky villa has certainly seen better days, as has the now entirely insalubrious neighborhood that surrounds it.

Baseball fans might note that **Shea Stadium**, home of the New York Mets, stands in the northerly section of the park. In 1965 it was the venue of a now legendary concert by the Beatles.

On the borough's northern side, facing the Bronx across the East River, **Astoria▶** is one of the world's largest Greek communities. Lining 31st Street and Ditmars Boulevard are countless Greek bakeries, cafés and restaurants, and even the graffiti on the walls is in Greek.

Not remotely Greek, though, is Astoria's **American Museum of the Moving Image▶** (36–11 35th Avenue; tel: 718/784-0077, www.ammi.org; *Open:* Wed and Thu 12–5, Fri 12–8, Sat and Sun 11–6.30. *Admission: moderate*), which occupies part of a working studio complex. During the 1920s, Paramount shot silent movies here with legendary figures such as Rudolph Valentino, Gloria Swanson and the Marx Brothers, before they relocated to Hollywood.

The museum shows cinematic classics and carries temporary exhibitions on various aspects of movie history. On permanent display is a large but only mildly interesting collection of film-making equipment, fan magazines, props, costumes, and vintage movie posters.

Heading back toward Manhattan is heavily industrialized **Long Island City**, which is forging a reputation as an artists' enclave. In its early days, the area of Long Island City known as Hunters Point was linked by ferry to Manhattan, encouraging business development here. Some of the old warehouses and factories have been turned into artists' studios.

In Long Island City is the riverfront **Isamu Noguchi Garden Museum▶▶** (32–37 Vernon Boulevard; tel: 718/204-7088, www.noguchi.org; *Open:* call for hours. *Admission: inexpensive donation)* devoted to the acclaimed sculptor. The son of a Japanese poet who emigrated to California, Noguchi's unconventional ideas were at first derided, but his extraordinary imagination and creativity is clear enough throughout the 12 galleries that chart his long career (Noguchi died in 1988, aged 84), and in the gardens that hold still more of his enigmatic creations.

▶▶ Rockefeller Center 151C2

47th–52nd streets, between Fifth and Sixth avenues
(www.rockefellercenter.com)
Subway: B, D, F, 1; 47th Street—Rockefeller Center

This is the world's largest commercial and entertainment complex, through which a quarter of a million people pass each day. The project changed the face of American urban planning from the 1940s on.

The center is named after the multimillionaire John D. Rockefeller, Jr., who was approached in 1928 by the Metropolitan Opera with a view to his developing a down-at-heel Midtown site, on land rented from Columbia University, as a new Opera House. Rockefeller agreed, but the Wall Street crash led to the shelving of the plans and left him with 11 acres (4.5ha) of land and a very large debt. In the country's first major pooled architectural project, Rockefeller commissioned several firms to erect 14 buildings on the site with the proviso that the structures form an aesthetically unified entity and that the complex should be a pleasing environment for working, eating, shopping and relaxing.

As a result, the art deco buildings themselves take a secondary role to the numerous cafés, restaurants, underground walkways and shopping plazas secreted in and around them, allowing a flow of light and easy movement of people. This became the blueprint for downtown urban renewal initiatives throughout the country. To reach the heart of the complex, enter from Fifth Avenue along the short Channel Gardens to the sunken **Plaza▶**, which holds an open-air restaurant and a winter-time ice rink and is presided over by Paul Manship's 1934 figure of *Prometheus*. Rising above Prometheus' head, the 70-story **GE Building** (better known by its original title, the RCA

ROCKEFELLER CENTER FACTS

Number employed in construction 1931–1940: 75,000.
Number of telephones: 100,000.
Number of elevators: 488.
Cost of buying Columbia University's leasehold in 1985: $400 million.

GERTRUDE STEIN ON THE RCA BUILDING, 1935

"The most beautiful thing I have seen."

Summertime brings bright umbrellas and a festive atmosphere to the sunken plaza amid the office buildings of Rockefeller Center

Building) is the heart of Rockefeller Center. Enter the lobby and note the murals by José Maria Sert—replacements for those of Diego Rivera, who refused to appease the anticommunist Rockefellers by removing a handsome likeness of Lenin.

The elevator's top stop is the **Rainbow Room** restaurant complex, where the reward for buying a meal is an opulent setting around a revolving dancefloor and fantastic views over Manhattan. Return to the lobby to collect a free map from the information desk, essential as you weave deeper into Rockefeller Center's impressive labyrinth.

Simple wanderings will reveal much of interest, but do not miss the **Radio City Music Hall**. The hall's 1932 gala opening was attended by the likes of Charlie Chaplin and Clark Gable, and it instantly became one of the great American entertainment palaces. More recently a favored location for live concerts and the occasional movie première, the 6,000-seat hall is still an art deco delight and can be seen on guided tours (tel: 307-7171, www.radiocity.com; *Tours:* Mon–Sun 11–3. *Admission: expensive*). Less glamourous but still in the realms of the showbiz world, the offices and studios of **NBC Television** (tel: 664-37000; can be viewed on hour-long guided tours, daily 9–5.

74

GETTING TO ROOSEVELT ISLAND
A road bridge crosses from Queens to Roosevelt Island, but to reach the island from Manhattan, use either the subway (lines B or Q) or (much the best choice) the cable car, which makes a 3-minute jaunt over the East River from a terminal at Second Avenue and 60th Street.

The Roosevelt Island cable car

▶ **Roosevelt Island**   187A2

Once given over to 27 hospitals that kept the incurably sick and insane (and the simply scandalous, such as Mae West) segregated from the rest of New York society, Roosevelt Island is today regarded as one of the most successful attempts at integrated mixed-income housing. Would-be residents now have to wait several years to get an apartment in the area. Besides near-total absence of crime, Roosevelt Island dwellers also enjoy automobile-free streets and a sight of the Midtown Manhattan skyline unsurpassed in most other locations in the city. For visitors, the peacefulness and the views (and the cable car that crosses to the island) are the only attractions, though the ruins of the old hospitals add a distinctly eerie note.

▶▶▶ **SoHo** 113A2
Named for being SOuth of HOuston Street (and bordered also by Canal, Lafayette and Sullivan streets), SoHo is dominated by large cast-iron factory buildings put up in the mid-19th century.

The determined efforts of conservationists saved the area and its unique buildings from demolition following a decade of neglect and after 10 years of colonization by up-and-coming artists who were attracted by spacious rooms lit by immense windows, SoHo entered a period of swift gentrification. Its loft-style apartments found favor with the city's rich and trendy—and with the art dealers who made the area internationally synonymous with contemporary art. With chic clothing stores and fashionable restaurants alongside scores of art galleries, SoHo is now transformed—but it is the dozens of remaining cast-iron buildings that shape its character.

Among the earliest examples, the **Haughwout Building** (488–492 Broadway) dates from 1857, rising in four tiers of elegant arched windows and Corinthian columns. On Greene Street, numbers 28–30 and 72–76 demonstrate the artistry that later ironwork facades acquired, while the **Little Singer Building** (561–563 Broadway) suggests the next great architectural step of replacing cast-iron floor supports with steel—the basis of the modern skyscraper.

Art lovers not satiated by SoHo's many galleries, may find still more stimulation inside the bright and boldly constructed building, seemingly composed of stacked rectangular boxes, at 235 Bowery (junction with Prince Street). This is the home of the **New Museum of Contemporary Art** (tel: 219-1222, www.newmuseum.org; *Open:* Tue, Wed and Fri–Sun 12–6, Thu 12–8. *Admission: inexpensive*), which stages six major exhibitions and five "media lounge" shows annually. Typically, these showcase emerging names and explore particular themes in diverse artistic fields. Works might range from painting and sculpture to multi-media creations including digital visuals and sound.

Creativity is all around you in SoHo

175

RICHARD HAAS' SOHO MURAL
Since 1973, at the intersection of SoHo's Prince and Greene streets, the neighborhood's bringing together of contemporary art and historic cast-iron buildings has been celebrated in a witty *trompe-l'oeil* by Richard Haas, which cleverly confuses the actual features of the buildings with painted representations.

You do not have to be an art dealer or critic to find New York's thousand or more art galleries fascinating. Many galleries are in Chelsea and SoHo—very much the international nerve center of contemporary art—though others are well established on the Upper East Side and around 57th Street. Visit the nonprofit galleries, too, publicizing the work considered too risky by the commercial galleries.

THE GALLERY GUIDE
The *New York Times*, the *Village Voice* and many special art publications carry art gallery listings, but the most comprehensive details are provided by *Gallery Guide*. A publication listing over 700 galleries and providing maps to help locate them, the *Gallery Guide* is published monthly and distributed free in galleries and a few selected bookstores. The thinner *New York Art World* has similar information. Many Chelsea galleries stock the free bimonthly gallery listing, *Chelsea Art*.

Upper East Side galleries The epitome of Upper East Side elegance and sophistication, the Paris-founded **Wildenstein & Co.** (19 East 64th Street; tel: 879-0500) specializes in French impressionist works, but its holdings extend from contemporary paintings to antique objets d'art. The diverse stocks of **Hirschl & Adler** are displayed in three separate galleries at the same address (21 East 70th Street; tel: 535-8810). The main gallery carries a broad selection of 18th- and 19th-century European pieces; Hirschl & Adler Folk gallery holds American folk art, from paintings to crafts, while **Hirschl & Adler Modern** gallery specializes in American and European names from the mid-1950s.

Focusing on modern American painters, the **Gagosian Gallery** (Madison Avenue, between 76th and 77th streets; tel: 744-2313) provides a museumlike exhibition space for lesser-known works by well-known names, such as Jackson Pollock, Willem de Kooning and Andy Warhol.

The pocket-sized **Jane Kahan Gallery** (922 Madison Avenue; tel: 744-1490) has a well-justified reputation for 19th- and 20th-century European works, Picasso among them. New York's oldest gallery, **Knoedler & Company** (19 East 70th Street; tel: 794-0550), helped develop many major private collections from the 1920s and continues to display works of note. **Margo Feiden** (699 Madison Avenue; tel: 677-5330) is lined by Al Hirschfeld's theatrical caricatures.

57th Street area galleries If you only have the opportunity to visit one 57th Street gallery, make it **Pace MacGill** (32 East 57th Street; tel: 759-7999). This deserves its place among the world's leading galleries for a stock that includes virtually every European and American name of major significance from the last 30 years.

A well established gallery spanning Cubism to Pop Art and beyond, the **James Goodman Gallery** (tel:593-3737) includes posters alongside its paintings and sculpture. For major American and European names, try the **Hammer Galleries** (33 West 57th Street; tel: 644-4400), which showcases 19th and (mostly) early- to mid-20th century paintings and drawings in an atmosphere closer to that of a fine art museum than a commercial gallery. Meanwhile, the **Jade Gallery** (413 West 50th Street; tel: 315-2750), along with many Western names, also represents artists from Latin America and Asia. Intriguing historical documents from the turbulent 1930s can be seen alongside examples of German expressionism at **Galerie St. Etienne** (24 West 57th Street; tel: 245-6734).

First established in SoHo, the **Mary Boone Gallery** (745 Fifth Avenue; tel: 752-2929) helped launch some of the brightest new names in American art, such as David Salle and Julian Schnabel.

Around the corner is the **Edwynn Houk Gallery** (745 Fifth Avenue; tel: 750-7070), exhibiting works by some of the world's best photographers; and the **Tibor De Nagy Gallery** (724 Fifth Avenue; tel: 262-5050) is a champion of emerging contemporary artists since the 1950s.

SoHo galleries Many early pace-setting SoHo galleries have closed or moved on. Among those remaining are

177

S. E. Feinman Fine Arts (448 Broome Street; tel: 431-6820), with emerging talent from the US and beyond, and **Margarette Roeder** (4th floor, 545 Broadway; tel: 925-6098) showing, among much more, artwork by composer John Cage and choreographer Merce Cunningham.

Chelsea galleries Much of the city's artistic energy is found in the former warehouses of Chelsea. Galleries here range from spacious and pricey **ACA** (5th floor, 529 West 20th Street; tel: 206-8080) to the non-profit **AIR** (Suite 301, 511 West 25th Street; tel: 255-6651) promoting exclusively work by female artists. Among others worth a look are **Cheim & Read** (547 West 23rd Street; tel: 242-7727), **Feigen** (535 West 20th Street; tel: 929-0500) and **Metro Pictures** (519 West 24th Street; tel: 206-7100).

Over the past couple of decades, numerous small galleries have opened in Chelsea, providing launch pads for many new names in the art world

South Street Seaport and the cargo ship Peking

▶ **South Street Seaport**   104B3

Eastern foot of Fulton Street (tel: 748-8600; www.southstseaport. org) Open: museum daily 10–5. Admission: inexpensive
Subway: 2, 3, 4; Fulton Street

A large collection of stores, seafood restaurants, bars, crafts centers and galleries make up the South Street Seaport district, which transformed an abandoned area beside the East River—the place where New York's 19th-century maritime trade flourished—into a history-themed pedestrian mall.

By day, however, most visitors come to Seaport itself to explore the vintage ships of the **South Street Seaport Museum** complex—which jump-started the area's gentrification some two decades ago—moored beside the South Street piers. The most interesting exhibit is the 1911 **Peking**, a four-masted cargo vessel that spent its glory days shifting nitrate from South America to the US and made several roundings of Cape Horn. Climb aboard and descend to a lower deck where a pictorial display recounts the ship's working life. Back on dry land is the **Museum Gallery**, which has a minor exhibition of maritime photos and ships-in-bottles and certificates and documents attesting to New York's historical place as one of the world's great seaports.

▶▶ **Staten Island**   48B1

A ride on the Staten Island Ferry (the panel opposite) is reason enough to make the crossing from the Financial District to the hilly chunk of land wedged between New Jersey and Brooklyn, but Staten Island has much more to offer than that. Settled by Dutch and French farmers in 1661 and an important British base during the Revolutionary War, the island has evolved into leafy suburbia with a tranquil mood that makes it seem a million miles from the hurly-burly of the rest of New York City. It also has some surprising collections among its museums.

The ferry docks at St. George is the island's least enthralling community. Two miles (3km) west (take bus S40 from the ferry terminal), Sailors' Snug Harbor is a

STROLL: WATER STREET
Water Street, between Wall Street and South Street Seaport, was New York's main riverside thoroughfare in the 19th century, lined by sailors' boarding houses, bars, and brothels.

better first stop. Founded in the 1800s as an institution for "decrepit and worn-out sailors," it is now better known as **Snug Harbor Cultural Center▶** (tel: 718/448-2500, www.snug-harbor.org; *Open:* daily dawn to dusk. *Admission: free*). Restoration has kept a number of its imposing 19th-century buildings intact.

It is farther south that Staten Island's real treasures are to be found (take bus S74). Visiting in 1991, the Dalai Lama himself described as "accurate" the stone cottage on Lighthouse Hill which is intended to replicate a Tibetan mountain temple and provide an apt home for the **Jacques Marchais Center of Tibetan Art▶▶▶** (tel: 718/987-3500, www.tibetanmuseum.com; *Open:* Wed–Sun 1–5. *Admission: inexpensive*), a wondrous stock of sculptured deities, ritual objects, incense burners and many other items from the world's Buddhist cultures.

Now the largest private gathering of such material in the western world, the collection was inspired by the discovery in 1880 by the young Jacqueline Norman Klauber (who later renamed herself Jacques Marchais) of 12 Tibetan figurines that her great-grandfather had brought back

THE CONFERENCE HOUSE
Students of international summirty might consider making a trip to the Conference House (tel: 718/984-0415; *Open* mid-Apr to mid-Dec, Fri, Sat and Sun 1–4). In September 1776, the stone house became the venue of the only peace talks attempted between the British forces and the American revolutionaries. The house served as a rat-poison factory before becoming a museum in 1926. The interior has period furniture and numerous items recording the revolutionary conflict, and the failed attempt to broker peace.

179

from a voyage to India and stored in the family attic. This experience stimulated a lifelong fascination with Buddhism and its sacraments, and she never missed an opportunity to expand the collection. Whether you are looking at a Buddhist Wheel of Life or musing over a yak butter burner, informative explanatory texts make sense of the exhibits, and illuminate their complex symbolism.

Around a mile (2km) south is **Richmondtown Historic Restoration▶▶** (tel: 718/351-1611, www. historicrichmondtown.org; *Open:* Jul and Aug, Wed–Sun 1–5, rest of the year Wed–Sat 10–5, Sun 1–5. *Admission: inexpensive*), which shows the fruits of half a century of gathering and restoring buildings dating from the 17th to the 19th centuries and equipping them with the original occupants' possessions. Local history buffs dressed in period costume lead tours around the old homes. These buildings range from a sparsely furnished Dutch building which doubled as local church and schoolhouse to a general store packed with 1840s consumer goods—all providing insights into earlier ways of life. Also within the complex, the Island Historical Museum presents a chronological record of Staten Island's growth, with many enjoyable exhibits from some of its early industries, from brewing to oyster harvesting.

The Staten Island Ferry terminal

THE STATEN ISLAND FERRY
The actual vessel is entirely ordinary, but the views from the Staten Island Ferry can be wonderful. The Statue of Liberty, Governor's Island, and the Verrazano-Narrows Bridge all appear as the skyscrapers of Lower Manhattan shrink into the distance and the green hills of Staten Island draw nearer. The ferry (pedestrians only) takes half an hour to make the 5-mile (8-km) crossing and the journey is free.

WILD STATEN ISLAND

The hilly, bucolic interior of Staten Island holds many acres of unspoiled land, parts of which can be explored on marked walking trails.
The Greenbelt (tel: 718/667-2165) spans wetlands, woodlands, streams, rivers and parks; organized weekend activities include riding and guided nature walks. The one-time mining of clay on Staten Island's southwest shore has helped create the 250 acre Clay Pit Ponds Preserve (tel: 718/967-1976), with pine woods and many man-made ponds that now provide wildlife habitats.

180

STATUE OF LIBERTY FACTS

Height: 151ft 1in (46m)
Weight: 450,000 lb (204kg)
Length of hand: 16ft 5in (5m)
Index finger: 8ft (2.44m)
Nose: 4ft 6in (137cm)
Waist (thickness): 3ft (10.7m)
Best movie role: in Alfred Hitchcock's *Saboteur*.
Biggest fictional blunder: Liberty's torch is described as a sword in Franz Kafka's *America*.

The **Alice Austen House▶** (tel: 718/816-4506, www. aliceausten.org; *Open:* Mar–Dec, Thu–Sun 12–5. *Admission: donation*), a seafront home on Staten Island dating to 1710, is filled with some of the 8,000 photographs taken by the untrained Alice over the 50 years to 1934. In 1951, *Life* magazine discovered and published some of her work. Her talents were soon recognized far afield, yet she spent her poverty-stricken old age in a workhouse.

Another small and equally unexpected collection is the **Garibaldi Meucci Museum▶** (tel: 718/442-1608, www.garibaldimeuccimuseum.org; Tue–Sun 1–5. *Admission free*), where Giuseppe Garibaldi—one of the founders of unified Italy—spent two years in the 1850s in the home of American-Italian Antonio Meucci. Garibaldi's place in history is assured, but fate was unkinder to Meucci, an inventor who developed a prototype telephone but failed to patent the idea. To reach both this and the Alice Austen House, take bus S51 from the ferry terminal.

▶▶ Statue of Liberty   48C2

There is no greater symbol of the nation and its promise of freedom and opportunity for all than the Statue of Liberty, which has held the flame of liberty above New York harbor since 1886. From Manhattan, a visit to the statue begins with a ferry ride from Battery Park Pier. Boats to the statue also stop at Ellis Island (see page 100).

For many years, visitors were invited to spend up to four hours climbing the interior of the statue to reach the crown, enjoying views to Manhattan and New Jersey, and be reminded of the dramatic scenes in Alfred Hitchcock's film *Saboteur*. A 1980s renovation lessened the ascent time but currently the only interior access is to the pedestal level, itself requiring a long climb. The reward is a view only slightly less splendid than that from the crown and the chance to peruse historical exhibits recording the creation of the statue and the effect it had on newly arrived immigrants when seeing it for the first time. Call for the latest information (the Statue of Liberty Ferry, tel: 269-5755; www.nps.gov/stli).

Liberty Island is in fact closer to New Jersey than to New York, but its statue is universally regarded as a fundamental part of the city

Originally intended to stand in Egypt, partly funded by a French lottery, and at first regarded in the US as a waste of money, the Statue of Liberty may be America's most famous landmark, but the story of its construction is much less straightforward than most people may realize.

Liberty in Egypt? A sculptor with a taste for monuments on the grand scale, Frenchman Frédéric Auguste Bartholdi visited Egypt and presented to the Egyptian sultan his plans for a gigantic figure of a robed female peasant holding a torch, to be sited at the entrance to the Suez canal.

The sultan rejected the proposal, but Bartholdi, on a trip to the US in 1871, found the perfect spot for his torch-carrying lady at the entrance to New York's harbor, 4,000 miles (6,400km) from her original intended location.

French friendship The idea of a gift from France to the US to mark the nations' shared belief in democracy had been around for some time, and Bartholdi's statue idea was taken on board by France's new Third Republic, busy modeling its constitution along US lines.

As a sign of friendship, both governments agreed that the work would be shared, Bartholdi producing the statue while its pedestal was made in New York. In France, a popular lottery raised 250,000 francs toward the project, but in the US, the idea was greeted with apathy.

As *Liberty Enlightening the World* (as the statue is officially titled) took shape outside Bartholdi's Paris studio—being too large to fit inside—the pedestal had barely left the drawing board, and the American press was full of satirical cartoons and articles condemning its expense.

Raising the money After Congress rejected a bill allocating $100,000 to the work, and the mayor of New York vetoed a plan for the city to donate $50,000, newspaper publisher Joseph Pulitzer attacked the miserliness of the nation's rich, and appealed for contributions—no matter how small—from ordinary Americans.

Packed into 214 crates, the finished statue arrived in New York in June 1885. Two months later, Pulitzer announced that the goal of raising the necessary sum of $100,000 had been reached.

The statue was hoisted onto its pedestal in May, 1886 and unveiled in October. The response of the public, as Pulitzer's newspaper recorded, was "one long cheer."

Liberty Enlightening the World—a powerful symbol of welcome to generations of new arrivals in New York Harbor

181

The Stock Exchange

▶ Stock Exchange 104B2

Broad Street near Wall Street (tel: 656-5167; www.nyse.com)
Subway: 4; Wall Street

Within the 1903 neo-classical facade that overpowers Broad Street is the high-tech money market of the New York Stock Exchange. Wearing the brightly colored jackets that indicate their particular job, brokers, reporters and pagers stride purposefully around the 37,000sq ft (3,437sq m) of trading floor, their successes and failures affecting the value of currency in pockets around the world. Since security concerns have made public tours a thing of the past, the exchange's part in plunging the world into the Great Depression can only be contemplated from outside; the widely-told story that stockbrokers jumped from its high windows on that fateful day in 1929, however, are entirely untrue.

▶ Theodore Roosevelt Birthplace 151A2

20th Street, between Broadway and Park Avenue (tel: 260-1616; www.nps.gov/thbp) Open: Tue–Sat 9–5.
Admission: inexpensive. Subway: 6; 23rd Street

The nation's future 26th president, Theodore Roosevelt, entered the world in 1858 in a Midtown brownstone, a building subsequently demolished but precisely reconstructed on its original site in 1923 to house a museum honoring the only president to have been a New York native. On display is an exhibition on Roosevelt's life, including hunting trophies and outdoor memorabilia.

▶ TriBeCa IFCB2

Subway: 1; Franklin Street

TriBeCa—the TRIangle BElow CAnal Street (bordered on the east by Broadway and continuing west to the Hudson River)—became the stamping ground of the artists who were priced out of their SoHo lofts (see page 175) as that district's property values soared throughout the 1970s.

Like SoHo, TriBeCa's old warehouses—formerly at the center of New York's dairy and poultry trade—offer apartments with ample space and natural light, making perfect studios. Also like in SoHo, however, TriBeCa's artists (except for the household names) have been long priced out of the huge lofts they made desirable in the first place, as TriBeCa real estate prices exploded in a climb only slightly slowed by the WTC disaster.

Besides providing as good a picture of New York-style urban regeneration as you are likely to find, a walk through TriBeCa uncovers something of note at almost every turn. Art galleries, much less slick than their SoHo counterparts, occupy many of the former industrial buildings. A notable example is the **Clocktower** at 108 Leonard Street. Dozens of pricey restaurants nourish fashionable faces while, at 37–41 Harrison Street, a primly restored row of early-1800s Federal-style town houses makes a wholly incongruous appearance.

▶ Trump Tower 151C2

Fifth Avenue at 56th Street
Subway: E, F; Fifth Avenue

High-profile property tycoon Donald Trump was the man brave enough to put his name to this garish glass tower: With its pink marble surfaces it is a monument to

A RADICAL EXORCISM AT THE STOCK EXCHANGE
The bulletproof glass screen that shields the trading floor of the Stock Exchange from the public gallery has been in place since 1967, the year when yippie (a twist on the term "hippie") Abbie Hoffman and friends tossed 300 one-dollar bills onto the trading floor. Traders went scurrying for the cash and one of Hoffman's coactivists described the incident as "exorcising the evil spirits of the Stock Exchange."

the booming economy of the early 1980s. Step inside for some serious window-shopping in the host of designer-name boutiques.

▶ Union Square   *IFCC2*

Between 14th and 17th streets
Subway: 4, 5, 6, L, N, R; 14th Street, Union Square

The thoroughfares of Broadway and 14th Street meet at Union Square, where the city's theater district was located during the late 1800s but which steadily moved farther north, leaving the broad square to become a left-wing political rallying point. Such was the potency and per-ceived threat of the workers movement that police mounted machine gun placements on surrounding buildings in 1927 in anticipation of a demonstration orga-nized to express anger at the execution of the anarchists Sacco and Vanzetti.

None of these events, or the decline that the square was subjected to during the 1970s, is apparent today in the busy but otherwise peaceful tract of land overlooked by two elegent art deco subway entrances and enlivened by a **Farmers' Market**, where fresh produce such as fruit, cheeses, bread and vegetables are sold from stalls each Wednesday, Friday and Saturday.

THE FORMER PAN AM BUILDING

Bauhaus architect Walter Gropius was among the team that designed the Pan Am Building on Park Avenue, adjoining Grand Central Terminal. The largest commercial office building ever constructed, it is also possibly the only one so closely resembling an aircraft wing. Following the demise of Pan Am, the Metropolitan Life Insurance company pur-chased the building in 1992 and set about removing its much-photographed Pan Am logo. The building itself remains as familiar a sight as ever, though still blocking the view up and down Park Avenue.

183

Inside or out, nothing is understated at Trump Tower

STROLL: DUANE PARK

By day, the streets around TriBeCa's Duane Park provide fruitful territory for a stroll. Head northward along Hudson Street, and turn off to explore Harrison and Leonard streets.

UN GROUNDS AND GARDENS

Besides its three main buildings, the 18-acre (7.3-ha) United Nations site also holds several sculptures, a small park and a rose garden. Two of the sculptures, Barbara Hepworth's bronze *Single Form* and Henry Moore's *Reclining Figure* commemorate Dag Hammarskjöld, Swedish UN Secretary General killed in a plane crash in 1961. More sculpture, each piece donated by a member state, lines the walk to and through the relaxing rose garden, where views reach across the East River to Queens and the southern tip of Roosevelt Island.

The General Assembly in session. The immense hall can accommodate delegations from up to 179 countries, and proceedings are conducted in six official languages

▶ United Nations 151C3

First Avenue, between 42nd and 46th streets (tel: 963-8687; www.un.org)

Tours daily, every half hour 9.15–4.45. Admission: moderate.

Subway: 4, 6, 7; 42nd Street—Grand Central

Given the problems blamed on its huge and infamously cumbersome bureaucracy, it might seem apt that the main building of the United Nations—the organization of world states formed in San Francisco in 1945 and operating on this plot since 1947—should be the entirely uninspiring Secretariat Building. This structure houses the UN's 16,000 administrative staff and rises for 39 marble-and-glass stories above the East River.

The UN's public entrance is through the General Assembly Building. The lobby carries temporary exhibitions on international themes, and from here a stairway leads down to the souvenir shop, post office (selling United Nations postage stamps, valid only on mail that is posted here), and also to a rather gloomy cafeteria.

To see any more of the UN, other than the grounds, gardens and the Delegates Dining Room (reservations essential), you have to take a guided tour. Departing from the lobby, the tours last around an hour and sweep through the various UN buildings, pausing on the way at displays on the work of the UN and at artworks donated by member states. None of these matches the emotional impact of the half-melted items culled from the ruins of Hiroshima and Nagasaki, which are also on display. Assuming no meetings are in session, the tour stops by the Security Council chamber—where the calmness imposed by the empty chairs and desks belies the fact that this is the only UN body with any teeth, able to impose economic sanctions and instigate military actions—and the General Assembly room, the very size of which suggests it can never be anything more than a debating chamber.

The gridlock that ensues whenever heads of state arrive to take their places at the United Nations now seems such an established part of New York life that it is easy to forget that the organization nearly opted for Philadelphia as its permanent home. What is more, present-day budget problems are causing the UN to reassess not only its expenditure but also its continued presence in the Big Apple.

The United Nations Charter was signed by representatives of 50 countries in San Francisco in April 1945, but the General Assembly held its first meeting in London in 1946, a year during which the scramble among several cities to become the organization's permanent base grew intense. San Francisco, Boston and Philadelphia were in the running before New York's application to become the UN's home was instigated by the city's most famous (some would say most infamous) planning department chief, Robert Moses, who promised that a successful bid "would make New York the center of the world."

Philadelphia or New York? Among those on the city's campaign committee was Nelson Rockefeller, of the Rockefeller banking dynasty, who was carving a political career for himself with the ambition of becoming president. Rockefeller persuaded UN officials to use New York as their base when sizing up the rival bids during 1946, but by December it seemed that Philadelphia would be chosen, and that city's authorities began preparing the future UN site. Meanwhile, property developer William Zeckendorf had been buying land alongside New York's East River for residential use. Rockefeller made Zeckendorf an offer he could not refuse for the land, presented the site to the UN officials and won the bid—the land being paid for with an $8.5 million grant from Rockefeller's father. The complex of buildings was completed in 1963, designed by an international team of architects led by William K. Harrison.

Mixed feelings Although not all New Yorkers could see the wisdom of diverting their taxes into easing the UN's arrival and providing incentives for its diplomats, the organization's presence took the city's prestige through the roof and injected millions into its economy.

Overstaffing and well-publicized expenses abuses caused streamlining to be ordered in 1992, and the UN Children's Fund and UN Development Program considered leaving base for rent-free accommodations elsewhere. Meanwhile, in a move certain to gain favor with New Yorkers (and encourage their support in a forthcoming election), Mayor Giuliani announced in 1997 that UN officials would no longer be able to claim diplomatic immunity when issued with parking tickets.

185

Considered by many to be New York's most boring building, the UN Secretariat towers above the East River and is home to the organization's huge administrative machine

Gracie Mansion, official residence of the mayor of New York, echoes the opulent feel of the Upper East Side

MUSEUM MILE
Almost all of New York's finest museums are on a stretch of Fifth Avenue that has become known as Museum Mile. From 79th Street going north, you will find the Metropolitan Museum of Art, the Guggenheim Museum, the Cooper-Hewitt National Design Museum, the Jewish Museum and the Museum of the City of New York. Just outside the officially defined mile are the Frick Collection on 70th Street, the Whitney Museum of American Art on Madison Avenue and Museo del Barrio on 104th Street.

▶▶▶ Upper East Side   151D3

Nowhere in Manhattan is the sheer pleasure of being incalculably wealthy so clearly evident as amid the mansions, high-rent apartment houses and ultra-chic shops of the Upper East Side, synonymous for a century with the kind of lifestyle only a bottomless bank account can buy.

There was a vacant space until the creation of Central Park and Manhattan's steady northward population shift made it ripe for development. The Upper East Side's first homes were modest affairs alongside new elevated train lines that ran above Park Avenue, and the streets to its east, erected in the 1870s.

By the 1890s, the city's wealthiest people began eyeing the two-block corridor formed by Fifth and Madison avenues. The richest of the rich erected grand mansions in styles ranging from mock-Gothic to imitation Italian Renaissance along Fifth, while the merely very rich moved into the fine brownstone town houses constructed along Madison.

With a few exceptions, such as the 64-room former home of Andrew Carnegie (now the Cooper-Hewitt National Design Museum) and that of Henry Clay Frick (site of the Frick Collection), the Fifth Avenue mansions were demolished during the 1920s to make way for the luxury apartment houses that stand here now, their windows giving priceless views over Central Park and their entrances guarded by white-gloved doormen.

Through the 1950s, the Madison Avenue brownstone buildings were steadily converted to stores and offices,

Walk

Art and elegance

Giving a taste of the Upper East Side's elegance and taking in several interesting but often overlooked buildings, this walk also includes a couple of important art collections.

Begin on 65th Street at **Temple Emanu-El**, a 1929 synagogue with space for 2,500 people. Its design incorporates Romanesque and

Temple Emanu-El

Byzantine features, a mixing of East and West.

Two blocks east and to the north is the **Seventh Regiment Armory** with a drill hall for shows and sales.

Ahead, on Park Avenue, is the **Asia Society** building (page 65), west of which stands **St. James Episcopal Church** (1884), with its two tiers of stained-glass windows and impressive reredos.

Facing Fifth Avenue, the former mansion home of Henry Clay Frick holds the **Frick Collection**, mostly of European Old Masters (page 110). By contrast, four blocks north and to the east, the very best of modern American art is the specialty of the **Whitney Museum** (page 191).

and now fashionably groomed locals patronize the art galleries, antique shops and designer clothing outlets of one of the nation's most exclusive—and expensive—commercial strips.

Strolling Madison Avenue dreamily window-shopping and eavesdropping on neighborhood banter is the perfect way to acclimatize yourself to Upper East Side life.

Additional reasons to come to this area are the so-called Museum Mile (see the panel), and Gracie Mansion—the official residence of New York City's mayors since 1942 (see page 111).

"He adored New York City. He idolized it out of all proportion." These lines from the opening of Woody Allen's Manhattan *could easily be applied to the director himself, whose movies have regularly celebrated New York and its inhabitants—and done so more convincingly than perhaps any other movie-maker.*

REBEL WITH A CAUSE
After the much publicized wrangling with ex-wife Mia Farrow, Allen made the news again in 2000 when he opposed a developer's plans to build a high-rise apartment building on top of a bank in his own neighborhood at Madison Avenue and 91st Street. Allen made his shortest movie, just under three minutes long, to illustrate his case to the city's landmarks preservation committee, describing it as "the first movie I ever made for a cause." On Mondays, Allen can sometimes be found playing jazz clarinet at Café Carlyle, in the Carlyle Hotel, Madison Avenue at 76th Street (tel: 744-1600).

In 1942, the six-year-old Allen Konigsberg rode the subway from Brooklyn with his father and emerged onto 42nd Street. He would later recall that he was "in love with Manhattan from the earliest memory."

Home to New York By the mid-1950s, Konigsberg had become Woody Allen and was working as a TV gag-writer in Los Angeles when (legend has it) he proposed by phone to his Brooklyn sweetheart because he needed someone to go with to see *Casablanca* at the weekend.

Meanwhile, Lenny Bruce and Mort Sahl had reshaped stand-up comedy and paved the way for the stage-shy Allen to progress swiftly from playing tiny Greenwich Village nightspots to becoming a major figure on the national comedy circuit.

A television appearance by Allen led to his (by then ex-) wife mounting an unsuccessful $1 million lawsuit for defamation of character, but Allen's antiwife jokes did not prevent him from remarrying, this time to an Upper East Sider through whom he claimed to have assumed "citizenship of Manhattan."

WOODY ALLEN'S MANHATTAN

The movies Allen's first movie to give New York a starring role was *Annie Hall* (1977). In it Allen cast himself as a stand-up comic and writer devoted to New York. Two years later, from its George Gershwin soundtrack to its monochrome photography, *Manhattan* was as much an ode to New York as it was a tale of the "emotional alienation of the Manhattan intelligentsia." Key scenes unfolded in Central Park, the Whitney Museum of American Art and the New York Aquarium.

Perhaps Allen's best 1980s New York movie, however, was *Hannah and Her Sisters* (1986), with its complex dilemmas of upper-middle-class Manhattan intellectuals. *Annie Hall* star Diane Keaton returned for the genial *Manhattan Murder Mystery* (1993) and Allen's prodigious output continued with New York-set movies such as *Bullets Over Broadway* (1994), the musical *Everyone Says I Love You* (1997), *Celebrity* (1998), *Small Time Crooks* (2000), 1940s film noir tribute *The Curse of the Jade Scorpion* (2001) and *Anything Else* (2003).

▶▶ The Upper West Side 151D1

Between the modernism of Lincoln Center and the turn-of-the-century mood of the Columbia University campus, the largely residential Upper West Side has remained solidly bourgeois over the past hundred years.

Still standing in a neat cluster around 72nd Street are some of the city's first luxury apartment houses. The Dakota, the earliest of them all, is described on page 96. Another one which is well worth a second glance is the Kenilworth Apartments, at the corner of Central Park West and 75th Street. The limestone twirls decorating its facade bring fresh meaning to the term "wedding-cake architecture." Elsewhere, gracefully aging town houses cover large sections of the area and, close to the Hudson River, several streets contain picturesque Queen Anne-style homes.

While its buildings remain, recent decades have seen marked changes in the Upper West Side's social make-up. The park-facing apartments along Central Park West have always been occupied by the well-to-do, but much of what became Lincoln Center was a slum during the 1950s, and not by accident was it chosen as the site of the 1960 movie *West Side Story*.

THE NICOLAS ROERICH MUSEUM
Born in Russia in 1874, Nicolas Roerich's life was devoted to art, archeology and philosophy. In 1929, his "Peace through Culture" banner, intended to indicate and safeguard cultural monuments and institutions during times of war, earned him a Nobel Peace Prize nomination. The Nicolas Roerich Museum (319 West 107th Street; tel: 864-7752, www.roerich.org; *Open* Tue–Sun 2–5. *Admission: free*) remembers this remarkable person with his books, possessions and many of his enigmatic paintings, often depicting a lone figure striving to find enlightenment amid Himalayan landscapes.

189

Lincoln Center's arrival was followed by an influx of academics and media folk—many of them fleeing the rising rents of Greenwich Village. They have made the Upper West Side a liberal and cultured enclave boasting bookstores, cafés and some fashionable bars. Other new arrivals are high-earning professionals with young children, taking advantage of the neighborhood's proximity to the green vistas and playgrounds of nearby Central Park and Riverside Park.

The American Museum of Natural History is one of the Upper West Side's main draws for visitors. From it you are well placed for further exploration on foot. Aim also to investigate the curious Nicolas Roerich Museum, on the northern edge of the Upper West Side (see panel).

Central Park lake. Prestigious apartment houses arrayed along here have much-prized views over the park

New York

A 1939 OPINION
Appreciation of the
Custom House's Beaux-
Arts style seems to be a
recent phenomenon. In
the 1939 WPA (Works
Progress Administration)
Guide to New York the
building is described as
"somewhat ponderous in
its neo-classical
treatment."

190

*Though no longer used
by US Customs, the
lavishly built Custom
House at Bowling Green
stands as testimony to
the prosperity that
maritime trade once
brought to New York*

▶ US Custom House 104A2

Broadway at Bowling Green (tel: 514-3700)
Open: daily 10–5. Admission: free
Subway: 4; Bowling Green

On the site of Fort Amsterdam, Manhattan's first permanent European settlement, the 1907 former US Custom House is an eloquent Beaux-Arts statement designed by the previously unknown Cass Gilbert.

The Custom House cost a staggering $7 million, but at the time of its construction, customs revenue was the biggest contributor to the Treasury's coffers. New York's customs—with the city established as a major seaport—were the most lucrative of all.

Heavily endowed inside and out with symbols of maritime trade, the building has at its entrance several Corinthian columns topped by the head of the Roman god of commerce and holds a frieze etched with dolphins, anchors, masts and other nautical emblems.

Raised on pedestals on the Custom House's steps, four limestone sculptures by Daniel Chester French (best known for his statue of Abraham Lincoln in Washington, DC) represent the four great trading continents: Asia contemplating her navel, Europe looking to the past, Africa an unknown quantity—and America, lively enough to leap from her seat and sprint across Bowling Green. Inside, the building is capped by an impressive rotunda and decorated by a series of 16 frescoes by Reginald Marsh, commissioned by the Works Progress Administration, a government office that created work for American artists and writers during the Depression. It shows the travels of American explorers and—much more interestingly—an ocean liner docking in New York, with Greta Garbo among the disembarking passengers.

The US Custom Service moved in 1973, and the building was closed. One section, ironically in a building packed with markers to the glories of commerce, reopened as the city's bankruptcy court. Since 1994, the US Custom House has held the National Museum of the American Indian (see page 164).

▶▶ **Whitney Museum of American Art** *187B1*
Madison Avenue at 75th Street (tel: 800/WHITNEY;
www.whitney.org) Open: Wed, Thu, Sat and Sun 11–6, Fri 1–9
Admission: moderate. Subway: G; 77th Street
In one form or another, the Whitney Museum has ignored
fashion, upset critics, baffled the general public, and been
single-minded in its devotion to supporting emerging
American artists for eight decades. It now finds itself in
possession of some of the most important names—and
works—of 20th-century art.

Wealthy would-be sculptor Gertrude Vanderbilt
Whitney began supporting young artists in the 1910s,
purchasing and displaying their output at her Greenwich
Village studio. During the 1920s, she presided over the
Whitney Studio Club, a celebrated art forum that displayed works by Edward Hopper, Stuart Davis and John
Sloan. These and other Whitney-backed artists emerged
as major creative forces in contemporary American art,
though they did not do much to impress the Metropolitan
Museum of Art, who rejected Whitney's offer of her personal collection in 1929. The snub encouraged Whitney to
found her own museum, which moved to its present
home—a severe rectangular block of granite-clad
reinforced concrete designed by Marcel Breuer—in 1966.

First held in 1932 (and continuing in odd-numbered
years), the Whitney Biennial continues to be a controversial, invitational exhibition of the country's latest
trends—often meeting the mixed response that greeted
Gertrude Whitney's earliest buys. Despite the museum's
attention to emerging artists and its strong temporary
exhibitions, it is the long-established names that provide
the main appeal for first-time visitors. The Permanent
Collection galleries are a roll call of American greats and
include such influential figures as Claes Oldenburg, Mark
Rothko, Jasper Johns, Roy Lichtenstein, Andy Warhol,
Willem de Kooning, and Jackson Pollock. Within this
area, three galleries are devoted to equally important
artists with close links to the Whitney: Alexander Calder,
Georgia O'Keeffe, and Edward Hopper.

*Most of the big names of
20th-century American
art are represented at the
Whitney Museum*

**THE WHITNEY BRANCH
MUSEUMS**
In 1973 the Whitney
opened its first branch
museum—staging free
exhibitions on special
themes—in the Financial
District. By the late 1980s
it had four such branches
elsewhere in Manhattan
(and another one in
Connecticut).

Sadly, the effects of the
recession have left just
one branch museum
remaining in the city: at
the Philip Morris Building,
120 Park Avenue.

►►► Woolworth Building
104C2

Broadway, between Barclay Street and Park Place
Subway: 2, 3; Park Place

Although once dwarfed—but certainly not outshone—by the nearby twin-towers of the World Trade Center, the Woolworth Building became the world's tallest building on its completion in 1913, when its 800-ft (240-m) high tower, with Gothic pinnacles, canopies and gargoyles, became an instant city landmark. The Woolworth Building retained its title of "world's tallest" until it was overtaken by the Chrysler Building in 1929.

Commissioned by Frank W. Woolworth as a headquarters for his ultra-lucrative chain of 2,000 "five-and-dime stores," the building was designed by Cass Gilbert (also responsible for the US Custom House, see page 190) and officially opened in April 1913 by President Woodrow Wilson. He flicked a switch in the White House to bathe the building—nicknamed "the Cathedral of Commerce" by a commentator of the time—in the glow of 80,000 light bulbs.

The exterior of the Woolworth building is certainly impressive, but the lobby—one of the richest in New York—with entrances on Broadway, Barclay Street and Park Place, is the real treat. Step inside to admire the blue, green and gold mosaics on the vaulted ceiling, wonder at the grand marble staircase, and look for the sculptured caricatures of Woolworth (depicted in the process of counting his nickels and dimes) and Gilbert (holding a model of the building), alongside other worthies.

F. W. WOOLWORTH
Rags-to-riches stories are seldom more spectacular than that of Frank Winfield Woolworth. He began his retail career as a humble clerk during the mid-1800s—an era when customers had to approach staff to ask about merchandise and, as likely as not, haggle over a price. In 1879, the first Woolworth "five-and-dime store" broke new ground by allowing customers to pick up and examine the stock, which was priced at either 5¢ or 10¢. By the time the Woolworth Building was commissioned, Woolworth presided over 2,000 stores and was able to uphold their no-credit credo by paying for the building in cash—a total of $13.5 million.

BATTERY PARK CITY
As the rest of Battery Park City (see pages 18–19) steadily recovers from the devastation of 11 September 2001, the riverside Esplanade remains a fine place for a stroll, particularly to watch the sunset over the Hudson River.

Symbol of a world-famous empire: the Woolworth Building

▶ World Trade Center Site   *104C1*

Bordered by Liberty, Vesey, West and Church streets.
Subway: 2, 3; Park Place

For anyone familiar with New York before 11 September 2001, it remains difficult to glance towards Lower Manhattan without being aware of the gap in the skyline once filled by the two World Trade Center towers. Rising 110 stories, the towers dwarfed their neighboring buildings that anywhere else would have been regarded as skyscrapers in their own right. Yet like an amputated limb, the missing towers still make their presence felt: Be it in the lasting agony of those who lost family and friends or in the much wider global consequences of their demise.

EXHIBITIONS
Nearby, St. Pauls Chapel became an impromptu rest center for emergency workers on that fateful day and both it and Trinity Church now have exhibitions on the former World Trade Center and the new Freedom Tower.

193

As the debris was cleared and life in Lower Manhattan returned to something approaching normal, what to do with the gaping site became a highly charged issue. On one hand, everybody was aware of the need to remember the dead, not least because in many cases, memories were all that remained (most who died were vaporized, leaving no remains; relatives were given urns of dust from the site in lieu of ashes). On the other hand, the 16-acre (6.5-ha) site formed one of the most commercially valuable plots of land in the world and was simply of too great an economic importance to be given over entirely to a memorial.

The culmination of many months of feuding and disagreement between architects and developers was a compromise plan, optimistically intended to combine office space with symbolism and aesthetics, for a structure to be known as the Freedom Tower. Largely based on plans by architect Daniel Liebskind, the tower is intended to rise to 1776ft (541m), matching the year of American independence, have lattice work upper portions that reflect the ironwork of the Brooklyn Bridge and be topped by a spire that echoes the arm of the Statue of Liberty. Nonetheless, agreement still remains elusive on the precise nature of the site's memorial to the 2,752 killed when the towers were felled.

The Freedom Tower is planned to be completed in 2009 and cost an estimated $1.5 billion. Predictably until then, much of the area looks exactly like what it is: a construction site, albeit one occasionally decorated with unofficial ad-hoc memorials to those who perished in the towers and those who sacrificed their lives in the rescue efforts to save others.

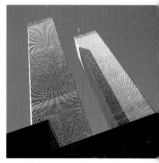

The WTC, impressive close up, offered great views from the 107th floor

Excursions

*Riverside living in the
tranquil surroundings
of the Hudson Valley.
It is hard to believe the
frenetic streets of New
York City are barely
30 miles (50km) away*

Excursions

Their affluent forebears may have had summer residences the length and breadth of the state, but many New Yorkers today go weak at the knees at the thought of leaving the familiar confines of the great metropolis.

Those who take the plunge, however, are rarely less than pleasantly surprised. Within an hour's drive of Manhattan lies a countryside thick with placid villages and abundant in blissfully rural vistas.

The Hudson Valley North of the city, the Hudson River flows through the 140-mile (225-km) long Hudson Valley (see pages 200–205). Once the major transit route into New York from New England, the river was of great strategic importance during the Revolutionary War, and several forts were founded along its course, one of which evolved into the famous Military Academy at West Point.

Though the battle sites remain, the valley no longer echoes to the sound of musket fire: Its verdant hillsides and farmlands, studded with vineyards and orchards, are the embodiment of pastoral tranquillity. These are the scenes that inspired the nation's first homegrown art movement, the Hudson River School; many examples of the artists' work can be seen in the region's museums.

Within the valley's nooks and crannies are many surprises: stately American Gothic homes, millionaires' mansions and the homes of Washington Irving (author of *Rip Van Winkle*) and Samuel F. B. Morse, the inventor of Morse code. The valley stops at the urban jungle (relatively speaking) of Albany, capital of New York State.

The Catskill Mountains Halfway up the Hudson Valley, the Catskill Mountains loom to the west (see pages 196–199). The highest peak in the Catskills, Slide Mountain, reaches only slightly above 4,000ft (1,220m), and rather than providing scope for climbers, the so-called mountains—their sides coated by pine forests and cut by tumbling streams—provide a postcard-perfect natural setting for the dozens of tiny communities enclosed in their folds. The rounded tops of the mountains are a legacy of the last ice-age, as are the deep gorges that sometimes hold spectacular waterfalls.

Photogenic views are abundant on the lanes that wind around the hills, and the Catskills' largest village, Woodstock, has a reputation for arts, crafts and culture stretching back to the early part of the century. With streets lined by clapboard homes, and dozens of galleries and craft shops displaying and selling locally produced works, Woodstock is a lovely place to succumb to the Catskills' rural pace, and its sidewalk cafés are prime vantage points for people-watching.

Long Island With its south coast bordered by the Atlantic Ocean and its north coast by Long Island Sound, the appropriately named Long Island (see pages 206–211) runs for 125 miles (200km) east from New York City, becoming progressively less populated as it does so.

Farming and seafaring were the traditional staples of Long Island life, but New Yorkers began frequenting the south shore's fine beaches a century ago: A group of pretty seaside villages called the Hamptons became a summer retreat for the wealthy, and to this day they remain a vacation destination for affluent beach lovers.

There are more excellent beaches along the protected dune-covered sand spit of Fire Island (part of it a popular gay getaway), though many of Long Island's more intriguing stops are on the north shore, where old whaling centers and immaculately preserved farming villages nestle among mansion homes built for families such as the Roosevelts and the Vanderbilts.

Clear skies, cool temperatures and warm colors make fall a good time for touring the Catskills

CAR RENTAL AND PUBLIC TRANSPORTATION
In the following pages, the excursions are described on the assumption that you are traveling by car. Note, though, that you will save money by renting a car outside New York City. All the main towns of the Hudson Valley and Long Island are well served by public transportation and have offices of the major car rental companies, so it makes sense to rent once you have arrived. A healthy alternative is to combine public transportation with exploration by bicycle. Bike-rental outlets are plentiful in most towns during the summer. To discover the best of the Catskill Mountains, however, you will certainly need a car.

Drive

Catskill Mountains

This drive goes from Kingston to Saugerties, twice crossing the ear-popping Catskill highlands and also passing some of the region's most interesting towns along the way.

The drive takes you through the colorful town of Woodstock and continues through several smaller towns, skirting forested hillsides beneath high peaks.

The breathtaking scenery is found on the drive's eastward leg, on Route 23A, as it climbs from Prattsville to Hunter—famous for its winter skiing and summer festivals. An alternative route from Prattsville would take you to East Durham, worth a detour for its two museums.

The final stretch of the drive descends sharply into the Hudson Valley toward the serene town of Saugerties. A lovely, seldom crowded place, with quaint antique shops and preserved homes, Saugerties is also within easy reach of Slabsides, the log cabin of venerated local naturalist John Burroughs.

All the important points of interest that you will pass as you travel along the route are covered in detail on pages 197–199.

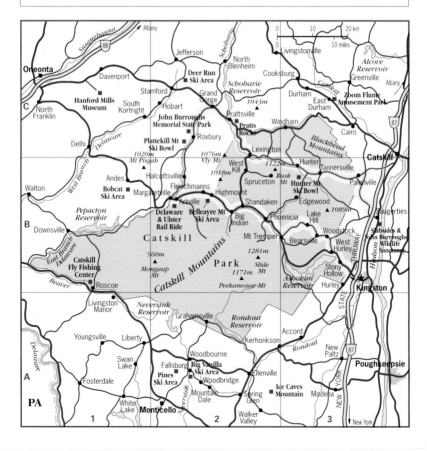

▶▶ Catskill Mountains 196

Kingston and Hurley While forest-covered hills and tiny villages secreted along winding lanes are what the Catskills are really all about, the region's largest town, Kingston▶▶, should not be overlooked.

Kingston began as a Dutch trading post in 1616. By the mid-1700s it had evolved into a significant commercial base and during the Revolutionary War it became the first capital of New York state.

At 312 Fair Street is the **Senate House State Historic Site▶** (tel: 914/338-2786, www.nysparks.ny.us; *Open:* mid-Apr–Oct, Mon, Wed and Sat 10–5, Sun 11–5, also open Memorial Day, Independence Day and Labor Day. *Admission: inexpensive*), which has been restored to its 1777 style to mark Kingston's two months as the seat of statehood; the senate swiftly moved south as the British approached from the north. An adjoining building displays a selection of paintings by locally born Hudson River artist John Vanderlyn as well as few by his peers.

The Senate House is one of several 17th- and 18th-century Dutch-built stone houses that occupy the Stockade District, within fortifications erected in 1658 to protect the town from Native American attack. Within easy reach are numerous old homes and the **Old Dutch Church▶** (tel: 914/338-6759; *Open:* Mon–Fri 9–2. *Admission: free*). Though built in 1852, the church was founded in 1659, and its cemetery bears Dutch tombs from that time.

Kingston's second historical area is the riverfront **Rondout** district, where the indoor and outdoor exhibits of the **Hudson River Maritime Museum** (tel: 845/338-0071; *Open:* May–Oct, Wed–Mon 11–5. *Admission: inexpensive*) chronicle the town's heyday as a boat-building and river trade center.

A few miles west of here, **Hurley▶** had a brief spell as the state capital during 1777 and retains its share of Dutch-built stone houses. Ten of these, on Main Street, open their doors to the public every year on the second Saturday in July.

NEW PALTZ
New Paltz, south of Kingston on Route 32, was settled in 1677 by a refugee community of French Huguenots. They were expert home builders and six of their houses remain in excellent condition along the appropriately named Huguenot Street. The local historical society leads tours of the homes (tel: 845/255-1660; *Open* May–Oct, Tue–Sun 10–4. *Admission: moderate*) furnished in period style and illustrating the trials and tribulations of local 17th-century life.

On Route 42 near Shandaken

Woodstock The best-known and busiest of the Catskill towns, **Woodstock▶▶▶** (8 miles/13km west of Kingston on Highway 212) gave its name to the legendary rock festival of 1969, even though the actual gathering took place 60 miles (100km) away. Nonetheless, if the festival had taken place here, it would have been well in keeping with the town's long-established Bohemian character.

HUNTER AND ITS FESTIVALS
New Yorkers know Hunter (north of Woodstock on Route 214) best as a ski resort, but when the snow leaves the slopes of Hunter Mountain the area kicks into its summer season with a series of festivals remarkable for their diversity. Early July finds an Italian festival, closely followed by a German Alps festival, and the first part of a country music festival. August sees the National Polka Festival, a Celtic festival, the second part of the country music festival, and a Golden Oldies festival. Rounding out the season is the Mountain Eagle Native American Indian Festival, in early September.

In the early 1900s, an Englishman inspired by the Utopian ideals of John Ruskin and William Morris founded the **Byrdcliffe Arts Colony** (tel: 914/679-2079; www.woodstockguild.org/byrdcliffe) in the hills around Woodstock. Artists and artisans arriving to live and work in the studios helped create a rich program of cultural events in the village, a tradition which still continues into the present day.

West from Woodstock Continuing deeper into the Catskill hills, the roads weave and pass tiny villages such as **Phoenicia** and **Shandaken**, where white-water rafting and a rich sprinkling of gourmet-class French restaurants are the main sources of local income. Both appeal to well-heeled weekending New Yorkers, who regard this area as their own piece of heaven. On the western side of the Catskills, **Arkville** offers a touch more diversity with the **Delaware & Ulster Rail Ride▶** (tel: 845/586-3877, www.durr.org; *Open:* late-May–Oct, Wed–Sun 10–5. *Admission: moderate*), which operates over a 12-mile (19-km) segment of a historic railroad that makes a jaunt to Halcottsville and back several times a day.

Roxbury and Prattsville North of Arkville, **Roxbury** acquired the **Jay Gould Memorial Reformed Church** in 1892. This imposing structure of limestone and oak was erected by the children of the unloved robber baron

Gould, who was born here in 1836. A worthwhile call is to the **John Burroughs Memorial State Park▶** (tel: 518/827-6111, www.nysparks.ny.us; *Open*: grounds daily dawn to dusk. *Admission: free*), 2 miles (3km) west. Here the Catskills' foremost naturalist was born in 1837 and buried in 1921. Burroughs accompanied the likes of Theodore Roosevelt, Thomas Edison and Henry Ford on camping trips into the Catskills and introduced the wonders of its nature to many more in his informative writings.

Named after local tannery-owner Zadock Pratt, **Prattsville▶▶** claims to be the first planned community in the country and backs up this assertion with some excellently maintained 1830s houses. One of them, the home of Pratt himself, stores the local history collections of the commendable **Zadock Pratt Museum▶** (tel: 518/299-3395, www.prattmuseum.com; *Open*: May–Oct, Thu–Mon 1–4.30. *Admission: inexpensive*).

In **East Durham** on the Catskills' northern edge, you will come across an entertaining collection with something to catch the interest of almost everyone. There are a variety of farm tools, fossils, Native American artifacts, military paraphernalia and miscellaneous household furnishings displayed in the **Durham Center Museum▶** (tel: 518/239-8461; *Open*: Apr–Oct, Wed, Sat and Sun 1–4, Thu 1–4, 7–9. *Admission: free*). The building itself is a former schoolhouse which was built in 1825.

In complete contrast, the watery rides of the **Zoom Flume Water Park▶** (tel: 800/888-3586, www.zoomflume. com; *Open*: Jun–Labor Day, Mon–Fri 10–6, Sat and Sun 10–7. *Admission: expensive*) close by on Shady Glen Road are the perfect way to keep cool on a hot day. Take a picnic lunch and some children with you and make the most of it.

PRATT ROCKS
Just outside Prattsville, on Route 23, are the Pratt Rocks, which carry engravings depicting Pratt and his horse. They were commissioned by Zadock Pratt during the 1860s, to enable an itinerant stone-cutter to earn the money to pay for lodgings.

Left, below, and bottom: aspects of Woodstock, the classic Catskills town

199

Drive

Hudson Valley

Ever-changing views of the Hudson River and its beautiful tree-studded valley will guarantee lasting memories of this drive.

See map opposite.

Take two or even three days to make the most of the route, visiting some of the valley's many unique communities and historic homes—some of which have been a feature of the Hudson Valley region since its earliest European settlement.

The drive ends at Albany, New York's capital and one of the few Hudson Valley towns where modern buildings are as much in evidence as those from times long past.

The points of interest you will pass along the route are covered in detail on pages 200–205.

The Philipsburg Manor, north of Tarrytown: scenes of rural New York life during the 17th century

▶▶ Hudson Valley

Yonkers to Tarrytown Although it is unrepresentative of the pastoral scenes farther to the north, industrial **Yonkers** should be your first stop out of New York City on the Sawmill River Parkway or via Metro North (taxis at every train stop will transport you locally for a few dollars).

The evocative Hudson River School landscapes gracing Yonkers' **Hudson River Museum▶** (tel: 914/963-4550, www.hrm.org; *Open:* May–Sep, Wed–Sun 12–5, Fri 12–8, rest of the year Wed–Sun 12–5. *Admission: inexpensive*) will whet your appetite for what lies ahead.

Nearby, a taste of Hudson Valley history is provided by the stone-built **Philipse Manor▶** (tel: 845/965-4027, www.philipsemanorfriends.org; *Open:* Apr–Fri 12–5, Sat and Sun 11–5, reduced hours rest of year. *Admission: free*), where Frederick Philipse III—grandson of a Dutch settler who made a fortune through shipping and slavery—led a life of ease until he was imprisoned during the Revolutionary War for supporting the British.

Farther north on Route 9, just south of Tarrytown, a neo-Gothic castle, complete with battlements, towers and spires, stands beside the river, screened by woodlands. Known as **Lyndhurst▶▶▶** (tel: 914/631-4481, www.lyndhurst.org; *Open:* daily mid-Apr to mid-Oct, Tue–Sun 10–5, rest of year Sat and Sun 10–4. *Admission: moderate*), the exuberant structure is among the finest examples of American Gothic architecture and is the work of the genre's leading practitioner, Alexander Jackson Davis. Built in 1838, Lyndhurst was purchased by the despised robber baron Jay Gould in 1880. To his credit, Gould maintained the structure well, and his descendants lived here until 1961. The castle is filled by a collection of Victoriana.

As Lyndhurst was nearing completion, author Washington Irving moved into a less ostentatious dwelling at nearby **Sunnyside▶▶** (tel: 914/631-8200, www.hudsonvalley.org/web/sunn-main.html; *Open:* Mar, Sat and Sun 10–4, Apr–Dec, Wed–Mon 10–5. *Admission: inexpensive*), where he added Dutch gables and a Romanesque tower to the original 17th-century farmer's cottage. Guided tours explore the rooms where the creator of *Rip Van Winkle* and *The Legend of Sleepy Hollow* spent the later years of his life.

Off Route 9 north of Tarrytown is **Philipsburg Manor▶▶** (tel: 914/631-8200, www.hudsonvalley.org/web/phil-main.html; *Open:* Mar, Sat and Sun 10–4, Apr–Dec, daily 10–5. *Admission: inexpensive*). This building is a reconstruction of the 17th-century mill at the heart of the Philipse family's empire. With livestock in the yard and the gristmill and granary in operation, the tours led by guides in 1750s attire are informative and fun.

201

Above left: Sunnyside, home of author Washington Irving, is one of several preserved buildings near Tarrytown

Little more than a pitchfork's throw from the manor, the **Old Dutch Church▶** (tel: 914/631-1123; *Open:* mid-May–Oct, Mon, Wed and Thu 1–4, Sat and Sun 2–4) was built at the direction of Frederick Philipse I in 1697. Alongside those of numerous Dutch settlers the cemetery holds the tombs of Andrew Carnegie and Washington Irving. The headless hero of Irving's *Legend of Sleepy Hollow* arose from his slumbers here.

Tarrytown to West Point On the Hudson's west bank, accessible via the Tappan Zee Bridge (1-287 west) Route 9W passes close to the village of **Nyack▶**, birthplace of the great American realist artist Edward Hopper in 1882. The artist spent much of his life here, at what is now the **Hopper House Arts Center** (82 North Broadway, tel: 845/358-0774, www.edwardhopperhouseartcenter.org; *Open:* Thu–Sun 1–5. *Admission: donation*). His finest canvases are hung in prestigious museums elsewhere, but devotees will find a few of his local landscapes here, plus a large number of souvenir prints and books.

Farther north off Route 9W is the **Stony Point Battlefield State Historic Site▶** (tel: 914/786-2521, www.nysparks.state.ny.us; *Open:* mid-Apr–Oct, Wed–Sat 10–5, Sun 1–5, also Memorial Day, Independence Day and Labor Day. *Admission: free, museum inexpensive*), the remains of a British fort attacked and captured in a midnight raid by General "Mad" Anthony Wayne in 1779. A visitors' center describes the battle and its significance. Beyond Stony Point, Route 9W climbs into the **Hudson Highlands**: An area of rare beauty, where the river narrows and the sheer tree-clad valley walls are studded with exposed rock.

Route 218 wends a scenic route above the river, passing through the **United States Military Academy at West**

The campus of the Military Academy at West Point. Visitors here can stroll in the footsteps of many famous Americans

Point▶. Since 1802, West Point has sought to instil discipline, moral fiber and leadership qualities into its cadets. Numerous presidents, generals and astronauts have graduated from here; even among the drop-outs there have been some famous names, such as Edgar Allan Poe and the late Timothy Leary, the LSD guru of the 1960s.

Ports of call here include the **West Point Museum**, (tel: 914/938-2638, www.usma.edu; *Open:* daily 10.30–4.15. *Admission: free*) with mementos—guns, flags, medals and more—from every conflict that has ever involved the US; the remains of the Revolutionary-era **Fort Putnam**, perched 450ft (140m) above the Hudson; and the **Drill Ground** (known as the "**Plain**"), where some of West

The Monument to the American Soldiers in the grounds of the United States Military Academy at West Point

Point's 4,000 cadets may sometimes be seen marching along with their geometric precision.

West Point to Poughkeepsie At **Newburgh**, which is the next major settlement, George Washington occupied a stone dwelling, built by Dutch settler Jonathan Hasbrouck, at 84 Liberty Street during the 16 months between the British surrender and the signing of the peace accord in Paris. Preserved as **Washington's Headquarters/Jonathan Hasbrouck House▶** (tel: 914/562-1195, www.nysparks. state.ny.us; *Open:* mid-Apr–Oct, Wed–Sat 10–5, Sun 1–5. *Admission inexpensive*), the house is one of several 18th- and 19th-century homes that make a short stroll around the town time well spent.

A better picture of the stresses of the Revolutionary period is provided by the **New Windsor Cantonment State Historic Site▶▶** (tel: 914/561-1765; *Open:* mid-Apr–Oct, Wed–Sat 10–5, Sun 1–5, also Memorial Day, Independence Day and Labor Day. *Admission: inexpensive*), southwest of Newburgh near Vails Gate. Here, 10,000 of Washington's troops were accommodated in log cabins at the end of the war; only a speech by Washington himself quelled a mutiny in their ranks. During the summer months, local history enthusiasts re-create bygone scenes here, some of them firing replica Revolutionary-era weaponry. North of Newburgh lie the foothill villages of the Catskill Mountains. In contrast, on the east bank of the Hudson is **Poughkeepsie**. A venerable institution from Poughkeepsie's past is **Vassar College▶** (tel: 845/437-7000, www.vassar.edu), founded as an all-female college in 1861.

VASSAR COLLEGE
Strange as it may seen, profits from the production of beer helped fund Vassar College—founded in 1861 by local brewer Matthew Vassar. The intention of the rich and philanthropic Vassar was to offer women the liberal arts education that was available to men. The college did begin to admit men in 1969, although its student body remains overwhelmingly female. Besides male students, another comparatively recent addition is the Frances Lehman Loeb Art Center, built by architect Cesar Pelli, to house the college's artworks. Pelli is better known for the far grander World Financial Center in Manhattan.

203

THE SHAKERS

Founded in 1747, the Shakers—so named for the ecstatic trembling that followed their ritualistic dances—became one of the largest and most respected of the religious sects of the post-Revolutionary era. By the 1840s, more than 4,000 Shakers were living in twenty Shaker villages spread from Maine to Kentucky. Shaker skills and craftsmanship had enormous impact on rural America (their furniture is still highly coveted) and the sect's many inventions included the flat-headed broom, the wooden clothespin and the circular saw. Increasing wealth led to conflict within Shaker communities, which steadily declined from 1875. Many Shakers, however, retained their beliefs until death.

ALBANY'S EGGSHELL

What looks like a gigantic upturned eggshell in the center of Albany is in fact the home of ESIPA, or Empire State Institute for the Performing Arts (tel: 516/473-1061; *Open* daily 8.30–5). Inside, the eggshell has seating for 900 and a regular program of varied musical and theatrical events.

DIA-BEACON REGGIO GALLERIES

On the tree-lined banks of the Hudson River in the otherwise sleepy town of Beacon, the DIA-Beacon Reggio Galleries (tel: 845/440-0100; *Open* summer Tue–Mon 11–6, winter Fri–Mon 11–4. *Admission: moderate*) display the permanent collection of the ground-breaking Manhattan-based DIA: scintillating contemporary art in a memerable setting.

A 2-mile (3-km) detour south from Poughkeepsie on Route 9 leads to **Locust Grove**▶▶ (tel: 845/454-4500, www.morsehistoricsite.org; *Open:* Memorial Day–late Sep, 10–3. *Admission: moderate*). The house was bought in 1847 by inventor Samuel Morse, who enlisted the aid of Alexander Jackson Davis to transform it into a Tuscan-style villa. A pile of Morse's telegraph equipment shares the interior of the building with a diverting cache of Victorian furnishings.

Poughkeepsie to Albany Morse may be remembered by the code that bears his name, but he could not match the achievements of Franklin D. Roosevelt: destined to become the nation's longest-serving president, he was born in a clapboard house beside the Hudson in 1882, near the hamlet of Hyde Park, on Route 9 north of Poughkeepsie.

Roosevelt converted the house into a 35-room Georgian-style mansion in 1916 and used it to treat royalty and heads of state to Hudson Valley views. It is now preserved as the **Franklin D. Roosevelt National Historic Site**▶▶ (tel: 845/229-9115, www.nps.gov/hofr; *Open:* daily 9–5. *Admission: moderate*), and visitors can step inside and admire the Roosevelt taste in interior design.

Within the grounds is the **Museum of the Franklin D. Roosevelt Library**▶ (tel: 845/486-7770, www.fdrlibrary. marist.edu; *Open:* May–Oct, daily 9–6, Nov–Apr, 9–5. *Admission: inexpensive*), which stores the presidential archive and has an exhibition on Roosevelt's life and achievements. A shuttle bus continues to the **Eleanor Roosevelt National Historic Site**▶ (tel: 845/229-9115, www.nps.gov/elro; *Open:* May–Oct, daily 9–5, rest of the year Thu–Mon 9–5. *Admission: moderate*), used by Roosevelt's wife Eleanor as a summer resort and as a permanent home during her widowhood.

The **Vanderbilt Mansion National Historic Site**▶▶ (tel: 914/229-9115, www.nps.gov/vama; *Open*: daily 9–5. *Admission: moderate*) stands farther north. Frederick W. Vanderbilt, grandson of millionaire Cornelius Vanderbilt, lavished $2 million of the family fortune on this three-story Beaux-Arts mansion. Inside, the Persian rugs, Flemish tapestries, and other expensive features are on display. When Vanderbilt's niece could not find a buyer for the house in 1940, she donated it to the nation.

The most imaginative home in the Hudson Valley is not a multimillion-dollar mansion but **Olana**▶▶ (tel: 518/828-0135, www.olana.org; *Open:* Apr–Nov, Tue–Sun 10–5; Jan–Mar, Sat and Sun 11–4. *Admission: inexpensive*), on Route 9G southwest of Hudson. An inspired mix of Moorish and Middle Eastern building styles, Olana arose in the 1870s as the home of a leading Hudson River School artist, Frederick Church. Decorated with Islamic and Byzantine motifs, Olana's arched doors and windows frame lovely views. The interior is full of eastern treasures.

On the final stretch toward Albany, make an eastward detour to Old Chatham, a base of the religious community of the Shakers from 1787. The **Shaker Museum**▶▶ (tel: 518/794-9100, www.shakermuseumandlibrary.org; *Open:* May–Oct, Wed–Mon 10–5. *Admission: inexpensive*) has the most comprehensive collection of their simple and superbly crafted furnishings. There are eight buildings displaying numerous examples of Shaker achievements

The state government of New York has its offices in Albany's Empire State Plaza

in carpentry, metalwork and weaving. Other exhibits detail the history of the community and its beliefs.

Marking the northern end of the Hudson Valley is **Albany▶ ▶**, which boomed during the 18th century as a trade and transportation center, becoming New York's state capital in 1797. A restoration program has kept many of Albany's 19th-century buildings in good order, but what dominates downtown is the 1960s white marble modernism of **Empire State Plaza**, whose pedestrian way is decorated with sculpture. Take the elevator to the observation gallery on the 42nd floor of the plaza's tallest building, the **Corning Tower▶** (tel: 518/474-2418; *Open:* observation deck daily 10–2.30), for views over the valley.

At ground level, the plaza runs out beneath the pink granite exterior of the 1898 **New York State Capitol▶ ▶ ▶** (www.state.ny.us; *Tours:* Mon–Fri hourly 10, 12, 2, 3, Sat and Sun 11, 1, 3. *Admission: free*) built at a cost of $24 million and gaining French, Italian and Romanesque features as tastes—and architects—changed during its 30 years of construction. Guided tours wind up an elegant marble staircase to the restored legislative chambers.

Across the plaza is the **New York State Museum▶ ▶ ▶** (tel: 518/474-5877, wwwnysm.nysed.org; *Open:* daily 9–5. *Admission: free*), which uses exhibits and walk-through dioramas to describe the region's history, shedding light on subjects as diverse as the geology of the Adirondacks.

On show at the **Albany Institute of History and Art▶ ▶** (125 Washington Avenue, tel: 516/463-4478, www. albanyinsitute.org; *Open:* Wed–Sat 10–5, Sun 12–5. *Admission: inexpensive*) are Dutch settlement furniture, aristocratic portraiture and Hudson River School paintings.

THE SCHUYLER MANSION
If traveling through the valley has not exhausted your appetite for period homes, the pick of Albany's stately residences is the 1762 Schuyler Mansion (32 Catherine Street; tel: 518/434-0834, www.nys-parks.state.ny.us; *Open* mid-Apr–Oct, Wed–Sun 10–5, Jul and Aug also Tue 10–5. *Admission: inexpensive*), built for the well-connected Philip Schuyler, a successful businessman who served with distinction as an officer during the Revolutionary War.

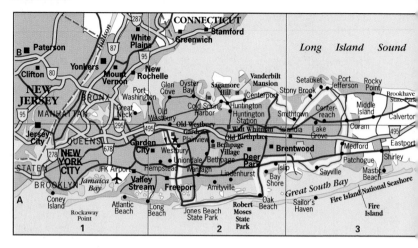

Drive

Long Island

This drive takes in some of Long Island's beaches, historic homes, and atmospheric fishing ports.

From the beautifully landscaped Old Westbury Gardens, the drive continues to popular Jones Beach before passing the south shore communities of Sayville and Patchogue. The route then passes tiny farming hamlets before reaching the picturesque villages of Setauket and Stony Brook on the north shore.

The Vanderbilt mansion can be reached down a side road off the main route, or you can continue direct to Walt Whitman's birthplace and the one-time whaling settlement of Cold Spring Harbor. The final stop is at Sagamore Hill, the stately home of Theodore Roosevelt. The points of interest you will pass along the route, as well as other highlights of a more extended visit to Long Island, are covered in detail on pages 207–211.

The beaches on Long Island's south shore are extensive enough to absorb any number of vacationing New Yorkers

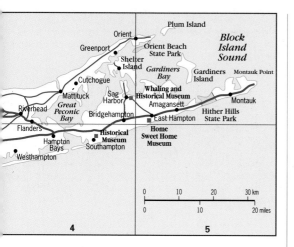

▶ Long Island

Old Westbury and Old Bethpage Much of western Long Island is now seamless suburbia crossed by freeways, but a century ago it was rural. John S. Phipps, the son of Andrew Carnegie's business partner, chose a plot near Old Westbury to built his rambling country estate. Phipps' Westbury House was completed in 1903. The grounds, known as **Old Westbury Gardens**▶▶ (tel: 516/333-0048, www.oldwestburygardens.org; *Open:* May–mid-Dec, Wed–Mon 10–4.15. *Admission: moderate*), are the main attraction for visitors: Landscaped and planted to perfection, the gardens have thousands of mature trees and an aromatic rose garden in their midst.

Long Island provides not only an escape from New York City but also, in **Old Bethpage Village**▶▶ (tel: 516/572-8400, www.oldbethpage.org; *Open:* May–Oct, Mon–Fri 10–5, rest of the year reduced hours. *Admission: inexpensive*), an escape from the present day. Crushed-oystershell lanes lead into this re-creation of an 1800s farming village,

207

THE WILLIAM FLOYD ESTATE

Close to Mastic Beach, where the road to eastern Fire Island meets the mainland, the William Floyd Estate (tel: 631/399–2030; *Open* year round, hours vary by season) is what is left of the plantation owned by General William Floyd, one of the signers of the Declaration of Independence. The simple house Floyd built in 1724 remains at the center of the 600-acre (240-ha) estate, greatly added to by successive generations of his descendants. The last of them lived here until 1975, while many of the others lie buried within the grounds in the family cemetery. The house's 25 rooms unfurl a fascinating tale of changing family fortunes.

The north shore of Long Island has great appeal for New Yorkers seeking a place in the country

typical of those that dotted Long Island long before the days of freeways. As the village's tailor, blacksmith, quilters and storeowners go about their daily tasks, it is hard not to be impressed by the thoroughness of it all.

Jones Beach and Fire Island Most New Yorkers hitting Long Island, however, are thinking not of old farming ways but about sunbathing on the south shore. On any summer weekend, **Jones Beach** is a picture of New York at play. Much the same applies to **Fire Island** (www.nps.gov/fiis), a renowned gay vacation area. The longest of the sandspits that flank the southern shore of Long Island, it is federally protected as **Fire Island National Seashore** (tel: 613/289-4810; *Admission: free*). The only section of the island reachable by car is **Robert Moses State Park** (tel: 613/660-0449; *Open:* daily dawn–dusk. *Admission free, fee for parking*), covering over 988 (400-ha) pristine acres at the island's western extremity. Adjacent, and acting as a visitor center and museum documenting lighthouse keepers, shipwrecks and sea rescues, is the **Fire Island Light Station** (tel: 613/661-4876; *Open* Apr–Oct, daily 9.30–5, winter Sat, Sun 12–4. *Admission: inexpensive*).

All of Fire Island is public land, although several sections are dominated by private resort communities. Day-trippers are not always welcomed with open arms at the more exclusive of them. One inviting destination for a day-trip, which can be reached by ferry from Sayville, is **Sailor's Haven►►** (tel: 516/589-8980). The fine beach, the nature trails weaving around the dunes, and the hardy vegetation forming the **Sunken Forest►** should not be missed. A visitors' center provides absorbing background material on Fire Island's subtle ecology.

The Hamptons East of Fire Island, the settlements collectively known as the Hamptons sat placidly at the center of windmill-studded farmland until the late 19th century, when wealthy New Yorkers discovered their vacationing potential and transformed them into highly desirable resorts. The Hamptons are still a getaway for the rich whose huge mansions stand close to fine beaches, chic boutiques and pricey restaurants. **Southampton►** is one of the Island's oldest towns and much from its past is assembled inside the 1843 whaling captain's home that now holds the **Southampton Historical Museum►** (tel: 631/283-2494; *Open:* summer Tue–Sat 11–5, Sun 1–5, reduced hours rest of year. *Admission: free*). The best-looking of the Hamptons, **East Hampton►►**, has narrow streets bordered by neatly trimmed hedges and picket-fenced cottages. Locally born actor and dramatist John

Howard Payne liked the place so much that he composed the most sentimental of songs, "Home Sweet Home," here, a fact duly acknowledged by the preservation of his house as the **Home Sweet Home Museum**▶ (tel: 631/324-0713, www.easthampton.com/homesweethome; *Open:* daily 10–4, *closed* holidays), which is mostly filled with a collection of 18th-century ceramics.

On Main Street, the 1784 **Clinton Academy**▶ (tel: 516/324-6850, www.easthamptonhistory.org/pages/clinton.html; *Open:* Jul and Aug, daily 10–5, Jun and Sep,

Cross the Robert Moses Causeway to reach the south shore

Sat and Sun 10–5. *Admission: free*), once a revered seat of learning, now has exhibitions on varied facets of local life.
Sag Harbor Unless you want to make the 20-mile (30-km) drive to the eastern end of Long Island (see panel), head northwest from East Hampton to **Sag Harbor**▶▶. Though few people would believe it on first sight, this sleepy waterside community was once a busy port, second only to New York City in its importance. Until 1871 it boasted the world's fourth largest whaling fleet.

A whale's jawbone frames the doorway of the former Masonic Temple, which is now the town's **Whaling Museum**▶▶ (tel: 631/725-0770; *Open:* mid-May–Sep, Mon–Sat 10–5, Sun 1–5. *Admission: inexpensive*), where piles of scrimshaw and nautical objects are stacked to the ceiling. The 1789 **Custom House**▶ (tel: 631/692-4664; *Open:* Jul and Aug, daily 10–5, reduced hours rest of year. *Admission: free*) is another survivor of Sag Harbor's seafaring heyday, as is the **Whaler's Church**▶, built in 1841 in a curious Greek-Egyptian style. As if to mark the decline of Sag Harbor's sea trade, the church's steeple—long a landmark for seamen—was blown down by the hurricane of 1938.

Shelter Island A quick ferry ride north from Sag Harbor takes you to **Shelter Island** which is not only a shortcut to Long Island's north fork (a second ferry crosses to Greenport) but also an ideal spot to relax among narrow, weaving lanes that are flanked by attactive Victorian cottages. It was previously a haunt of 18th-century pirates.

LONG ISLAND'S EASTERN TIP
If you drive east from East Hampton to Montauk, you will kick yourself for not continuing a further 5 miles (8km) to Montauk Point, the last stop before the Irish coast. A lighthouse, built on the instruction of George Washington in 1797, sits at the easternmost point. The rewards for braving vertigo and dizziness to climb its 138 steps are views of Rhode Island and the Connecticut coast.

Sagamore Hill was completed in 1885 for the only US president to have been born in New York City, Theodore Roosevelt; the cost of the 22-room house was $16,975

RIVERHEAD
One reason to visit Riverhead, a town off the main routes between the Hamptons and the north shore, might be the Suffolk County Historical Society (tel: 631/727–2881; *Open* Tue–Sat 12.30–4.30. *Admission: free*), whose exhibits range from local Native American cultures to whaling. Another reason could be the produce of the Palmer Vineyards (tel: 631/722-WINE; *Open* daily 11–6). If you are visiting in mid-August, Riverhead's Polish Street Fair and Festival should not be missed.

The north shore An exploration of Long Island's north shore is best begun at **Sagamore Hill▶▶▶** (tel: 516/922-4447, www.nps.gob/sahi; *Open:* daily 10–4. *Admission: inexpensive*), a three-story house set in 80 green acres (32ha) just east of Oyster Bay and completed in 1884 as the summer home of Theodore Roosevelt. Two floors of the main house hold roomfuls of Victorian furnishings and an extraordinary number of Roosevelt's hunting trophies. The spacious wood-paneled rooms provided the setting for Roosevelt's peace-brokering between warring Russia and Japan in 1905, for which he was awarded the Nobel Peace Prize. Further exhibits, and a short film detailing Roosevelt's life, can be viewed in the adjoining Old Orchard Home Museum, added by his son in 1938.

Continuing east on Route 25A is the **Whaling Museum** at **Cold Spring Harbor▶** (tel: 631/367-3418, www.cshwhalingmuseum.org; *Open:* Tue–Sun 11–5. *Admission: inexpensive*), which remembers the nine-ship whaling fleet based here during the mid-1880s. The exhibits include one of the few existing complete whaling vessels, and numerous smaller pieces—examples of scrimshaw, harpoons and other tools.

When the Cold Spring Harbor whaling fleet was still sailing the high seas, Walt Whitman—born in 1819, 2 miles (3km) away in Huntington—was busy overturning the rules of traditional verse to create *Leaves of Grass*, the work that sealed his place as a literary great. The two-story shingled dwelling built in 1816 by Whitman's father is now the **Walt Whitman Birthplace State Historic Site▶▶** (tel: 631/427-5240; *Open:* Memorial Day–Labor Day, Mon–Fri, Sat and Sun 12–5, 11–4, Sep–May, Wed–Fri 1–4, Sat and Sun 11–4. *Admission: inexpensive*), with exhibits recounting his adventure-filled life.

North of Centerport is the Spanish-style **Vanderbilt Mansion▶** (tel: 631/854-5555; *Open:* Tue–Sun 10–5, reduced hours rest of year. *Admission: moderate*), which belonged to William K. Vanderbilt II, great-grandson of Cornelius Vanderbilt. He combined his taste for opulent living with an interest in natural history, acquiring the 17,000 specimens of stuffed and mounted creatures that make a strange addition to the antiques and original furnishings on display here. The adjacent Vanderbilt Planetarium has views of the heavens, which fail to match up to those across Long Island Sound.

Stony Brook and Setauket An almost too perfectly preserved village, **Stony Brook▶▶** was saved from neglect by wealthy philanthropist Ward Melville during the 1930s. Melville also financed the **Long Island Museum of American Art, History and Carriages▶▶▶** (tel: 631/751-0066, www.longislandmuseum.org; *Open:* Wed–Sat 10–5, Sun 12–5. *Admission: inexpensive*), a complex that focuses on 19th-century Long Island life. Pride of place goes to the vintage carriages and the paintings by William Sidney Mount, a Stony Brook resident who emerged as one of the country's most original and daring artists during the mid-1800s. Mount acquired lasting fame by capturing rural scenes on canvas, and was the first major painter to produce sympathetic images of African-Americans.

Close to Stony Brook is the pretty village of **Setauket▶**, which was a hotbed of espionage during the revolutionary years of the late 1700s, and the birthplace of what is said to have been the nation's first spy cell. One technique employed to outwit the occupying British troops was the conveying of messages using a local housewife's clothesline. The combination of clothing on the line corresponded to a prearranged code and did most damage—as far as the British were concerned—when used to alert George Washington to the approach of the French Expeditionary Force in 1780.

A TRIP TO CONNECTICUT?
Should the combination of Long Island's sea air and nautical museums give you the urge to take to the waves, you can seize the opportunity at Port Jefferson, 3 miles (5km) east of Setauket. From here, a ferry (taking both cars and pedestrians) makes the 20 mile (30-km) crossing of Long Island Sound to Bridgeport in Connecticut, several times daily.

Framed by formal gardens, the 24-room Vanderbilt Mansion near Centerport sits at the heart of a 43-acre (17-ha) estate and provides a taste of high-class living, although most visitors come for the excellent planetarium and natural history exhibits

Accommodations

The one thing all New York hotels share is inflated prices. True bargains can be extremely difficult to find; and when you do, you sometimes wish you hadn't. The hotels listed in this book are the best in all price categories—even the budget choices are a step above cheap.

Budget hotels Any hotel room priced under about $200 is unlikely to offer anything more than the basic necessities: a roof over your head and a mattress under your back, and the bathroom maybe a shared.

That said, hotels at the rock-bottom end of the market are safe and clean and have air-conditioning. Not all have in-room phones or cable TV.

Basic comforts For $200–300, you can expect a comfortable room with cable TV and a bathroom and telephone. Rooms at this tier are more elegantly furnished and a good range of complimentary soaps and shampoos should be found in the bathroom, and occasionally a complimentary newspaper will be delivered to your door each morning. A concern for design and architecture and quality linens may also be evident.

Spoiling yourself To taste the New York good life means that you can kiss goodbye to at least $300 a night. Do this, and you will be able to stretch out on a giant-sized bed in a large room, with a fully equipped, often marble, bathroom.

Further spending will be encouraged by in-room CD players, DVD players and access to a library of movies on demand through the hotel, plus many other extras and 24-hour room service. There should be a knowledgable concierge available to recommend sightseeing trips, restaurants, galleries and shows and to assist with reservations and tickets.

HOTELS: THE FACTS

The NYC & Company Visitor Information Center (810 Seventh Avenue, 3rd floor, between 52nd and 53rd streets, tel: 484-1222; www.nycvisit.com) publishes a free guide to hotels listing their addresses, phone numbers and prices, and indicating their location on a map. More opinionated descriptions of New York hotels can be found on pages 262–268.

You will need to have a taste for opulent living, and ample funds, to enjoy a stay at the large and very plush Helmsley Palace on Madison Avenue

Accommodations

The Warwick is just one of many comfortable hotels conveniently located in northern Midtown, where some of the city's top luxury establishments are also to be found

213

Hidden extras Although prices may seem frightening enough already, every hotel has to add on a string of taxes: New York City hotel tax (5 percent), sales tax (8.25 percent) and a $2–$5 occupancy tax, per room, per night.

Therefore, what might seem an $80 bargain will actually turn out to cost $92.60, and planning your budget for a $250 room will land you with a bill close to $285.

Quoted rates do not include tax, and do not always include breakfast either. Some hotels have restaurants, but going for breakfast at a nearby coffee shop or diner is always cheaper and a quintessentially New York way to start the day.

Special deals Slightly better news on the financial front is that hotel prices are often lower on weekends, when many establishments seek to tempt suburb dwellers to spend some time and money in the city by offering special cut-rate weekend deals.

Such packages can bring savings of up to 40 percent on regular prices and are chiefly advertised in New York area newspapers. It is always worth enquiring whether a package is available. Longer-term visits will often also attract reduced rates: A few hotels give discounts for stays of two weeks or more.

Seasonal factors New York never runs short of visitors, but the peak tourist seasons match the clemency of the weather. The prime months for this are April, May and June. In the fall, many hotels are filled by delegates who attend the numerous business conventions held in the city, and the months up to Christmas are spectacularly busy.

So, make it a point never to turn up in New York without prearranging accommodations, at least for your first night, and do so well in advance of the date you expect to arrive.

DISCOUNTED ROOMS
In the hospitality industry, hotel rooms (like airplane seats) are considered extremely "perishable" because as soon as the night is over, the potential revenue for the room is lost. Hotels.com operates like an airline broker for hotel rooms, making last-minute reservations for people in the city's best properties, often at seriously discounted rates. Several other websites like expedia.com and priceline.com provide a similar service.

The Upper East Side is a fittingly exclusive setting for the art deco Carlyle, a truly grand hotel

CREDIT CARDS

Most hotels accept credit cards as payment and, in fact, require your card details on arrival to cover incidentals. All major cards are widely accepted.

THE RAINES HOTEL LAW

In an effort to cut down the level of alcohol consumption among the city's down-and-outs, the Raines Hotel Law of 1896 made it illegal to sell liquor in New York on a Sunday, except in hotels to accompany meals. To circumvent this law, every seedy bar with a few spare rooms declared itself a hotel and offered inedible sandwiches to its oblivion-seeking customers. The law was soon repealed.

Reservations and payment To secure a room in advance, you will be asked to place a deposit. The simplest way of doing this is by quoting your credit card number by phone (by email or fax). To be on the safe side, it is best to reconfirm your reservation as close to your arrival date as possible.

Payment for your full stay (or at least a large part of it) is sometimes expected on arrival by credit card, traveler's check, or cash (though carrying large amounts of money is not advisable in New York).

Areas of the city Manhattan is quick and simple to travel around, so you can be selective about where you stay. By far the densest concentration of hotels is in the section of Midtown Manhattan bordered by 44th and 57th streets, where some of the grandest and priciest hotels can be found, in a knot around Grand Central Terminal and at the southern end of Central Park. The cheaper Midtown hotels (mostly around Times Square) can be unappealing, and you will get better value elsewhere.

South of Midtown Manhattan, where noise and traffic levels are more bearable, residential areas such as Chelsea and Gramercy Park hold several hotels full of character with attractive rates.

A handful of classy hotels with sky-high rates sit in the moneyed environs of the Upper East Side. On the other side of Central Park, the limited number of hotels on the Upper West Side are better value, especially if you like a large room, but are usually less elegant.

In Lower Manhattan, many high-rises in the Financial District are aimed at the expense-account traveler. SoHo and TriBeCa have chic boutique hotels that cater to the fashionable and affluent who desire a downtown aesthetic. Some affordable, and interesting, lodgings are dotted (albeit very thinly) through these neighborhoods and Greenwich Village.

Bed and breakfast Bed-and-breakfast accommodations are an increasingly popular alternative to staying in a hotel, but prices are not significantly lower: Such is the demand for accommodations of every kind in a city where real bargains are hard to come by.

New York B&Bs fall into two categories. "Hosted" means that guests occupy a spare room or two in the apartment of a New Yorker who will provide at least a modest breakfast. Hosted B&Bs can be a source of useful insider information on the city, but there is always the risk that you might find yourself at odds with the host. With "unhosted" accommodations, guests get the run of a New York apartment whose owner is not in residence.

B&B prices vary according to the neighborhood and facilities. Many B&Bs are in outlying locations, so bear this in mind when making reservations. A hosted bed and breakfast is generally a cheaper option ($60–$150) than its unhosted equivalent ($80–$200). Rooms should be booked well in advance for the widest choice, although you can book the day before, if necessary. Among a growing number of bed and breakfast agencies are City Lights (PO Box 20355, Cherokee Station, New York, NY 10028; tel: 737-7049) and Urban Ventures (PO Box 426, New York, NY 10024; tel: 594-5650).

STUDENT DORMS
Further inexpensive accommodations are available (during short holiday times) in the student dorms of New York University. There is a minimum stay of three weeks and the cost per week is around $70. This kind of room is extremely limited and is quickly snapped up. If you are interested, consult the New York telephone book and contact the housing office listed under the university entry.

215

Cheap and cheerful If hotels and B&Bs are beyond your budget but you still wish to see the Big Apple, the city has three YMCAs that, for slightly less than the cost of the cheapest hotel room, offer single, double and family rooms plus a range of facilities to men, women and family groups. The West Side YMCA occupies an elegant historic building at 5 West 63rd Street (tel: 787-4400).

You do not have to be a youth to stay at Hostelling International—New York's stylish and well-equipped New York hostel (891 Amsterdam Avenue; tel: 932-2300), although you do have to be a member of the International Youth Hostel Federation. Prices depend on whether you opt for a dormitory bed or a private room, but either cost substantially less than hotels and B&Bs. It is wise to make reservations in advance.

Although hotels are plentiful in New York it is best to make reservations well in advance to avoid paying over the odds

Food and drink

The city that never sleeps it may be, but New York is also a city that never seems to stop eating. This gastronomic obsession is easily explained: No city on earth has such an abundance or such a variety of food available—from burgers, blintzes and catfish to dim sum and sushi—around the clock and at prices most people can afford.

Meals on the move The busier the street, the more vendors it will have. Most street vendors serve hot dogs—even the humble frankfurter in a bun has a place in New York culinary legend, and is a must-eat snack when visiting Coney Island (see page 75)—and also knishes (a doughy pastry filled with potatoes), bags of roasted chestnuts and huge soft pretzels, crusted with salt—each for around $2 (more in the pricey heart of Midtown Manhattan).

You are never far from the next snack in Manhattan

Another common sight are falafel (small deep-fried croquettes made of spiced, ground chick peas) carts and, occasionally, soup vendors. In the morning, you'll often see stands stuffed with breakfast pastries, oversized bagels and the like—breakfast-on-the-run.

In the Financial District, those working in the industry grab their midday meal from rows of ethnic vendors lining the main thoroughfares. These pushcarts are convenient and quick, and hot piles of meat or seafood and noodles are sold for only a few dollars.

The deli: a New York institution Street vendors apart, what New York has more of than any other American city is delis. The old-timers of the breed, known for their mile-high sandwiches stuffed with Eastern European meats such as pastrami, are nowadays few and far between. However, they have given their name to a variety of food sources all over the city where overstuffed sandwiches are served to eat in or to go.

More recently, Korean immigrants have given the word "deli" a whole new meaning, installing salad bars holding trays of cooked meats, seafood dishes, stir-fries, hot and cold vegetables, casseroles, salads, fruit and even sushi.

TIPPING
In any eating place that has waiter or waitress service, you are expected to leave a tip. Restaurant and coffee-shop staff depend on tips for a large part of their income, which is why the majority will eagerly attend to your needs. The precise amount that you leave should be judged according to the standard of service, but a tip of 15–20 percent of the bill is considered average.

Just fill a plastic container and pay by the weight. Depending on the price (per pound) and how much you want to eat, you can have your fill for between $4 and $10. Many establishments have tables, but you may prefer to eat in the open air on the nearest bench while doing a spot of people-watching.

Most New York delis also serve a mind-boggling variety of sandwiches. Along with the traditional corned beef and pastrami on rye, you can also get heros (submarine sandwiches), as well as sandwiches based on food specialties of the individual deli owner's native land. In delis owned by Greeks and Middle Easterners, for instance, you may find gyros—spit-roasted beef or pork stuffed inside a pita bread envelope. Even ordinary sandwiches, such as turkey or tuna fish, are often unbelievably thick—at least an inch of meat as filling.

Bagels are served everywhere with many weird and wonderful toppings, but it is hard to beat the traditional New York way of eating them: hot out of the oven and smothered in (or with just "a schmear" of) cream cheese.

Every New Yorker has a favorite deli. Once you have found yours, start exploring the other deli specialties such as thick soups, chicken soup with the dumplings known as matzoh balls, sponge cakes and mile-high meringue pies and blintzes—similar to crêpes—wrapped around cream cheese or fruit fillings. And don't forget to try the famous New York cheesecake.

Diner or coffee-shop breakfasts If you are not in a rush, linger over breakfast in a coffee shop or diner. Such establishments are as prevalent as delis and street vendors and draw an equally devoted clientele. Sit at a table or at the counter and choose from a menu which is likely to include sausages, bacon, lox (smoked salmon), pancakes, waffles, French toast, eggs and omelettes with a host of mix-and-match fillings. Coffee-shop breakfasts are often served with home fries and toast. Often your cup of coffee will be refilled for free, for as long as you like to linger there.

EATING WITH CHILDREN
New York can be a wonderful and exciting place for children to eat. There are scores of diners, theme restaurants, pizzerias and casual ethnic eateries from which to choose. Even the city's best restaurants have a reputation for being accommodating to well behaved youngsters. If a children's menu is not offered, don't be afraid to ask for something simple; New Yorkers are not shy when it comes to ordering in restaurants.

217

A New York legend—the original Jewish deli

A coffee-shop breakfast, consisting of eggs, toast, "home fries" and coffee, will cost around $5. There are also many cafés that serve somewhat healthier alternatives like homemade muffins, oatmeal, granola with fresh fruit and fresh squeezed juices.

Lunchtime fare Lunchtime in New York usually begins at 11 and ends around 2, though it isn't hard to find something to eat throughout the afternoon. Sandwiches and salads are popular, and several establishments, such as the **Cosi Sandwich Bar** and **Mangia** food stores, have turned sandwich and salad making into an art. Here you can find items such as fresh mozzarella and sun-dried tomatoes on a baguette and smoked turkey and avocado on Russian black bread; sometimes these sandwiches are so large you can barely fit them into your mouth. Cosi's many branches continually bake their own delicious bread before your eyes. The **Daily Soup** chain serves a wide variety of homemade soups as an alternative to the sandwich.

Among New York's sandwich specialties are the grilled "Reuben" (corned beef with Swiss cheese and sauerkraut on rye bread) and the "Club" (turkey with bacon, lettuce and tomato on toasted white bread). Coffee shops also serve salad plates that could feed an army and offer variations on the plain and simple hamburger such as bacon-and-cheese burgers, chilli-cheese burgers and pizzaburgers, as well as one made from ground chicken.

An even cheaper lunch may be found at a neighborhood pizza joint, where slices are sold with your choice of toppings. Several pizza parlors also offer Italian hero sandwiches filled with meatballs, chicken cutlets, or eggplant and overstuffed calzones with cheese, broccoli, spinach or sausage fillings.

Many New York restaurants, whatever their culinary leaning, offer specially priced lunch menus or lunch buffets for under $12, which not only means good eating at a great price but also makes lunchtime a golden opportunity to begin your investigation of the city's innumerable ethnic cuisines. Seldom will you have the chance to sample so wide a choice of restaurant fare at such affordable prices. Some of the city's finest restaurants also offer very reasonable prix fixe deals at lunch, and during Restaurant Week in mid-June the top eateries' 3-course menus are priced to correspond to the year ($20.01, $20.02 etc) with many extending the promotion through the summer.

Italian restaurants Throughout New York City, Italian restaurants can be relied upon for excellent food at very fair prices. If you are interested in good food, then try to avoid Little Italy, where the atmosphere and the prices are designed exclusively for tourists. In its highest form,

Chinese specialties

Italy's *alta cucina* carries a heavy price tag, but outside its homeland, you won't find such impressive renderings.

Little Italy's prices are also higher than they deserve to be. However, if money is no object and you are neatly dressed, head instead for the gourmet Italian restaurants— try **Babbo, Lupa** or **L'Impero**.

Chinese food A short distance from Little Italy are the restaurants of Chinatown, which are unmatched for value. Because their trade is largely drawn from New York's Chinese community, the eateries can stay in profit without compromising their quality to suit western tastes.

Nobody should leave New York without dropping into a Chinatown restaurant for dim sum. Usually served until mid-afternoon on weekends, dim sum comprises steamed dumplings and baked buns filled with meat, seafood and/or rice and noodles. Diners choose from trolleys pushed between the tables: just point at what looks good.

When you cannot eat another thing, let the waiter or waitress know and the bill will be assessed by the number and shape of the empty plates on your table.

Return to Chinatown at night, when the dinner options span Cantonese, Hunan and Szechuan specialties as well as some obscure regional cuisines.

Japanese food New Yorkers first got excited by sushi and sashimi during the late 1970s when a rash of new restaurants appeared. These were intended to serve the city's fast-growing Japanese population but found themselves besieged by locals entranced by the exotic combination of raw fish and vineyard rice. The city is still an excellent place for sushi and sashimi (ask any New Yorker for their suggestions). Some of the city's best restaurants such as Nobu serve an international gourmet clientele—but little gems like **Jewel Bako**, with its East Village location, are local sushi superstars.

Affordable food to suit most tastes

MEALTIMES
To avoid crowds, or to avoid having a restaurant to yourself, be aware of the city's popular dining times. Most coffee shops open for breakfast around 6am and are at their busiest around 8am. By 10am, the pace has slowed as most New Yorkers are already planning their lunch. Some people eat their midday meal as early as 11.30am but around 1pm is more common. By 2.30 or 3pm coffee shops start preparing for the dinner rush, from around 5pm to 7pm. In restaurants, lunch hours tend to be similar to those of coffee shops but the peak restaurant dinner period is between 7 and 10.30pm. Some of the noted after-theater dining spots do most of their business between 11pm and midnight.

Head for 6th Street in the East Village for a dazzling array of Indian restaurants

Korean and Indian Korean is the other Asian cuisine firmly established in New York, even though few out-of-towners ever stumble on the Korean business district. Here, within a few blocks of the Empire State Building, off Fifth Avenue in the West 30s, a large number of Korean restaurants maintain around-the-clock service.

With its emphasis on barbecued beef and pork, Korean eating might be less gastronomically adventurous than Chinese or Japanese, but anyone with a liking for spicy meat should enjoy Korean *jeyuk gui*, strips of barbecued pork smothered with a very hot sauce and the huge variety of *kimchee* (pickled condiments).

Indian food has been popular in New York for decades. The section of 6th Street, between First and Second avenues in the East Village is packed with mostly mediocre Indian restaurants. Another more authentic and better quality group is to be found in Midtown Manhattan, around Lexington Avenue, between 27th and 30th streets.

Spanish and Greek New Yorkers often combine dining out with a trip to the theater, but not if they are planning to tackle one of the gargantuan helpings of paella (which might well take most of the evening to devour) served at the convivial Spanish restaurants dotted throughout the city, with several notable examples in Greenwich Village and Chelsea.

Outside the huge Greek neighborhood in the Astoria area of Queens, Greek food is getting much easier to find. Simple Greek dishes such as spinach pie and moussaka often appear in Greek-owned coffee shops.

CROSSOVER CUISINES
New York's ethnic cuisines are quick to mix with one another. To become a gastronomic explorer at the frontiers of culinary adventure (which is sometimes a long way from culinary excellence), seek out the city's Cuban–Chinese restaurants, Kosher-Italian delis and Chinese-Mexican fast-food outlets, among dozens of eclectic combinations.

South American and Caribbean food You're assured of a lively evening in any of the city's increasingly well-regarded Brazilian restaurants. *Churrascarias*, where waiters circle the room with mammoth skewers of meat, usually offer all you can eat at great prices. Several Puerto Rican restaurants are along 116th Street in East Harlem, and they will be more than happy to serve you barbecued pig (the island's national dish).

Less daunting Puerto Rican specialties are also served, but East Harlem can be intimidating after dark. Therefore it is more sensible to restrict your food forays into the area to lunchtime.

Eastern Europe In the Yorkville district, in the 1970s and 80s streets of the Upper East Side, several Hungarian, German and Czech-Slovak restaurants are reminders of the Eastern European communities that settled here before departing for the suburbs. Look no farther for rich, heavy soups, stuffed cabbage and extremely large portions of goulash.

Similarly solid but tasty fare turns up in the Ukrainian eateries of the East Village as well as in the Polish cafés that survive on the Lower East Side. In Brighton Beach's Russian restaurants, meanwhile, be ready for a Cyrillic menu or choose from a buffet table—however be prepared to dodge the vodka-sozzled dancers as you are doing so.

A variety of cheeses, smoked meats and other delicacies displayed at a delicatessen in Greenwich Village

221

Recipes from the regions With the foods of the world providing such competition, the regional cuisines of the nation battle hard to be noticed. Nonetheless Cajun, Tex-Mex and southwestern cooking all have their devotees. Fried catfish, grilled swordfish, jambalaya, gumbo soup and even stuffed armadillo are among their offerings.

Being hungry in Harlem is a perfect excuse to discover soul food. Order a plateful of fried chicken or beef ribs coated in gravy, and don't skimp on the side dishes, such as black-eyed peas, corn bread and grits.

Vegetarian food Although New Yorkers may love their steak, they are also known to start (and follow) healthy trends. The food offerings available to vegetarians are numerous and varied. Ethnic restaurants, particularly Southern Indian and Chinese, have much to offer. Most upscale restaurants offer at least one or two vegetarian entrées and many of the city's best have vegetarian tasting menus available when a comparable meat menu is offered.

Steak houses New York steak houses, either local legend or nouveau, are packed with Atkins's dieters and carnivores feasting on large, thick and juicy hunks of charcoaled prime beef. A la carte side dishes, like baked potatoes or creamed spinach, are popular accompaniments. Chicken and salmon are often alternative menu choices.

The crème de la crème At the top end of the dining spectrum, New York's finest restaurants not only employ some of the world's best chefs, they also engage the top waiters, managers and leading interior designers.

To experience New York eating at this rarefied level requires much more than mere appetite and a big bank balance. You will also need to make a reservation (for some, a month in advance). Although the dress codes have relaxed in may places, at certain others, unless you are an extremely famous face (and sometimes even then), you may be shown the door if you are not dressed in your best for the occasion.

Expensive restaurants sometimes allow you to sample their premier offerings with fixed-price *menus dégustation,* or "tasting menus." These menus enable you to try several dishes at a price below what it would cost to order them à la carte.

Coffee and tea Coffee is usually freshly brewed and available in regular and decaffeinated forms. Cappuccino, caffe latte and espresso coffee, costing around $3–$5

222

A revered New York institution: the steak house

per cup, are especially popular at chain neighborhood coffee shops. Coffee of a lesser quality may be ordered to go from delis and street vendors, at prices graded according to the size of the cup or container. In New York always ask for "regular" coffee if you want milk but no sugar—to get a sweetened brew, ask for "regular with sugar."

Coffee shops such as Starbucks specialize in serving several different fine coffee blends (and usually a variety of teas and soft drinks) and vie for business with local shops. In addition to a variety of strengths, at most you can get your coffee sweetened with specialty syrups such as hazelnut or caramel. Order your drinks at the counter and wait whilst it is being prepared, then, if you are planning to have a break, take it to any seat that's free. A number of coffee houses are good places to linger.

Alternatively, many bookstores such as the Barnes & Noble chain, have in-store cafés: a perfect place to sit and browse through a book or magazine while you sip your coffee.

There are few more welcoming sanctuaries from the mayhem of Manhattan's streets than the city's elegant tea-rooms (often in deluxe hotels) between 2 and 5pm on a weekday afternoon. At this time, for a price ranging from $15 to $20, you can partake of tea—the list of blends usually spans Chinese, Indian and Russian—and nibble selectively from a silver tray laden with chicken, ham and smoked salmon sandwiches, chocolate cakes, delicate pastries and scones topped with thick Devonshire cream.

For something different, try the **Wild Lily Tea Room** in Chelsea or the fairy-talelike tea at **Mackenzie-Childs** on Madison Avenue. For real extravagance, try afternoon tea at the **Four Seasons**.

Both iced coffee and iced tea are great drinks for cooling you down whilst sightseeing on a hot day in the city. Most delis in New York serve hot tea, although it is seldom brewed from loose leaves. Some restaurants now offer an impressive selections of teas, sometimes proffered by a tea sommelier for you to sniff before you make up your mind.

Sample the wide variety of worldwide fare available in New York

New York

Relaxing outside the Victory Café on the Upper East Side

NEW YORK'S NEW BEERS
Partly as a reaction against mass-produced beers, microbrewed beers (produced in small batches, often by the bar that serves them) have become increasingly common since the mid-1990s. Hops enthusiasts can sample the likes of Brooklyn Brewery Black Chocolate Stout, Weinhard's Red, Rockefeller Red, Hudson River Porter, Gotham City Gold, Empire State Bitter and Lady Liberty Light. At the Fraunces Tavern (see page 107) they can imbibe the creamy Swig Tavern Keeper, supposedly similar to that brewed when George Washington propped up the bar.

Juice bars Gaining in popularity among some of the more health-conscious New Yorkers and even those who just like the beverage, nutritious fruit juices are sold in the city's specialized juice bars and at smoothie stands. As well as fresh orange, grapefruit and carrot juice, some juice bars offer power-packed juices blended from parsley, ginger, spinach and root vegetables and smoothies often contain milk and fruit; expect to spend $4 for a glassful.

Bars and beers Bars, which are open from around midday to the early hours (legally they must stop serving at 4am), range from the chummy neighborhood variety to those patronized almost exclusively by a particular social set—be it stockbrokers, art dealers or punk rockers. For more insights into the diversity of New York bars, see pages 114–115.

Most bars, especially larger ones and those with outdoor tables, have waiter or waitress service, though usually you can go to the bar and order drinks directly from the bartender—as you can if you sit at the bar. In all bars, the bartender will expect you to leave a tip of 15–20 percent when buying a round of drinks or when leaving.

Mass-market beers such as Budweiser, Miller and Rolling Rock are served in virtually every bar. Many establishments also carry a commendable selection of bottled European beers (occasionally found on tap).

Adventurous beer-drinkers should also investigate the output of the nation's many microbreweries: Locally brewed Brooklyn Beer and Anchor Steam Beer, brewed in California, are commonly found.

Sports bars New Yorkers can watch the playoffs in sports bars with multiple extra-large television screens. Some favorite ones in the city include **Sporting Club** (99 Hudson Street at Franklin Street), baseball-mad **Mickey Mantle's** (42 Central Park South), **Runyons** (932 Second Avenue, between 49th and 50th streets), **Scruffy Duffy's** (743 Eighth Avenue, between 46th and 47th streets), **Time Out** (349 Amsterdam Avenue, between 77th and 78th streets) and the **Back Page** (1472 Third Avenue, between 83rd and 84th streets).

Wines and liquor Alongside beer, New York bars will also be able to serve you from a selection of wines from the United States and Europe—many of which are available by the glass. The more elegant the bar, the more extensive (and expensive) its wine stocks will be. Some good restaurants produce wine lists on regularly updated computer printouts. Behind every bar will be a very well-stocked rack of liquor, including malt whiskies, Russian vodka and various bourbons, as well as more unusual drinks.

Cocktails Any bar describing itself as a cocktail lounge—particularly in parts of Midtown Manhattan and in the Upper East Side—is likely to be either a watering hole for the wealthy or a meeting place for the current "in-crowd." For eavesdropping on high-society gossip, cocktail lounges are unrivaled, but to spend an evening inside one you will need to be very well dressed (in black if you're downtown) and not afraid to spend $10 or more on a single drink—and on no account should you topple drunkenly from your stool.

Theme bars There are many interesting spots that are off the beaten path and offer quirky themes along with strong cocktails. **Idlewild** (145 East Houston Street), named for New York's old airport, is set up like the interior of an aircraft, complete with reclining seats and servers in groundcrew uniforms.

VINTAGE CLASSICS
Hotel bars provide exhausted sightseers with some of the best places in Manhattan. The **Plaza Hotel's Oak Bar** (Fifth Avenue and 59th Street) continues to age well with its posh, dark-wood furnishings; it draws sophisticates, shoppers and celebrities. The **Carlyle** (35 East 76th Street) contains the charming **Bemelman's Bar** with whimsical animal murals, painted by Ludwig Bemelman and live jazz piano music at night. At the art deco-style **Essex House** (160 Central Park South), **Journeys** bar is pure English country-style with rich carved wood, sporting scenes on the walls and a large fireplace. One of the most elegant, venerable spots in New York to have a glass of wine (or a cup of tea) remains the lobby bar of the **Algonquin Hotel** (59 West 44th Street), with its many literary associations.

Since 1913, the Grand Central Oyster Bar and Restaurant has been serving celebrities, commuters and visitors alike

THE WINTER ANTIQUES FAIR

One way to keep warm in New York during January is to pay a visit to the Winter Antiques Fair, held at the Seventh Regiment Armory (see page 187). With all of New York's antiques dealers and antiques lovers gathered under one roof, you might not be able to afford anything, but eavesdropping on the chit-chat can be fascinating. There are plenty of fine antiques to admire, too.

Union Square now teems with shoppers choosing fresh produce at the popular Farmers' Market, which is held several times a week

Shopping

From the ultra-exclusive antiques shops of the Upper East Side to the trendy boutique clothing stores that proliferate in Lower Manhattan, New York is not only the most exciting place in the world to buy things, but also the easiest and sometimes even the cheapest. Not surprisingly, New Yorkers often like to "shop till they drop."

Antiques The New York millionaires who plundered the treasures of Europe and the Far East to furnish their mansions contributed to the city's emergence as the center of the international antiques trade. There is still plenty to drool over in the upscale antique shops of the Upper East Side. The more affordable stuff, meanwhile, can be found on Atlantic Avenue in Brooklyn. The West Village and Tribeca—as well as Lafayette Street—have antiques and modern furniture shops, too.

In Greenwich Village, **Kentish Galleries** (36 East 12th Street) stocks seven floors of 18th- and 19th-century furniture; its jewelry counter at Bergdorf Goodman sells Edwardian and Victorian pieces. **Les Pierre Antiques** (369 Bleecker Street) has three crowded floors of 18th- and 19th-century French country tables.

Among the city's top-range antiques shops, **A La Vieille Russie** (781 Fifth Avenue at 59th Street) highlights the achievements of czarist Russian craftsmen with Fabergé enamelware, jewel-encrusted icons, snuff boxes, clocks and assorted silverware.

Japanese prints, books and ornaments (18th and 19th century) are among the Far Eastern treasures that can be found at **Things Japanese** (60th Street, between Park and

Lexington avenues). Connoisseurs of art deco find plenty to please amid the pricey rarities at **Delorenzo** (Madison Avenue, between 75th and 76th streets).

The enormous **Gallery 532 Tribeca** (142 Duane Street near Church) is the best place for art deco settles, bookcases, dining tables and chairs, plus lighting, art and decorative work. **City Barns Antiques** (269 Lafayette Street at Spring Street) has a fine selection of Heywood-Wakefield pieces.

For contemporary catch-all shops, try **Terrance Conran** (407 East 59th Street), **ABC Home & Carpet** (888 Broadway Street at 19th Street and 20 Jay Street in DUMBO, Brooklyn) and **West Elm** (West 18th Street and 75 Front Street, DUMBO, Brooklyn) for inexpensive yet well-designed pieces. **Moss** (46–150 Greene Street at Houston) sells contemporary decor objects. **Wyeth** (315 Spring Street at Greenwich Street) is a find for vintage 20th-century furniture and furnishings, many of which have been refinished with a "distressed" look.

A change of identity? Anything is possible in the stores of Greenwich Village

If you lack the nerve to pose as a genuine customer in the more exclusive antique shops, you might aim instead for the friendlier environs of the **Manhattan Art & Antiques Center** (1050 Second Avenue, between East 55th and East 56th streets). At the **Laura Fisher Gallery**, one of the center's 194 separate stores, you will learn more about American quilts than you thought you could know. **Flying Cranes** has rare Japanese pieces from the Meiji period.

Another low-key spot high on potential is the **Chelsea Antiques Building** (108–110 West 25th Street), where 150 dealers are spread across twelve floors and sell items ranging from 18th and 19th-century furnishings to toys and books.

The mood in SoHo antiques outlets, typically set in warehouse-like stores, is much less stuffy than that of the Upper East Side shops and the prices are lower (but by no means a bargain). Among the inventory of **Back Pages** (Green Street, between Prince and West Houston streets) you will find Wurlitzer jukeboxes, vintage pool tables and vending machines. Big Apple detritus forms the eclectic stock of **Urban Archeology** (239 East 58th Street and 143 Franklin Street in Tribeca). This is just the place to pick up a bizarre bathroom fitting or a vintage barbershop chair.

Books New Yorkers's love to read. A proliferation of **Barnes & Noble** and **Borders'** superstores cover all bases and offer pleasant environments (many with cafés) in which to browse and read. There are an equal number of independent booksellers that tailor their collections with more personality. Try **Three Lives & Co.** (154 West 10th Street at Waverly Place) in the West Village or **St. Marks Bookshop** (31 Third Avenue at 9th Street) in the East Village. Featuring used and remaindered books, and also review copies, **The Strand** (828 Broadway) is a New York institution.

Specialty bookstores also abound. If your interest lies in people's lives, check out the **Biography Book Shop** (400 Bleecker Street). For mysteries and crime try **Murder Ink**

BUYING RECORDS AND CDS

With 75,000sq ft (6,700m) of floor space, the Virgin Megastore (Broadway, between 45th and 46th streets) claims to be the world's largest music and entertainment store. As you pore through rack after rack of records, CDs and cassettes, and pass through a classical section that includes space for a concert pianist, the claim is easy to believe. A second outlet can be found on Union Square. Only slightly smaller are the several branches of Tower (692 Broadway; Trump Tower, 725 Fifth Avenue; and Broadway at 66th Street).

(2486 Broadway) or **Partners & Crime** (44 Greenwich Avenue). The shelves are stacked high with children's books at **Books of Wonder** (16 West 18th Street). The country's largest selection of gay and lesbian books is stocked at **A Different Light Bookstore** (151 West 19th Street) and the oldest at the **Oscar Wilde Memorial Bookstore** (15 Christopher Street). **Bluestockings** (172 Alen Street at Stanton Street) is the city's bookstore dedicated to women. **Labyrinth** (34 West 112th Street) is a large academic bookstore.

CDs and records CDs and tapes can be found to fit all tastes amid the eclectic and vast stocks of **Tower Records** (Broadway at 4th Street), **J&R Music World** (23 Park Row, in the Financial District), **Virgin Megastore** (1540 Broadway at West 45th Street and 52 East 14th Street at Broadway) and those listed in the panel on this page. **Other Music** (East 4th Street, between Lafayette and Broadway streets) carries all manner of hard to find music from modern mixes from Japanese artists to indie bands and French free jazz.

Clothing New York is a fashion capital. Every major designer has an outlet here.

Those clothes-conscious people who do not need to worry about their credit limits—or about being patronized by snooty staff—do much of their shopping in the designer-name stores of Midtown Manhattan and the Upper East Side.

These areas are cluttered with the stores of world-famous names such as **Giorgio Armani** (Madison Avenue at 65th Street), **Gucci** (there are two shops on Fifth Avenue at 54th Street—numbers 685 and 689), **Hermès** (57th Street, between Madison and Fifth avenues), **Louis Vuitton** (Fifth Avenue at 55th Street) **Prada** (Fifth Avenue and 56th Street) and **Yves St. Laurent** (Madison Avenue at 71st Street).

A typical New York window-display

MUSEUM SHOPS

Many museums have excellent shops. The Museum of Modern Art (pages 158–160) and the Guggenheim Museum (pages 122–124), in particular, are excellent places to find art books, unusual badges, T-shirts and other souvenirs marking their major exhibitions. A branch of the Guggenheim Museum in SoHo (575 Broadway) also has a good range of art-related merchandize, and the Cooper-Hewitt Museum (page 95) has tomes covering all aspects of the decorative arts.

One pedigree designer you should visit for the setting alone is **Polo/Ralph Lauren** (Madison Avenue at 72nd Street). The company occupies a French Renaissance-style Upper East Side mansion that is a showpiece in itself. Another is **CommedesGarçons** (22nd Street and Tenth Avenue), whose trend-setting futuristic store in Chelsea resembles an attraction at an amusement park.

The person of more average income and in search of quality clothing should aim instead for the scores of discount outlets, where designer clothing is piled high, unceremoniously discounted and sold for as little as half its regular price. Among them are **Loehman's** (101 Seventh Avenue) and **Daffy's** (18th Street and Fifth Avenue), selling an amazing array of discounted merchandize for men and women. The best of the bunch is **Century 21** (22 Cortlandt Street) in Lower Manhattan, for top-shelf brands for men and women. Note that there are typically inadequate or no dressing rooms at these stores.

Up-and-coming designers and those who cater to a savvy yet average-income shopper sell up-shop downtown in SoHo, the East Village and the Lower East Side. The sweet success of some has turned these neighborhoods into stylish enclaves for uptown ladies seeking downtown looks, too.

In SoHo **Kate Spade** (454 Broome Street), a wildly popular designer, sells bags and other accessories, available in a wide range of colors and styles. Style-conscious men will love **Jack Spade** (56 Greene Street) for coats and totes and French influenced **Sean** (132 Thompson Street), where proper cotton shirts come in an array of colors. Try **Seize sur Vingt** (243 Elizabeth Street) for impeccable details on updated yet classic clothes, while **Scoop** (532 Broadway) carries trendy lines for women and, at this store, also for men. **Kirna Zabête** (96 Greene Street) is a mini department store selling edgy fashions for urban hipsters.

Just East of SoHo is the fashionable neighborhood of NoLiTa, where independent designers peddle their wares in tiny shopfronts. Check out **Language** (238 Mulberry Street) for stylish designs, as well as beautiful objects for your home. **Calypso** (280 Mott Street) sells bright island-wear and the place for "of-the-minute" shoe styles is **Sigerson-Morrsion** (28 Prince Street).

Lower Manhattan is a good area for bargain clothing stores and stalls such as this one on West Broadway

For true bargain hunters there's Orchard Street on the Lower East Side, where stores can be found selling leather accessories, shoes and some designer duds at discount prices. (But be warned that most of Orchard Street shuts down on Saturday.)

American sportswear Nothing is more emblematic of American fashion than jeans. The new **Levi's Store** (536 Broadway) and the uptown branch (Lexington Avenue) have a great selection of denim, jackets and stylish shirts.

Sportswear giant **Tommy Hilfiger** (372 West Broadway) has a SoHo shop frequented by trendy kids and young adults. The masters of catalog casual, **J. Crew** (99 Prince Street), boast five shops citywide that hawk weekend-wear year-round. **Old Navy** (503 Broadway), a member of The Gap family, has mostly sporty styles at coupon-cutting prices.

Department stores Immortalized in movies, fiction and folklore, Manhattan's department stores are the stuff of legend. Generations of New Yorkers have grown up unable to imagine life without these totems to 20th-century consumerism, and while they are superficially similar, each one has a character and cachet very much its own and its own band of loyal supporters.

Among them is **Macy's** (34th Street and Sixth Avenue), famously described as the world's largest department store. The claim seems justified as you wind up its 10 floors and find half a million mostly mainstream items for sale.

By contrast, **Bloomingdale's** (Third Avenue at 59th Street) is a wonderful store in which to buy cosmetics, accessories, men's and women's fashions, and much more. Although it is not cutting edge, Bloomies does feature a wide range of designers, in a wide range of prices.

Bloomingdale's was the first New York department store to feature now-stablished designers such as Yves St. Laurent, Calvin Klein and Ralph Lauren, and it supports many newer ones as well. There are also departments dedicated to electrical gadgetry, furniture and fine-food.

More opulent still is **Bergdorf Goodman** (Fifth Avenue, between 57th and 58th streets). Here the fashionable ladies of the Upper East Side shop beneath crystal chandeliers for clothes, jewelry, perfumes and other luxury items. Downtown shoppers make the trek for the right outfit or to register for tableware in the home department, Their husbands, meanwhile, sift through the $100-a-piece tie racks in the most elegant men's store, **Bergdorf Goodman Men**, directly across Fifth Avenue.

Spread over nine artfully designed floors, **Barneys** (660 Madison Avenue) offers all the stylish and successful Manhattanite could wish for: cutting-edge designer names by the score, high-end beauty products and a small

spa treatment room, beautiful jewelry and accessories and some classic New York attitude. Barneys is also justifiably proud of its window displays—especially at Christmas.

The ultra-chic Meatpacking District department store **Jeffrey** (14th Street and Ninth Avenue) sells prohibitively priced avant-garde designer outfits. The antidote to all this trendiness is **Saks Fifth Avenue** (Fifth Avenue, between 49th and 50th streets), which offers tasteful, stylish and high-quality clothing, shoes and cosmetics, in an orderly setting with efficient service.

Jewelry Dozens of jewelers occupy Manhattan's "diamond district," which fills a block of 47th Street immediately west of Fifth Avenue. This wholesale jewelry trading district is where diamonds are cut and polished, jewelry is repaired, gems are set and deals are done above the ground-level stores. More famous stores include **Tiffany & Co.** (Fifth Avenue, between 56th and 57th streets), with three floors of highly desirable pieces, not all of which cost the earth, and the more conservative **Cartier** (Fifth Avenue at 52nd Street), worth a call not least for the landmark mansion that it occupies. The contemporary, Eastern-inspired designs of **Me & Ro** (239 Elizabeth Street) have a celebrity following.

Shoes Shoe stores abound in New York, and if you cannot find what you want (whether it's handmade Italian loafers, kitten heels or streetwise sneakers), you are simply not trying. Aside from numerous upscale outlets in Midtown and on the Upper East Side and the extensive stocks of most department stores, many discount stores on Broadway, between Houston and 14th streets offer good deals in footwear. Manhattan also has two "shoe districts," where you will see rows of shoe stores—on West 8th Street and on 34th Street, between Fifth and Sixth avenues. **Jimmy Choo** (645 Fifth Avenue) and **Manolo Blahnik** (15 West 55th Street) are the favored stores for ultra-sexy stilettos.

Everything under one (huge) roof: Macy's

PERSONAL SHOPPING
If the prospect of roaming the city's department stores fills you with dread, consider consulting a personal shopper, who will select items especially for you. All you have to do is make an appointment and pay for the goods—the personal shopper is complimentary. Telephone for details: Bergdorf Goodman (tel: 872-8757); Bloomingdale's (tel: 355-5900); Macy's (tel: 695-4400); Saks Fifth Avenue (tel: 753-4000).

Nightlife

New York nightlife is never boring, and it's more plentiful and more diverse (and often of a higher standard) than almost anywhere else in the world. To enjoy it, all you need is energy and, in most cases, plenty of money.

Most New York-based publications carry extensive nightlife listings. The most thorough are *Time Out New York, New York Magazine*, the *Village Voice* and the Friday and Sunday editions of *The New York Times*. For new movies and plays, the *New Yorker* is also an excellent source of opinionated reviews and information.

Theater From the *Ziegfeld Follies* to *Hairspray*, the theater has been an integral part of New York nightlife for years. The section of Broadway nearest Times Square—dubbed "The Great White Way" for its multitude of lights—has long been established as the flag-carrier of big-budget American theater.

Although ticket prices can be high (as much as $100), a good reason for splurging on a night inside one of the 34

official Broadway theaters is to enjoy the sumptuous auditorium and get a taste of the history and folklore that every Broadway playhouse has in abundance.

Regularly hosting the city's major shows are the **Eugene O'Neill Theater** (230 West 49th Street), probably the biggest and best of the neighborhood playhouses; the **Broadway Theater** (1681 Broadway); the **Neil Simon Theatre** (250 52nd Street); the **Palace Theater** (1564 Broadway); the **Richard Rogers Theater** (226 West 46th Street); and the **Roundabout Theatre Company**, which is housed in the American Airlines Theater (227 West 42nd Street).

The **New Victory Theater** (209 West 2nd Street; tel: 646/223-3020) is wonderfully restored, and the only theater devoted to putting on performances geared toward children and families.

Another venerable New York dramatic institution is the **Public Theater** (425 Lafayette Street; tel: 260-2400). Here you will discover provocative new plays and controversial adaptations of the classics in six separate theaters. The Public Theater hosts the New York Shakespeare Festival in Central Park for over seven weeks each summer.

After 16 years of closed, vandalized doors, the historic **Biltmore Theater** (263 West 47th Street) was recently rehabilitated by the Manhattan Theatre Club, which produces acclaimed new work there from established and emerging playwrights.

THEATER TICKETS

For most Broadway and Off-Broadway productions, New York theater goers usually order tickets by phone (Tele-Charge tel: 239-5258 and Ticketmaster tel: 307-7171) or buy tickets through a ticket agent (listed in the *Yellow Pages* and local newspapers) rather than going to the theater box office. Although, cheap "rush hour tickets" may be available at the box office the day of the show.

TKTS

Half-price day-of-performance tickets are sold from Manhattan's TKTS Discount Theatre Centres (payment by cash or traveler's checks only; there is a surcharge). There is almost always a long line of people, especially at the Times Square outpost, so be prepared to wait.

Times Square: Duffy Square (47th and Broadway), *open* Mon, Tue, Thu, Fri, Sat 10–2, 3–8, Wed, Sat 10–2, 3–8 and Sun 11–8.

South Street Seaport (at corner of John and Front streets), *open* Mon–Fri 11–6, Sat 11–7 and Sun 11–3.30.

Nightlife

Smaller than their Broadway counterparts, Off-Broadway theaters (seating 100–499) are a little more adventurous offering an excellent choice of musicals, comedies, revivals, classics and new works that few cities can equal. Top playwrights and leading professional actors are no strangers to Off-Broadway productions, and many of the more successful make the transition to Broadway.

A wide range of plays and shows can be seen at all of the Off-Broadway theaters. Many leading Off-Broadway theaters can be found in the East and West Village, and they include the **Orpheum** (Second Avenue at 8th Street; tel: 477-2477), **New York Theatre Workshop** (79 East 4th Street; tel: 460-5475) and the **Cherry Lane Theater** (38 Commerce Street; tel: 989-2020). This theater was originally built in 1817 as a silo for a local farm.

In the fall of 2004, look for **Dodger Stages**, a complex of five new Off-Broadway theater, dance and performance venues below ground at the former Loews movie theaters at Worldwide Plaza (West 50th Street, between Eighth and Ninth avenues).

You can go further afield and sample an Off-Off-Broadway venue. The dozens of tiny Off-Off-Broadway theaters (seating under 100) are housed in places like converted churches or vacant schoolrooms. Here daring and experimental plays are performed by unknown but often very talented actors. It is seldom necessary to pay more than $15 for a seat, and ticket availability will be less of a problem than seats for a Broadway hit. These also stage performance art and alternative cabaret. Among the best bets are **The Ohio Theater** (66 Wooster Street; tel: 966-4844), **HERE** (145 Sixth Avenue; tel: 868-4444) and **PS122** (First Avenue at 9th Street; tel: 477-5829).

THEATER INFORMATION
Besides the listings in the *New Yorker*, *New York Times*, and *Village Voice*, 24-hour recorded information on what is playing where, and on ticket availability, can be found by calling the NYC/ON STAGE hotline (tel: 768-1818).

SHAKESPEARE IN THE PARK
The Public Theater's former director, Joseph Papp, instigated the popular "Shakespeare in the Park" series: the bard's plays in Central Park's open-air Delacorte Theater (near the 81st Street entrance on the Upper West Side) between June and August. Tickets are free but limited to two per person. A very long line begins forming around noon—entertainers stroll and everyone chats and picnics: The tickets are distributed at 6pm.

233

Bright lights in the theater district

The golden age of neon may be long since gone, but the gaudy excitement of Times Square remains legendary

Movies Cinema and New York have a mutual love (see pages 14–15 and 188). Besides its guest-star status in countless films, the city is also a great place to watch movies. Not only do most high-budget Hollywood features get their first screenings here in state-of-the-art movie theater complexes, but dozens of smaller movie houses specialize in new independent films and rarely seen foreign films. Nostalgia buffs are in for a treat, with oldies—from cinema classics to kitsch 1940s musicals—regularly showing around the city.

Multiscreen complexes show the latest releases all over the city; most art house and revival cinemas are downtown in the Village, SoHo and TriBeCa. They include newly restored **Sunshine Theatre** (143 East Houston Street; tel: 330-8182), previously a yiddish vauderville house, the six-screen **Angelika Film Center** (West Houston Street at Mercer Street; tel: 995-2000); the **Anthology Film Archives** (Second Avenue at 2nd Street;

tel: 505-5181); **Film Forum** (Houston Street at Varick Street; tel: 727-8110); **The Screening Room** (Varick Street; tel: 334-2100); and the **Walter Reade Theater** (70 Lincoln Center Plaza; tel: 875-5600). A great nearby borough bet is the **Brooklyn Academy of Music's Rose Cinemas** (30 Lafayette Avenue, Fort Greene; tel: 718/636-4100).

Many city museums have projection facilities and mount film series linked to a particular exhibition. The **Museum of Modern Art** and the **Metropolitan Museum of Art** also have extensive film archives of their own, and the **Museum of Television and Radio** (see page 161) is another potential source of delight for moving images. During the summer Bryant Park (42nd Street and Sixth Avenue) has free outdoor film screenings on Monday nights.

Classical music From free open-air recitals to concerts featuring the biggest in big names, the serious music lover will find plenty to clap for.

Lincoln Center's Avery Fisher Hall is the home of the **New York Philharmonic**, whose season runs from mid-September to June (for information, tel: 875-5656). During July, the orchestra undertakes spectacular and free concert series in the parks of each of the city's five boroughs.

The walnut-walled **Kaufmann Theater** (East 92nd Street at Lexington Avenue; tel: 415-5500) is a hub of diverse classical music.

At Lincoln Center, **Alice Tully Hall** (tel: 875-5050) is another good place for chamber music, and all around the city numerous other venues regularly give all forms of classical music an airing. Historic **Carnegie Hall** (Seventh Avenue and 57th Street; tel: 247-7800) offers chamber music and solo recitals. A broad-ranging program is also offered at the **Town Hall** (43rd Street, between Sixth Avenue and Broadway; tel: 997-1003).

Music fans of meager means can try the compact **Merkin Concert Hall** (67th Street, between Broadway and Amsterdam Avenue; tel: 501-3330), which showcases more unusual fare such as ethnic music and choral groups for around $15. Scan the newspapers' listing sections for other free and moderately priced concerts, held at the Financial District's **St. Paul's Chapel**, the Upper West Side's **Riverside Church** and at the city's schools of music—the major one being the **Juilliard School of Music** at Lincoln Center.

Ballet and dance Based at Lincoln Center's **Metropolitan Opera House**, the **American Ballet Theatre** (tel: 477-3030) gets rave reviews for its interpretations of classical pieces. The season runs from April to June. The modern **New York City Ballet** is based at Lincoln Center's **New York State Theater** (tel: 870-5570). Their performances run from November to February and from April to June, with the *Nutcracker* on during the Christmas season. Tickets vary widely in price and sell out in advance. Sometimes you can pick up tickets at the box office on the day of the performance, or (sold at face value or less) outside the theater just before curtain time.

THE MOSTLY MOZART FESTIVAL
For six weeks each July and August, New Yorkers shake off their summer slumbers with the enormously popular Mostly Mozart Festival, held at Lincoln Center's Avery Fisher Hall. Featuring many star performers and conductors, the informal festival is also the only chance many people get to afford front row seats: for the festival, all seats are charged at a single (low) price.

THE NEW YORK FILM FESTIVAL
Each October, specially selected new American and foreign-made movies are shown at the New York Film Festival, held at Alice Tully Hall at Lincoln Center. The festival is organized by the Film Society of Lincoln Center, and tickets tend to be in short supply (tel: 875-5610).

Many of the world's finest dancers perform at the Met

THE FIRST MET
Generation after generation of New York's longstanding wealthy would demonstrate their social aloofness by occupying all of the few boxes available during the opera season at the Academy of Music (on Irving Place), leaving the *nouveau riche* of the mid- to late-19th century to face the social indignity of sitting below them. In retaliation, millionaires William Henry Vanderbilt and Jay Astor financed the first Metropolitan Opera House. The huge building that arose, opening in 1883, was criticized for its ugliness, but did provide the grand boxes from which the city's self-made millionaires could symbolically flaunt their affluence.

In summer, top international guest companies, such as the Bolshoi or the Paris Opera, often come for a two-week run. Bear in mind that the cheaper seats are very high and far from the stage, not really a great bargain in the theater.

Another important but much more intimate dance venue, **City Center** (West 55th Street, between Sixth and Seventh avenues; tel: 581-1212), hosts several innovative companies including the **Alvin Ailey American Dance Theater**; the **Paul Taylor Dance Company**; and the **Merce Cunningham Dance Company**. A new small but interesting venue is the **Doris Duke Performance Center Theater** (219 West 19th Street, between Seventh and Eighth avenues; tel: 924-0077), where the **Dance Theater Workshop** pioneers experimental dance. Bigger and more mainstream than the DTW, but smaller than the City Center, the **Joyce Theater** (175 Eighth Avenue; tel: 242-0800) has the Pilobus in residence among others. The promising talent of many future dance stars can be seen in the workshop performances of the prestigious **School of American Ballet** (tel: 769-6600) at Lincoln Center's **Juilliard Theater**.

Such is the excellent quality of its productions that dance-loving Manhattanites regularly cross the East River to attend shows at the **Brooklyn Academy of Music** (tel: 718/636-4100). The US's first center for the performing arts, the Academy was founded in 1861 and moved to its current site in 1908. Artists from Enrico Caruso to Laurie Anderson have graced its boards. Established as a major center of modern dance, the Academy hosts the celebrated Next Wave festival each autumn.

The Metropolitan Opera House

Opera During its late-September to mid-April season at Lincoln Center's vast **Metropolitan Opera House**,

the **Metropolitan Opera** company's performances (tel: 362-6000) are as much social as musical occasions, especially Monday evenings. The company is criticized as unimaginative but seldom turns in anything other than exceptionally polished performances. Tickets are steep and can be hard to get without booking a long time in advance. Standing room tickets are available.

Also based at Lincoln Center is the increasingly innovative **New York City Opera** (tel: 870-5570), usually performing at the **New York State Theater**.

Among a sprinkling of smaller opera companies, with lower prices and cozier settings, is the **Amato Opera Company** (319 Bowery; tel: 228-8200). From June to August, **New York Grand Opera** mounts free shows at the Central Park Bandshell (tel: 245-8837).

Comedy clubs New York's comedy clubs have given a break to the careers of Chris Rock, Jerry Seinfeld, Robin Williams and innumerable others over the years. Don't expect Las Vegas-style gags and routines—New York comedy clubs can be boisterous places and the crowds may be cruel if they dislike a particular comic.

Most clubs have two shows nightly. It is wise to make a

237

Music is a way of life for many New Yorkers. The city offers plenty of scope for talented performers

reservation for performances on Fridays and Saturdays. Expect to pay more (if you can get tickets) for a "name"; "open mike" nights (when amateurs take a turn, usually on Mondays) are almost always free, but you will still be expected to buy a drink.

The most extensive comedy club listings are carried by the *Village Voice*. With a range of well-chosen up-and-coming talent, and the occasional big name, the most reliable clubs are **Caroline's on Broadway** (Broadway, between 49th and 50th streets; tel: 757-4100); the **Comic Strip Live** (Second Avenue, between 81st and 82nd streets; tel: 861-9386); and **Stand Up NY** (78th Street and Broadway; tel: 595-0850).

For infectious downtown-style improv, visit the **Upright Citizens Brigade** Theater (West 26th Street, between Eighth and Ninth avenues; tel: 366-9176).

Nightclubs New York nightclubs are always in a state of flux. The last 20 years have seen the rise and fall of the jet-set Studio 54; the arty Mudd Club, which helped

Bright lights on the club scene

rejuvenate SoHo; and a batch of punky East Village clubs that reshaped many New Yorkers' notions of what a night out could be.

Despite arcane cabaret license struggles and the new anti-smoking rules, the city's nightclub scene thrives on. The action has shifted to fringier real estate on the west and lower east sides, but there are still scores of places of different kinds where you can pose, preen, or just dance well into the small hours.

For nonregulars, the biggest potential hazard at any club is the doorman, who will decide whether you are suitably attired or composed to be admitted. The arrogance of doormen is legendary, but don't take it personally—simply try somewhere else.

No nightclub worth its salt gets into gear before 1 or 2am in the morning (most are open until 4am and some until noon the next day). Arrive before midnight and you will probably have the place to yourself. One advantage of arriving early, however, may be a reduced admission charge. Drinks in nightclubs are more expensive than in bars, and sometimes extortionately so.

Many clubs have various types of entertainment, and therefore an entirely different crowd on particular nights of the week: always phone ahead to check. The best places to find information on the club scene are *Time Out New York* and *Paper Magazine*. New York nightclubs open, close, and change address with incredible rapidity; the following suggestions are intended as a representative cross-section.

Two overdone additions to the scene are the beyond-cavernous **Crobar** (West 38th Street, between Tenth and Eleventh avenues; tel: 629-9000) with diverse music and revellers nightly, and the 18,000-sq ft (1,672sq m) megaplex **BLVD** (Bowery at Spring Street; tel: 982-7767), which showcases a nightclub, a live music lounge and a luxe restaurant.

Sleuth the trendy Meatpacking District for the hidden yet crowded **APT** (419 West 13th Street, between Ninth and Tenth avenues; tel:414-4245), where style-seekers sip and shake the DJs of unsurpassed quality.

Around the corner, the lovely **Cielo** (18 Little West 12th Street, between Ninth Avenue and Washington Street; tel: 645-5700) serves up excellent club, house and a healthy dose of door attitude.

The swanky pick-up scene at **Plaid** in the old Spa space (East 13th Street, between Broadway and Fourth Avenue; tel: 388-1060) promises late-night carousing to rock and hip hop. Excellent Brazilian, bhangra and latin nights still prevail at **SOB's** (204 Varick Street at Houston Street; tel: 243-4940).

Gay guys can sweat the sleazy crowd at **The Cock** (188 Avenue A; tel: 777-6254), but lesbians should grab a *GO NYC* magazine at queer and alternative bars and shops to catch the latest night on the mercurial girl scene.

GAY AND LESBIAN NIGHTCLUBS
New York has many gay and lesbian nightspots, and many Lower Manhattan nightclubs are intended predominantly or exclusively for gay men or lesbians on certain nights of the week. The latest details can be found by reading the *Village Voice*, *New York Press*, *Time Out New York* and the many smaller gay- and lesbian-aimed publications found in specialty bookstores such as Different Light Books, 151 West 19th Street. Coffee shops in the West and East Village and Chelsea also carry free nightlife rags such as *HX* for men and *GO NYC* for women.

239

Radio City Music Hall is a popular rock venue

However, a new trend has evolved: the "lounge," a quiet place where the more sedate nocturnal New Yorker can just lounge and chat.

Rock music Rocks big names always include New York on their international touring schedules. Big venues like the **Beacon Theater** (Broadway at 75th Street; for ticket information tel: 496-7070), **Madison Square Garden** (Seventh Avenue, between 31st and 33rd streets; tel: 465-6741), or **Radio City Music Hall** (Sixth Avenue at 50th Street; tel: 247-4777) never disappoint.

Up-and-coming bands from the US and Europe who have outgrown the small club scene but are not yet ready for the large concert halls turn up most nights of the week in mid-sized venues such as the Bowery Ballroom (Delaney and Bowery streets; tel: 533-211), **Irving Plaza** (17 Irving Place; tel: 777-6800) and **Roseland** (52nd Street, between Eighth Avenue and Broadway; tel: 247-0200), the legendary ballroom of the Big Band era.

Other worthy venues include the happy and hectic lineup of alternative bands at the **Knitting Factory** (74 Leonard Street, between Broadway and Church streets;

ROCK MUSIC TICKETS

Tickets for major rock shows (usually $35–$75) and for most shows at medium-sized venues ($10–$30) can be booked by phone and paid for by credit card through Ticketmaster (tel: 307-7171).

tel: 219-3055), and the varied acts at the intimate **Joe's Pub** at the Public Theater (425 Lafayette Street; tel: 239-6200).

Brooklyn's burgeoning music scene entices indie rockers at **Northsix** in arty Wiliamsburg (66 North Six Street, between Kent and Whythe avenues; tel: 718/599-5103) and Park Slope's **Southpaw** (125 Fifth Avenue, between Sterling Street and St. John's Place; tel: 718/230-0236).

Plenty of exotically named hopefuls on the local scene can be heard every night for free, or a few dollars, in dozens of tiny clubs secreted throughout the East Village and SoHo. For details, read the ads in the *Village Voice* or look for the handwritten notices pinned up in local cafés and bars.

Talking Heads and Blondie were just two of the big names that emerged from the New York punk scene of the mid-1970s, which centered on the still-surviving **CBGB** (Bowery at Bleecker Street; tel: 982-4052). Unknown bands play here every night of the week, while performance art and readings are also billed at the **CB's 313 Gallery** next door (tel: 677-0455).

Independent musicians explore rock's avant-garde fringe at the **Knitting Factory** (74 Leonard Street; tel: 219-3055).

Jazz and blues Since the 1940s, New York has been well endowed with shadowy jazz clubs, usually occupying basements in Greenwich Village. Their floorboards have been trodden by many of jazz's most illustrious figures.

Most jazz clubs have two or three nightly shows. Cover charges range from around $10 to $20 or more and, depending on the venue and, sometimes, the band playing, you may have to pay per set, rather than for the whole evening. Sometimes there will also be a two-drink minimum charge (around $10 a piece).

The long-established and excellent **Village Vanguard** (Seventh Avenue at 11th Street; tel: 255-4037) epitomizes the dark-and-smoky Greenwich Village basement jazz club. Top names play here regularly. Major jazz stars are also frequent visitors to the atmospheric **Blue Note** (3rd Street at Sixth Avenue; tel: 475-8592), where cover charges can sometimes be very steep.

Among the city's newer jazz venues is the **Iridium Jazz Club** (1650 Broadway at 51st Street; tel: 582-2121), highly rated for its excellent roster of live acts. It offers three nightly jazz sets as well as a Sunday jazz brunch session.

An older venue in a fresh setting is **Birdland** (315 West 44th Street, between Eighth and Ninth avenues; tel: 581-3080) which aims to re-create the style of a 1940s supper club.

A popular jazz venue, Birdland is named after a club that was a 1940s legend

A lower-key Greenwich Village venue is the tiny **55 Bar** (55 Christopher Street; tel: 929-9883), where quality piano and bass duos, and more, thrive in an intimate atmosphere.

Also downtown is the lauded **Tonic** (107 Norfolk, between Delancey and Rivington streets; tel: 358-7501), which features avant-garde jazz without pretension. Or, get a side of Dixieland and Zydeco nightly (without a cover) at the **Cajun Restaurant** (Eighth Avenue at 16th Street; tel: 691-6174). The legendary Augie's, just shy of Harlem, has been retrofitted into the plush **Smoke** (Broadway and 106th Street; tel: 864-6622), offering savvy jazz fans hip and boisterous sets.

Blues and R&B, meanwhile, seldom come rawer than the nightly brouhaha at **Terra Blues** (149 Bleeker Street; tel: 777-7776). For more mainstream acts check out **B.B. King Blues Club and Grill** (243 West 42nd Street; tel: 997-4144), a large club where Roberta Flack and Little Richard have entertained.

Folk Greenwich Village was the epicenter of the early 1960s folk revival. Judy Collins, Bob Dylan and other legends started here. The days of hootenannie are long gone, but legendary folk venues such as the **Bitter End** (147 Bleecker Street; tel: 673-7030) remain, alongside newer ones such as the laid-back and divey **Freddy's Bar** in Brooklyn (Dean Street at Sixth Avenue, Prospect Heights; tel: 718/622-7035).

Country Listening to country music seems somewhat incongruous in ultra-urban New York, but the cozy, honky-tonk **Rodeo Bar** steps to the plate with great country, bluegrass and rockabilly acts. Would-be rednecks can also swill and stamp their city boots to live music at the rowdy **Hogs and Heifers'** new uptown location (First Avenue at 95th Street; tel: 722-8135).

Greenwich Village jazz: a costlier night out than 50 years ago, but the atmosphere remains the same

---

New York

FOR CHILDREN IN THE OUTER BOROUGHS

Brooklyn's Children's Museum (145 Brooklyn Avenue) is an architecturally innovative affair, with exhibits to encourage understanding of the basics of science and nature. Older children might prefer a romp through the vintage subway cars displayed at the New York Transit Museum (see page 76).

A ride on the Staten Island Ferry is enjoyable in its own right. Once ashore, the Richmondtown Historic Restoration (see page 179) has traditionally attired guides bringing local history to life in a colorful and informative way. Elsewhere, the Bronx Zoo (see pages 70–71) has a children's section; in Queens, the New York Hall of Science (page 171) has a mass of entertaining hands-on exhibits.

Alice and friends in Central Park

New York for children

A number of Manhattan museums have sections intended for children but only the **Children's Museum of Manhattan** (in the Tisch Building, 83rd Street, between Broadway and Amsterdam Avenue; tel: 721-1234) is specially designed: a wonderful play-as-you-learn facility using computerized interactive exhibits and displays. The Children's Museum's four floors of informative fun include the Creativity Lab with a drop-in program in art, science and reading and the Time-Warner Center for Media, where children can write, produce and star in their own videos.

Still with an educational role, the **American Museum of Natural History** (see pages 63–64), with its dinosaur skeletons, giant model whale, and scores of stuffed creatures, is usually popular. At the **Sony Wonder Technology Lab** (550 Madison Avenue and 56th Street), there are regular programs for children that explore animation and other media-related subjects with interactive computers and special workshops.

For city views, the **Empire State Building** is the star, and its nerve-shattering **New York Skyride** provides thrills. A boat trip (page 67) can be combined with a clamber around the historic ships of the **South Street Seaport** (page 178).

In Central Park, the main **Central Park Wildlife Center** is behind the Arsenal at 64th Street and Fifth Avenue (tel: 439-6500). Sea lion feeding times are at 11.30am, 2pm and 4pm. Storytelling takes place on Saturdays at the Hans Christian Andersen statue by Conservatory Water (tel: 794-6564 for details). On the northern edge of Central Park are the exhibits of the **Charles A. Dana Discovery**

243

Center (110th Street and Lenox Avenue), which explore environmental themes. Special events include beginners' birdwatching and walks.

For a treat, head to the first-ever **Scholastic Store** (557 Broadway, between Prince and Spring streets; tel: 343-6166) for books, toys and hoards of Harry Potter paraphernalia. The gargantuan **American Girl Place** (Fifth Avenue and 49th Street; tel: 877-AGPLACE) has a café, bookstore and musical theater and, of course, a shop for the popular dolls and ther accoutrements.

Above: Getting to grips with the game in Central Park

Above left: The Bronx Zoo, described on pages 70–71

Left: Rollerblading in Central Park

FREE IN THE OUTER BOROUGHS

Throughout the summer, the Brooklyn Arts Council (for details, tel: 718/625-0080) hosts free musical events at several locations, including Brighton Beach. The Bronx's Hall of Fame for Great Americans (pages 71–72) is always free, as is the Bronx Zoo (pages 70–71) fon Wednesday, although a voluntary donation is expected. In Queens, the New York Hall of Science (page 171) is free from 2–5 on Friday during Sep–Jun. Staten Island's Garibaldi Meucci Museum (page 180) has free admission, and there is no charge for the July concert series at Snug Harbor (tel: 718/448-2500).

Window-shopping, Manhattan-style: a live window display at Macy's department store

New York for free

Even paupers can have fun in the Big Apple. Many of New York's finest things—architecture, pulsating streetlife, distinctive neighborhoods, fantastic department stores can be seen without spending a cent. Study the suggestions below for even more ways to enjoy New York for free.

Free in Manhattan Several of the city's major museums described in the A-Z section of this book offer free admission on selected weekday evenings: the **Guggenheim Museum** (*Open* Fri 6–8pm. *Admission donation*); the **Museum of Modern Art** (*Open* Fri 4–7.45pm. *Admission donation*); and the **Whitney Museum of American Art** (*Open* Thu 6–8pm. *Admission donation*).

Among the smaller institutions with temporary shows, the **National Academy Museum** allows free entry to its exhibitions on Friday evenings (5–6pm), as does the **International Center of Photography** (*Open* Fri 5–8pm. *Admission donation*).

Museums and galleries to which admission is free are the **American Numismatic Society** (page 65); the **American Bible Society** (page 61); the **Forbes Magazine Galleries** (pages 107); the **Hispanic Society of America** (page 126); the **Museum of American Folk Art** (page 155; a suggested donation of $3); the **Museum of American Illustration** (see page 62); the **Nicolas Roerich Museum** (page 189); and the **New York City Police Museum** (page 165).

Visiting **Federal Hall** (page 102) and the **General Grant Memorial** (page 110) costs nothing, and both **Lincoln Center** (page 134) and the **Stock Exchange** (page 182) offer free guided tours. When tickets are available, you can listen for free to delegates' speeches at the **UN General Assembly** (page 184).

Free musical and theatrical entertainment can be found in the summer in **Central Park** (tel: 360-2777), in **Prospect Park** (tel: 718/855-7882), at **Rockefeller Center** (tel: 632-3975), on the plazas of **Lincoln Center** (tel: 875-5456), and at **South Street Seaport** (tel: 732-8257).

Travel Facts

Arriving and departing

By air Flights into New York
land at John F. Kennedy Airport
(tel: 718/244-4444; in Queens, about
15 miles/24km east of Manhattan), at
La Guardia (tel: 718/533-3400; also in
Queens, 8 miles/13km east of
Manhattan), and at Newark (tel:
973/961-6000; in New Jersey, about 15
miles/24km west of Manhattan). La
Guardia Airport is almost exclusively
for internal flights.

As part of its drive against terror,
the FAA has introduced additional
security checks for internal flights, so
arrive at the airport in plenty of time
for your flight. You must have gov-
ernment-issued ID with you. You will
not be able to take on board anything
that could be used as a weapon
(including items such as golf clubs or
insect repellent), so if in doubt, leave
it behind.

Wherever you land, travel into
Manhattan is fairly straightforward
if somewhat time-consuming.
Depending on traffic, travel from
the airport to the city can take from
30 minutes upwards. Each airport has
a Ground Transportation desk where
you can check routes, times and fares
into the city.

Besides the public transportation
services detailed below, taxis operate
from each of the three airports and
should be taken from the clearly sign-
posted official taxi dispatch lines
outside the terminals. Any taxi driver

Use only licensed yellow cabs

who approaches you in person is
likely to be unlicensed. Never ride in
independent cabs; stick with yellow
cabs, and look for the medallion—the
official flat bronze-colored disk
affixed to the vehicle's hood.

Taxi fares from the airports into
Manhattan are high: around $45–$55
(road and bridge tolls are extra) from
Newark, $30–$40 from La Guardia.
From JFK there is a flat fare of $45
plus tips and tolls. "Share and Save"
group rates are available 8am to midnight at Newark and La Guardia;
make arrangements with the airport's
taxi dispatcher. Bear in mind, too,
that traffic can be dense around
each airport and can add further to
taxi charges.

From JFK AirTrain JFK ($5)
run to the nearest subway station,
which is Howard Beach, leaving a
60-minute ride into Manhattan. Other
buses link the airport to other subway
lines, intended for New Yorkers who
want to get home without changing
lines. (See **Public transportation** on
pages 252–254.)

New York Airport Service Express
Bus (tel: 718/875-8200) has separate
buses leaving every 20–30 minutes
between 6.15am and 11.10 to Grand
Central Terminal, Port Authority
Station or Penn Station. The $13 ticket
is sold at the Ground Transportation
desk and by the driver.

Many tourists and locals carrying
luggage use van services provided by
Super Shuttle (tel: 800/258-3825).
Purchase a ticket from an agent at the
Ground Transportation desk near the
baggage claim. The vans run on
demand but most frequently from
7am to 11.30pm and stop at
Manhattan hotels.

From Newark Olympia Airport
Express (tel: 908/354-3330) operates
to Midtown Mantattan destinations
($12), generally between 4am and
11pm. As at JFK, Super Shuttle operate shared vans to all Manhattan
destinations for $15–$19. Linking
Newark and Penn Station, the
Airtrain (800/AIRRIDE) operates at
least hourly from 5am to 2am.

From La Guardia Local buses run to
the rest of Queens, but the best way
to reach Manhattan is with a New
York Airport Service Express Bus

Helicopters provide a speedy but costly way to sightsee or reach the airport. Most travelers prefer to use the bus

(718/875-8200) for $10–$12. Alternatively, and for destinations outside Midtown, use Super Shuttle vans (800/358-5825) charging $15–$22.

By boat New York's great days as a seaport may be long gone, but the QE2 keeps the tradition and the sheer luxury of transatlantic ocean-liner travel very much alive. After the ocean crossing from Southampton, you will glide into New York beneath the Statue of Liberty, travel a short distance up the Hudson and put ashore at Midtown Manhattan's gleaming Passenger Ship Terminal, which is situated on Twelfth Avenue, between 50th and 52nd streets.

By bus Long-distance buses into New York complete their journeys at the country's largest and busiest bus station: Port Authority Bus Terminal (tel: 564-8484), which stretches between 40th and 42nd Street on Eighth Avenue.

By train Most local commuter trains pull into Grand Central Terminal, at 42nd Street, between Lexington and Park avenues: for more information

on the Terminal, see pages 166–167. Amtrak's long-distance train service arrives at New York's other station, Penn Station, at 31st Street and Eighth Avenue. For Amtrak information, tel: 800/872-7245.

The Port Authority of New York-New Jersey metropolitan region governs the airports, train and bus stations. For more information about your arrival or departure gate, visit www.panynj.gov.

Car rental
With traffic lights on almost every block, a lack of affordable parking and the constant threat of gridlock, Manhattan—and New York City generally—is a difficult place in which to drive. For excursions outside the city,

247

however, a rental car is almost essential. A few taxi rides cost less than a space in an overnight parking lot, so no Manhattanite drives a car in the city unless absolutely necessary. If you are planning an excursion, it is more practical to rent a car just before departure.

You will save money but not time if you travel out of the city by public transportation and then rent a car in a smaller town. The majority of international car-rental companies have desks at the airports and offices in the city, where you can collect a prebooked car or rent one on the spot. Renting a car at an airport branch is usually less expensive than at the same agency's Manhattan branch.

The address of the nearest major car-rental outlet can be found by calling the following toll-free numbers: Avis (tel: 800/230-4898); Budget (tel: 800/527-0700); Hertz (tel: 800/654-3131); National (tel: 800/227-7368). Many more rental firms are listed in the *Yellow Pages*, though the international companies are often safest.

New York has outlawed the sale of the Collision Damage Waiver

Life on the move in New York City

(CDW), which is an optional form of insurance that can add considerably to costs. In New York you pay only for the first $100 of damage to a rental car. Check also whether or not the vehicle has to be returned with a full tank of gas.

Anyone under the age of 25 and/or without a credit card may have problems renting a car in New York.

In the unlikely event of your rental car breaking down, simply phone the car rental firm you rented from. Should you break down far from a phone, stay with your vehicle and wait for a police officer to come by.

If a passing motorist stops to offer help, there is every chance that the approach will be genuine—but treat the offer with caution. Usually, the best help such a person can provide is to make a telephone call on your behalf, probably from their cellphone.

Climate

Although there is an occasional bone-chilling winter day, with winds blasting in off the Hudson, snow is not often a problem in the city. The skyscrapers trap enough heat to melt most snowfalls, otherwise city officials are always ready with snow

plows and salt. Summer is the only unpleasant time of year, especially the humid, hot days of July and August, when many New Yorkers vacate the island for summer homes. Most hotels are air-conditioned, but if you're traveling in summer and choosing inexpensive accommodations, it is a good idea to check beforehand whether your room has an air conditioner. Air-conditioned stores, restaurants, theaters and museums provide respite from the heat; so do the many green expanses of parks. Subways and buses are usually air-conditioned, but subway stations in summer can be as hot as saunas.

For advice on when to travel outside New York City, where summer activities can be much more pleasant, see the panel on page 194.

Crime

New York has become a much safer city in recent years. The crime rate has dropped 70 percent since 1993. However, as in any large city, caution is still advised: Don't leave money and valuables in your hotel room and inquire whether the hotel has a safe. Keep track of your wallet or purse. Don't go into dark or deserted areas, epecially at night and past midnight take a taxi instead of a subway train. With less traffic, the ride will be much faster and cheaper than it is during the day.

Lost or stolen traveler's checks are relatively easy to replace (read the instructions when you buy the checks and make a note of all the relevant details).

Driving tips

It is never a good idea to bring a car into Manhattan—not least because New Yorkers drive like maniacs, and parking can be very expensive. Where less-expensive parking lots do exist, they are rarely the most central or convenient. Free parking on the street is almost impossible to find in Midtown, except on Sunday mornings. If you *do* bring a car into Manhattan, note that parking infringements attract stiff fines or worse (your car could be towed), so always read the signs carefully. Never park within 10ft (3m) of a fire hydrant. If possible, avoid leaving

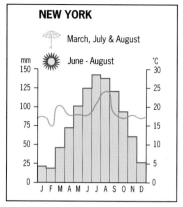

any valuables in the car: if you can't take them with you, make sure that they are out of sight.

If you decide to venture beyond the city to the Catskill Mountains, the remoter parts of the Hudson Valley, Long Island, New Jersey (see pages 194–211) or even farther afield, then wheels of your own become essential.

There is a speed limit of 65 mph (104kph) in force on interstates and on some state roads there may also be a minimum limit. In built-up areas, lower speed limits are indicated. It is not unusual for hefty fines and prison sentences to be imposed for driving under the influence of alcohol. New York City now has a policy of confiscating drunk drivers' cars—permanently.

Tolls are charged for some Manhattan bridges and tunnels, and for some stretches of road in the Outer Boroughs.

If you are a member of one of the automobile clubs, such as the AAA, be sure to have its emergency road service phone number handy in case of a breakdown.

Emergency telephone numbers

For **ambulance**, **police** or **fire**, dial 911 (no money required) and ask for the relevant service.

Other emergency numbers include **Crime Victims Hotline** (tel: 577-7777), **New York Gay and Lesbian Anti-violence Project** (tel: 714-1141), **Sex Crimes Report Line** (tel: 267-7273).

Lost property

Lost at JFK Airport, La Guardia Airport, or Newark, contact your airline. Lost in a taxi, tel: 692-8294. Lost on a bus or the subway, tel: 712-4500.

Media

New York has hundreds of TV and radio channels and newspapers and magazines. Free publications aimed at visitors litter every hotel lobby of varying degrees of accuracy and usefulness. Also free and more useful are *Village Voice* and *NY Press*. Other sources of information are the weekly *Time Out* and *New York* magazine. For a full run-down on the city's media, see pages 132–133.

Money matters

Automated-teller machines (ATMs) are everywhere. You can use virtually any bank or credit card (providing your card has been programmed with a personal identification number, or PIN) anytime at any one of the 24-hour machines which can be found in and outside of banks, in supermarkets, corner delis and department stores.

Most US banks charge $1.50 per transaction, while free-standing ATMs in stores will typically charge $2, in addition to any charges your own financial institution may make. Check in advance on limits on withdrawals within specific periods.

Elevated subway in Williamsburg

American Express Company's **Express Cash** system lets you withdraw cash and/or traveler's checks from a worldwide network of 57,000 American Express dispensers and participating bank ATMs. You must enroll first (call 800-CASH-NOW). Withdrawals are charged to a designated bank account. You can withdraw up to $1,000 per seven-day period on the basic card, more if your card is gold or platinum.

Alternatively the Travel Funds Card can be preloaded using any credit card and used to get cash at any American Express ATM, or to pay many bills.

At AmEx offices, cardholders can also cash personal checks for up to $1,000 in any seven-day period; of this $200 can be in cash, more if available, with the balance paid in traveler's checks, for which all but platinum cardholders pay a 1 percent fee. Higher limits apply to the gold and platinum cards.

Older travelers

There are a number of organizations in the United States that older travelers will very find useful. One such group is the **American Association of Retired Persons** (AARP). You have to pay a small membership fee, but once you have joined, discounts are available on a wide range of services, including flights, car rental, hotels and motels, plus various other vacation-related deals. Anyone over 50 can join by contacting AARP, 601 East Street, NW, Washington DC, 20049, tel: 888/687-2277, or visit www.aarp.org for more details.

If you are intending to claim a discount, it is advisable to mention it at the time of booking to ensure that one is on offer, although it might be limited to only certain days and times. You may also be asked to provide some evidence of your age. Even if you are not a member of a particular group, it can be worth asking about senior citizen discounts, as special rates may be applicable. The usual qualifying age for discounts normally range from 50 to 65.

Opening hours

New York store opening hours vary greatly. Many big stores will open on weekdays and Saturdays from 9am to 8pm, but smaller or more specialty stores in night-owl areas, such as Greenwich Village and the East Village, may open as late as 11am or noon and close at 9 or 10pm. On Sundays, opening times are from 11 or 12 till 6 or 7. However, in a city as large as New York, you are likely never to be stuck for somewhere to shop.

Museum opening times also vary. Many are open from 10 or 11am to 6pm on weekdays and Saturdays (although there are several that close on Mondays). Some also open on Sundays, and several keep late hours on Tuesdays or Thursdays.

Bank opening hours are Monday to Friday from 9am to 3 or 3.30pm (6pm on Thursday at some branches).

Places of worship

New York's places of worship are many and varied. These include:
Baptist: Memorial Baptist Church (141 West 115th Street).
Episcopal: Cathedral of St. John the Divine (112th Street, junction with Amsterdam Avenue).
Jewish: Temple Emanu-El (1 East 65th Street).
Methodist: Christ Church United (Park Avenue and 60th Street.
Roman Catholic: St. Patrick's Cathedral (Fifth Avenue and 50th Street).
Most of the above, and others, are described in the A to Z section of this book and on pages 120–121. Your hotel will be able to advise of those in your neighborhood, and the telephone book carries a comprehensive list. Several companies including **Harlem Spirituals** (tel: 391–0900) offer Sunday gospel trips to Harlem.

Police

"New York's Finest," the city's police, are usually helpful and efficient. Besides patroling in cars, officers are regularly seen on the street, and the police are well represented in crowd situations.

If you are unfortunate enough to be the victim of theft, you may want to

CONVERSION CHARTS

FROM	TO	MULTIPLY BY
Inches	Centimeters	2.54
Centimeters	Inches	0.3937
Feet	Meters	0.3048
Meters	Feet	3.2810
Yards	Metres	0.9144
Metres	Yards	1.0940
Miles	Kilometers	1.6090
Kilometers	Miles	0.6214
Acres	Hectares	0.4047
Hectares	Acres	2.4710
U.S. Gallons	Liters	3.7854
Liters	Gallons	0.2642
Ounces	Grams	28.35
Grams	Ounces	0.0353
Pounds	Grams	453.6
Grams	Pounds	0.0022
Pounds	Kilograms	0.4536
Kilograms	Pounds	2.205
U.S. Tons	Tonnes	0.9072
Tonnes	U.S. Tons	1.1023

MEN'S SUITS

U.S.	36	38	40	42	44	46	48
U.K.	36	38	40	42	44	46	48
Rest of Europe	46	48	50	52	54	56	58

DRESS SIZES

U.S.	6	8	10	12	14	16
U.K.	8	10	12	14	16	18
France	36	38	40	42	44	46
Italy	38	40	42	44	46	48
Rest of Europe	34	36	38	40	42	44

MEN'S SHIRTS

U.S.	14	14.5	15	15.5	16	16.5	17
U.K.	14	14.5	15	15.5	16	16.5	17
Rest of Europe	36	37	38	39/40	41	42	43

MEN'S SHOES

U.S.	8	8.5	9.5	10.5	11.5	12
U.K.	7	7.5	8.5	9.5	10.5	11
Rest of Europe	41	42	43	44	45	46

WOMEN'S SHOES

U.S.	6	6.5	7	7.5	8	8.5
U.K.	4.5	5	5.5	6	6.5	7
Rest of Europe	38	38	39	39	40	41

Driving in NewYork is best left to the experts

visit a police station to report the theft—mainly to validate your claim for insurance proposes as, realistically, there is little hope of finding the stolen item.

Every New York neighborhood has a police station. To find the one nearest you, dial 374-5000. If you need the police in an emergency, dial 911. To reduce your chances of needing police assistance, see the **Crime** section on page 249.

Post offices

New York's main post office, at Eighth Avenue, between 31st and 33rd streets, stays open around the clock, every day of the week. Elsewhere in the city, larger post offices are open Monday to Friday from 8am to 6pm and Saturday from 8am to 1pm. Smaller post offices keep shorter hours.

Stamps can also be bought, sometimes at inflated prices, through vending machines found in some stores and in many hotel lobbies.

Public transportation

If you are planning to spend most of your time in Manhattan, you will be much less reliant on public transportation than you might expect. Not only are distances small, but much of Manhattan is best seen on foot. However, if you are in a rush, planning to visit the Outer Boroughs, or simply commuting between uptown and downtown, you will need to make use of the city's buses, subway or taxis.

City buses Much slower than the subway trains, New York buses at least allow passengers to view the city as they travel through it, and many find them less intimidating than the subway system. The bus network is comprehensive (free maps are available from the tourist information offices listed on page 256), and the majority of routes run north–south and east–west (crosstown), with free transfers between another bus or subway ride.

Bus stops themselves are close to street corners—marked by a blue sign and a yellow painted section of curb—and most have a route map and frequency schedule for the buses that use that stop. The route is displayed on the front of each bus.

Most buses stop every two or three blocks; those marked "limited" (which only run at rush hour) make fewer stops, usually only at major intersections. As with the subway, there is a flat fare (currently $2) for all journeys. This can be paid with a swipe of a MetroCard (see below), in coins (exact change only; no dollar bills) or with a subway token (see below), either of which should be put into the box beside the driver.

When using your MetroCard, whether on the bus or the subway, you will be entitled to a free transfer to another bus or subway ride. This is automatically encoded on the card and valid for two hours. If you use coins or a token, ask the driver as you get on the bus for a transfer slip.

Especially during rush hours, New York buses can become packed; crosstown buses make only slightly better headway than pedestrians. If you are wedged in a crowded bus and think your stop may be coming up soon, start making your way toward the exit doors (which are in the middle of the bus—though you can also get off at the front door where you entered) in plenty of time; otherwise there is every chance you will not reach the doors before they shut and the bus moves on. A bell signal strip runs along both sides of the bus, but it is rare for the bus not to make each stop in busy periods.

The subway The much-maligned New York subway system is a swift, inexpensive and largely efficient way to get about the city.

A tangle of lines denoted by numbers and letters, the subway system map (available free from subway station token booths and from the tourist information offices listed on page 256) initially seems hopelessly confusing. In fact, the system is relatively easy to use provided you remember that "Uptown" trains go north (toward the Upper West and East sides and Harlem) and "Downtown" trains travel south (toward Lower Manhattan). Any train labeled "Brooklyn Bound" is indeed bound for Brooklyn but will make stops in Lower Manhattan on the way.

What can be more confusing is the choice between "Express" and "Local" trains. While local trains stop at all stations on a particular line, express trains stop only at selected stations (see pages 54–55). Board an express train by mistake and you can sometimes find yourself some distance from where you want to be, and possibly in a dangerous neighborhood. If this happens, cross over to the other platform and take the next train back.

It is a good idea to know which line and direction you want before entering the station and follow the relevant signs to the platform. If you are not sure which train to take, consult the wall maps in the station, inquire at the ticket booth, or ask a passerby for advice. New Yorkers are usually sympathetic and pleased to help visitors find their way. Even New Yorkers become baffled when trains are rerouted or stop running due to frequent construction projects (especially on weekends).

Listen closely to the announcements made over the public address system. Each train has the relevant letter or number and its destination shown along its side, in a color that corresponds to the colors on the subway map.

During the day, trains arrive every 10–15 minutes (more often in rush hours). Between midnight and 5am (the service operates around the clock), the usual wait is around 20–30 minutes.

253

City streetlife takes many forms in the Big Apple

To enter the subway system, you will need to swipe your MetroCard through an electronic reader or drop a subway token (which currently costs $2) into a slot, and then pass through a turnstile. MetroCards and tokens can be bought from the booths found at every station (many booths are open 24 hours) and also from a few major museums. Electronic MetroCards are generally a more cost-effective way to pay for multiple trips and particularly useful for tourists.

The MTA sells three kinds of gold plastic MetroCards: unlimited rides, pay-per-ride and the Fun Pass. For $21, you can buy a card that lets you take an unlimited number of trips in a 7-day period (a saving if you plan to take at least 13 trips). Turnstiles will allow only one person at a time to swipe in on the unlimited ride card (you cannot swipe an unlimited card again for 18 minutes to prevent fraud), so each person in your party must have one if you are riding together. With a pay-per-ride card, which can hold from $4 to $80 dollars, you can swipe in as many people as you like on one card, as long as it has enough credit to cover each $2 fare. The $7 Fun Pass allows one day of unlimited travel for one

Street advertising is an art form New York could call its own

person (from first use to 3am the following day). With the MetroCard, you can transfer free from bus to subway or subway to bus within two hours.

The subway, like other locations in New York and other large cities, does have its share of pickpockets—but providing you remain with the crowds and stay alert, you should have no problems with serious crime (see pages 54–55 for tips on traveling around the city and the Crime section on page 249).

Taxis
New York taxis are expensive and liable to be stuck in traffic for long periods of time. Sometimes cabs are the most time-efficient way to get where you are going, however, especially at night. When you want one, raise your hand to hail the next empty one to pass by. You know a cab is empty if the "taxi" sign on its roof is lighted.

Always wear the seatbelts provided—the security barriers can be lethal to teeth in sudden stops—and get a receipt from the driver before leaving. If you leave something in the cab, the receipt could help in getting it back.

Use only the official "medallion" cabs. These are yellow with "NYC Taxi" stenciled on the side, a light on the roof and a medallion on the hood. Any other vehicle looking for passengers will be unlicensed (known colloquially as a "gypsy cab") and should be ignored. Official taxi charges currently begin at $2.50 and gain 40¢ for every fifth of a mile traveled and 20¢ for each minute stopped in traffic. There is a 50¢ surcharge between 8pm and 6am; a 15–20 percent tip is the norm.

Rest rooms

Public rest rooms in New York run the gamut when it comes to cleanliness. Facilities in Penn Station and Grand Central Terminal are pleasant enough; those in Port Authority bus terminal much less so. Do not use rest rooms in subway stations. Instead, try Midtown department stores such as Macy's, Lord & Taylor and Bloomingdale's, museums, and large hotels. Public atriums, such as the Citicorp Center and Trump Tower, also provide reasonable public facilities.

Restaurant rest rooms are usually for patrons only. If you're dressed well and look as if you belong, you can just sail right on in. Movie theaters, Broadway theaters and concert halls have limited amenities, and there are often long lines before performances, as well as during intermissions.

Student and youth travel

Students in full-time education and anyone under 26 may qualify for discounted flights offered by travel agents that specialize in youth and student travel. Students carrying International Student Identity Cards (ISICs) will be entitled to reduced admission to many New York museums and other attractions.

While not exclusively for young and student travelers, the city's YMCAs and youth hostels (see page 215) offer inexpensive accommodations and a chance to socialize with other young visitors from around the world.

Times Square—the heart of the city that never sleeps

Telephones

You'll find pay phones in the street, in hotel lobbies, in train and bus stations, in bars and restaurants and in most public buildings.

Almost without exception, hotel room telephones have much higher charges than those of public telephones. Sometimes hotels even charge for dialing toll-free numbers.

Emergency calls (dial 911); calls to the operator (dial 0); the international operator (dial 800/874-4000); and calls for directory assistance (411) are usually free from payphones.

Throughout this book, toll-free numbers are given where available. The predominant area code (212) for Manhattan is omitted on the asumption that your call is from another 212 number. Some newer Manhattan numbers use 917 or 646—when calling these numbers from a 212 number (or vice versa), a "1" plus the full area code must be dialed. Area codes in the Outer Boroughs are 347 and 718.

255

Policemen will be happy to help

Time

New York uses Eastern Standard Time, three hours ahead of the West Coast, five hours behind the UK.

Tipping

How much you tip is entirely up to you, but the usual rule in a restaurant or coffee shop is to leave the person who served you 15–20 percent of the total bill. (An easy way to calculate the approximate amount is to double the sales tax figure—8.25 percent—shown at the bottom of the bill.)

Do not leave a tip at any food outlet where you serve yourself or where the food is sold to go.

After a taxi ride, it is customary to tip the driver around 15 percent of the fare. The amount need not be exact, however, and most people (if the amount works out within reason) allow the driver to keep the change from whatever bills they've handed over in payment.

Tipping hotel porters is also expected. Again, the amount you tip is entirely discretionary, but plan on $1–$2 per bag. If a porter simply helps move your luggage from the lobby into a taxi outside the hotel, a total of $1–$2 should usually be sufficient. Leave the chambermaid between $1 and $3 per day; if the service provided was particularly good then consider leaving more .

Tourist information

The multilingual staff of the New York Convention and Visitors Bureau (NYCVB), 810 Seventh Avenue, between 52nd and 53rd streets (tel: 800/NYC-VISIT for ordering printed materials or 484-1222 to speak to a counselor; Mon–Fri 8.30–6, Sat and Sun 9–5) can answer inquiries, provide free bus and subway maps, and have racks of leaflets detailing restaurants, hotels, and tourist attractions. They also operate kiosks at the southern tip of City Hall Park and in Harlem at 163 125th Street.

The New York Division of Tourism (1 Commerce Plaza, Albany, New York, NY 12245, tel: 518/474-4116 or 800/225-2697) offer help and information not only on Manhattan but on a state-wide basis—useful if you are planning excursions.

Tours on foot

There are many guided walking tours on offer in New York. Among them, the **Museum of the City of New York** (tel: 534-1672) and **New York City Cultural Walking Tours** (tel: 979-2388) visit the city's architecture, landmarks and historic sites.

The **Big Apple Greeters** (tel: 669-8159) will match your particular interest in the city with a local who can tell you all about it on a 2- to 4-hour jaunt. The service is free and tips are not accepted. More walking tours are suggested in the panel on page 56.

Travelers with disabilities

In New York, facilities for travelers with disabilities are not only impressive, but also improving all the time. By law, public buildings have to be at least partially wheelchair-accessible, and all must provide accessible restroom facilities. Almost all New York buses have rear-door "elevators" for wheelchair-users, and most also have a "kneel" step to make it easier to get onto the bus from the curb. The subway, however, is nearly impossible to use for those in wheelchairs.

Trains and airlines are obliged to provide services for travelers with disabilities if requested, and Amtrak has earned a reputation for doing this well. Though less comfortable than the trains, Greyhound buses are more frequent and will allow a companion to travel free provided that you have a doctor's certificate stating that this is necessary. Some major car-rental companies can arrange vehicles with hand controls provided they receive advance notice.

For brochures and further information, contact the **Mayor's Office for People with Disabilities** (100 Gold Street, Second floor, New York, NY 10038, tel: 788-2830). Blind or visually impaired visitors may appreciate a visit to the **Andrew Heiskell Braille and Talking Book Library** (40 West 20th Street, tel: 206-5400), a public library with a large collection of Braille, large-print and recorded books, housed in a layout specially designed for easy access by the visually impaired.

The Society for Accessible Travel and Hospitality (SATH) is a non-profit making organization, which was founded in 1976. It provides detailed information on a number of issues, including traveling with specific disabilities and a list of tour operators specializing in this field. SATH members also receive other benefits such as a newsletter and magazine. Visit their website at www.sath.org or contact them at 347 Fifth Avenue, Suite 610, New York, NY 10016, tel: 447-7284, fax: 725-8253.

The **Big Apple Greeters**, volunteers who show visitors around the city (see **Tours on foot** page 256), also extend their service to those with disabilities.

Web sites

Many New York museums, tourist attractions, newspapers, hotels and restaurants have their own websites, the addresses of which can be found with most search engines. They can also be found using the search feature on the more general sites listed below. Many of these are extremely helpful for travelers and may allow you to make reservations using a credit card.

www.nycvisit.com is the website of the New York Convention and Visitors Bureau (see **Tourist information**) and has a useful selection of general visitor information.

www.ci.nyc.ny.us is billed as the official New York City website, run by the local government, and covers areas such as transportation, health and safety, as well as tourist attractions.

www.newyork.metro.com is a good site for entertainment, shopping and nightlife.

www.iloveny.com, a service provided by the New York Division of Tourism, offers suggestions on what to do across the whole of New York.

www.nytoday.com is a very large site put together by the *New York Times* and is, therefore, very strong on the latest news and features from the Big Apple.

www.villagevoice.com, by the magazine of the same name, covers a very broad range of topics, but is good for tips on nights out.

Subways are the fastest way to get around New York

Further reading

Architecture Manhattan is home to some of the world's most famous buildings so it isn't surprising that there is a wealth of books to be read about them. To start, pick up a copy of *The Empire State Building*, by John Tauranac; or *Divided We Stand: A biography of the World Trade Center*, by Eric Darton. *The AIA Guide to New York City*, by Elliot Willensky and Norval White, is the definitive guide to the city's many buildings. *Central Park: the Birth, Decline, and Renewal of a National Treasure*, by Eugene Kinkead, describes the evolution of the famous city landmark.

Current affairs *The Mole People*, by Jennifer Toth, concentrates on New York's subculture, namely the homeless people who live in the abandoned tunnels underneath the city. *Den of Thieves*, by James B. Stewart, concerns the notorious Wall Street conspirators of the 1980s. *Goldman Sachs: The Culture of Success* by former vice president Lisa Endlich is an account of the rise of the investment banking firm.

Memoir and biography Some of the best early full-length accounts are Christopher Morley's *New York*, a mid-1920s essay; *Walker in the City*, by Alfred Kazin; Eileen Myles' *Chelsea Girls*; and *Manhattan When I Was Young*, by Mary Cantwell. In *New York in the 50s*, Dan Wakefield recalls his early days spent with such notables as Jack Kerouac and James Baldwin. Anatole Broyard describes his coming of age in *Kafka Was the Rage* while Willie Morris writes about moving to New York from Mississippi and becoming the editor of *Harper's* magazine in *New York Days*. More recently, Max Frankel published his memoir *The Times of My Life and My Life with the Times* about his career with the venerable *New York Times*; *Bloomberg by Bloomberg* is the story of the mayor's world-famous career; and *Arguing the World* is Joseph Dorman's recollection of the political views and discussions of his contemporaries David Bell, Irving Howe, Irving Kristol, and Nathan Glazer. *Fiorello H.*

La Guardia and the Making of Modern New York, by Thomas Kessner, is a biography of the city's Depression-era mayor, while *Rudy Giuliani, Emperor of the City*, by Andrew Kirtzman is about New York's previous mayor. *The Power Broker* by Robert Caro is a fascinating biography of Robert Moses, one of city's influential parks commissioners. Follow a celebrity through several decades in *The Andy Warhol Diaries*.

History For a fine introduction to the history of the city, read the heavily illustrated *Columbia Historical Portrait of New York* by John Kouwenhoven. Pulitzer Prize-winning *Gotham: A History of New York City to 1898*, by Edwin Burrows and Mike Wallace, is a comprehensive study of the city's early development. *In The Kingdom and the Power*, Gay Talese gives you a behind-the-scenes look at the *New York Times*. For insight about New York's other famous publication, *The New Yorker* magazine, read Brendan Gill's *Here at the New Yorker*. Also, don't miss E. B. White's 1949 essay, *Here is New York*, found in many anthologies. *Gay New York* is a history of gay life in the city before 1940 by George Chauncey. Jan Morris reconstructs the city in *Manhattan '45*. Herbert Mitgang's *Once Upon A Time in New York* is about the rivalry between Jazz-Age mayor Jimmy

Walker and governor Franklin Roosevelt, and *The Future Once Happened Here*, by Fred Siegel, is about the policies and philosophies of mayor Rudy Giuliani. Nathan Glazer's *Beyond the Melting Pot* is about ethnic change in New York. William Corbett's *New York Literary Lights* is an encyclopedia of anything literary in New York. *The Great School Wars*, by Diane Ravitch is a history of New York City's public school system. For labor history, see *Working Class New York* by Joshua B. Freeman.

Theater Theater lovers may want to read *Act One*, the autobiography of playwright Moss Hart; *Bring on the Girls* and *Performing Flea*, P. G. Wodehouse and Guy Bolton's entertaining account of their years spent writing for musical comedy; *Rewrites* by Neil Simon; *Hot Seat*, by Frank Rich; and *It Happened On Broadway*, by Brooks Atkinson. For up-to-date essays on the city's theater scene, try Mark Steyn's *Broadway Babies Say Goodnight*; David Mamet's *The Cabin*; William Goldman's *The Season*; or Walter Kerr's *The Theater In Spite of Itself* and *The Decline of Pleasure*.

Literature Perhaps because so many writers have lived in New York City, there is a wealth of fiction set here.

From a restaurant meal to a shoe-shine… don't forget that tipping is expected

Winter's Tale by Mark Helprin uses surreal fantasy to create a portrait of New York's past. Novels set in 19th century New York include Henry James' *Washington Square*, Edith Wharton's *The Age of Innocence* and *The House of Mirth* and Stephen Crane's *Maggie, A Girl of the Streets*. O'Henry's short stories depict the early years of the 20th century, while Damon Runyon's are set in the raffish underworld of the 1930s and '40s. F. Scott Fitzgerald (*The Beautiful and the Damned*, 1922), Betty Smith (*A Tree Grows in Brooklyn*, 1945) John Dos Passos (*Manhattan Transfer*, 1925), John O'Hara (*Butterfield 8*, 1935) and Mary McCarthy (*The Group*, 1938) also wrote about this city. Truman Capote's 1958 novella *Breakfast at Tiffany's* is a favorite.

More current New York stories include *Bonfire of the Vanities*, by Tom

259

260

Americana for sale in a flea market in Little Italy

Wolfe; *The Mambo Kings Play Songs of Love*, by Oscar Hijuelos; *The New York Trilogy* by Paul Auster; *Underworld*, by Don DiLillo; *The Alienist*, by Caleb Carr; *Manhattan Loverboy*, by Arthur Nersesian; *Glamorama* and *Bright Lights, Big City* by Jay McInerney; and *People Like Us*, by Dominick Dunne.

The experience in Harlem of African–Americans has been chronicled in Ralph Ellison's *Invisible Man*, James Baldwin's *Go Tell It on the Mountain* and Claude Brown's *Manchild in the Promised Land*. *When Harlem Was in Vogue*, by David Levering Lewis, is set in 1920s. A more recent account about the life of a Haitian immigrant is *Breath, Eyes, Memory* by Edwidge Danticat.

For portraits of gay life, try David Leavitt's *The Lost Language of Cranes*; Larry Kramer's *Faggots*; and Sarah Schulman's *After Delores* and *People In Trouble*.

The history of New York's Jewish population can be traced through such books as *World of Our Fathers*, by Irving Howe; *Call It Sleep*, by Henry Roth; *The Promise*, by Chaim Potok; *New York Jew*, by Alfred Kazin; *Enemies, A Love Story*, by Isaac Bashevis Singer; *Our Crowd*, by Stephen Birmingham; and *The Jew of New York*, a comic book-style account by Ben Katchor.

National Book Award winner *Charming Billy* is Alice McDermott's story of an Irish-American family living in Bayside, Queens, and Frank McCourt's autobiographical *Angela's Ashes* and *'Tis* recount the tale of his life between the two continents.

Mysteries set in New York City range from Dashiell Hammet's urbane 1922 novel *The Thin Man*, to Rex Stout's Nero Wolfe mysteries to the more recent *While My Pretty One Sleeps*, by Mary Higgins Clark.

Billboard in Midtown westside